Happy Hooking

The Art of

Anchoring

Third Edition

By

Alex Blackwell

USCG Lic. Master Mariner

&

Daria Blackwell

USCG Lic. Captain

Alex & Daria Blackwell

Please Note

Every boat, every skipper, every anchor, every bottom, and every weather factor is different, so our methods may not be best for you or for your boat. Please consult manufacturers of the tackle you are considering for their specific recommendations.

We do not and cannot accept any liability or responsibility whether expressed or implied for how or if any piece of equipment or method performs or is applied. There are inherent dangers to boating and every skipper and crew member must accept these prior to embarking onto a boat.

Errors in product descriptions are unintentional and subject to correction.

Whereas we do write about and mention specific brands and equipment and may recommend one piece of equipment over another and have received items of equipment at no cost to us from manufacturers, we are under no contractual or other obligation to any one or other manufacturer or reseller. Our statements of suitability are based entirely on our own experience and failing that, on the experience of other testers.

ISBN Number: 9781795717410

Happy Hooking ⚓ The Art of Anchoring

From Alex:

This book is dedicated to the memory of Middleton Joseph Blackwell, without whose encouragement and love for the sea and life in general I may not have chosen the path I walk today, to my mother Meike Blackwell, for opening our eyes as children and supporting our every decision throughout our lives, and to Aunt Klara and Uncle Hans Gaffron from whom I learned respect and love for the ocean and for the abundance of life beneath its waves.

Above all, this book is dedicated to my wife, partner, sailing companion, soul mate, and co-author Daria, without whom none of this would ever have come true.

From Daria:

I dedicate this work to all our friends without whose questions we may not have recognized a need for possible answers and without whose stories and insights this would have been a much shorter edition.

And most of all, thanks to Alex, my partner in life's adventures.

Alex & Daria Blackwell

Happy Hooking ⚓ The Art of Anchoring

In Appreciation:

We would like to express our gratitude to those who took the time to review and critique our manuscript or provide us with equipment to test, photographs, and other materials. Among them were several anchor manufacturers, all of whom have made a huge personal commitment to improving boaters' safety by producing and continually improving their products.

We are firmly of the opinion that one learns most from one's own mistakes, and we certainly have made our portion of them. We also believe you can learn much from the mistakes made by others. So we thank all the cruisers who shared their anchoring stories with us to give us the benefit of their well-earned wisdom.

Alex & Daria Blackwell

Happy Hooking ⚓ The Art of Anchoring

Table of Contents

Alex & Daria Blackwell

Introduction

Unless you are far offshore, at some point you are going to need to park your boat. This may be because you want to or because you need to. In either case you have three choices. You can go to a dock, which lacks many of the plus points of being away from land. You can pick up a mooring, which often has a number of challenges and unknowns associated with it. Or you can drop a hook (common term for anchor), which just happens to be our preferred choice.

Securely anchored in a peaceful anchorage.

Just like knowing how to stop your car before you start is perhaps the most important part of driving, anchoring is perhaps the most important skill you can and should acquire in boating. Anchoring a boat can be a lovely dance in a harbor or a painful and often embarrassing display of *Homo sapiens'* inability to plan or communicate. In the following, we will endeavor to help you find a combination of tackle and technique best suited for your circumstances when anchoring your vessel.

For our purposes, we will define anchoring tackle as the combination of gear used to attach your boat to the bottom. The tackle will always include an anchor, which is meant to dig into and hold onto the bottom, and a rode that connects the anchor to the boat. The rode can be chain, rope, or a combination of the two.

Traditional anchoring tackle

What should you expect of an anchoring system? An anchoring system should:

- ⚓ Set quickly,
- ⚓ Hold securely
- ⚓ Connect anchor to boat reliably...with no weak links.

By outlining how different anchors work, considering the pluses and minuses of different adjunctive pieces of equipment, and reviewing the current thinking about how to select an anchorage and deploy this equipment, we hope you will be armed with enough information to make more informed decisions about what might work best for you.

We will also give you some pointers on related subjects, as well as some thoughts on ensuring that your stay in an anchorage among other boats is peaceful and enjoyable. We will even try to help you with your etiquette and communications skills.

Our suggestions are based on our personal experiences on the smaller and larger boats we have sailed or driven over the course of years. Although we have been fortunate to have been exposed to a broad range of conditions, we know that with so many outside factors having an influence, we can never know it all. Yes, we have dragged anchor, we have lost an anchor, we have pulled up something we shouldn't have, and we have been to places where our anchor just would not hold. Each time we questioned our competence and each time learned some valuable bit of information that made us that much more knowledgeable about how to handle a similar situation the next time. What we learned from all those experiences made us want to investigate further and share our findings with you.

Besides conferring ability to enjoy swinging at anchor in some secluded cove, the skill of securely connecting your boat to the bottom has some important safety implications. Even if you do not plan to anchor overnight, safety reasons – such as keeping your vessel from running aground in bad weather or in emergency situations like engine or steering failure – dictate that you should be prepared and know how to anchor your boat when you need to. At times like these you will be glad you have your gear ready to go as well as the experience to deploy it.

We hope to give you the confidence to drop your hook, enjoy nature and take it easy for a spell, fish in a noted spot without drifting away, weather a storm in a protected anchorage, or save your boat from ending up on the rocks. Anchoring with assurance gives you the ability to enjoy cruising, fishing, swimming, lunch aboard, the sunset cocktail, or an overnight stay. It also increases your range, letting you cruise longer distances and explore new places.

To a novice, anchoring may seem simple and the attention we give it may seem like overkill at first. Yet, it is important to review the characteristics of the tackle (the gear used to attach your boat to the bottom: anchor, chain, rope, swivels, shackles, etc.) and how the gear you have matches up with different anchorages, conditions and particular vessels. We will try to help you understand how to approach the decision making for your own unique situation. Yes, it can be simple, but only after thinking it all through.

Please bear in mind that every boat, every skipper, every anchor, every bottom, and every weather factor is different, so our methods might not be best for your situation. If you are in doubt, please consult a local expert for advice prior to setting out and never expect a 'lunch hook' to suffice for overnight or heavy weather anchoring.

If you could take only one piece of advice from these pages, perhaps you will remember what Tommy Moran, an old salt in the West of Ireland, advised time and again:

> *"Anchor as though you plan to stay for weeks,*
> *even if you intend to leave in an hour."*

If you add to that some sound advice from our good friend Dr. Philip Meakins, you should be in good shape should an unexpected situation arise:

> *"Your vessel should always be ready to clear out at a*
> *moment's notice, so have your exit strategy well prepared."*

Cruising is what many of us live for or at least dream about. Even some of the most heavily built up areas have many unspoiled bays and coves just waiting to take us away from reality. We assume that one of the reasons that waterfront property is so valuable is because of the ambience provided by cruisers anchoring their boats near shore. On that note, when we anchor off a multi-million-dollar estate we enjoy the same views and sunsets as they do – usually without as high an expense. Anchoring safely enables us to enjoy the best parts of cruising.

Our adventures have taught us to stay cool under pressure, work together as a team and always be prepared with an exit strategy should we need it. Advance planning is the key to Happy Hooking. Always ask, "What if?" Review all the possibilities and the chance of being caught unaware will be reduced.

> *Happy Hooking!*

Definition per Wikipedia:

> *'Anchors achieve holding power either by "hooking" into*
> *the seabed,*
> *or via sheer mass, or a combination of the two.'*

Part 1: 'Hooking Gear' – Anchors

"There are probably more types of anchors available now than any normal person will ever have a chance to try out (normal being like most us who are not employed to actually conduct anchor tests). My first anchor was an iron window weight I found behind the house when I was a young child. Though some may disagree with this statement, for me an anchor is anything you can deploy to securely attach your boat to the bottom of the stream, lake, ocean or other body of water your craft happens to be floating on. In the muddy-bottom lake near where we lived, this window weight held my ten-foot canoe quite admirably."

"During my first summers off Cape Cod poking around in a nutshell-sized rowing boat in a protected inlet, I progressed to a suitably heavy rock. The rock was quickly replaced with a plow anchor by my aunt who happened to own the dinghy and had this notion that my rock might not hold. Perhaps coincidentally, the rock was having an adverse effect on the dinghy's bright work. Though not nearly as heavy as my rock, I soon learned that this anchor did indeed do a better job of connecting 'my' boat with the bottom."

"This was the beginning of my lifelong pursuit of making sure our boat stayed where it was supposed to;" Alex.

We are fortunate to be living at a time when significant advances have been made in anchoring technology. We are no longer talking about weights on a rope. We are now into the age of technologically superior anchor performance. A great anchor is your best insurance policy.

5

Chapter 1. Anatomy of an Anchor

Basic anchor design crosses the different categories of anchors. The anchor fluke or blade is what is intended to bury into the seabed. The very tip of a fluke is sometimes called the bill or the toe. Hook anchors have two or more flukes, as per the illustration below.

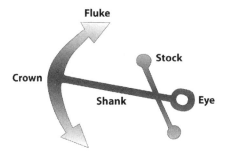

The stock (crossbar) is usually at right angles to the fluke(s). It turns the anchor to an attitude that enables the flukes to dig into the sea bed. Stockless anchors, as the name suggests, do not have a stock. They rely on other methods to ensure appropriate orientation as they address the bottom.

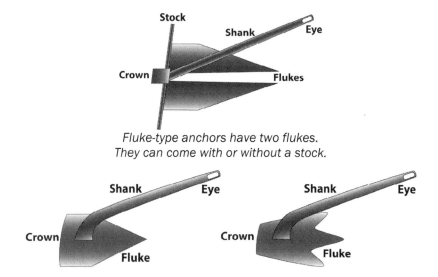

Fluke-type anchors have two flukes.
They can come with or without a stock.

Most modern anchors, including the plows, scoops, and claws have a single fluke and no stock.

Hooking Gear ⚓ Anchors

The shank or shaft is connected at the crown to the fluke(s). There is an eye on the end of the shank, which is the attachment point for the rode. There is sometimes an eye at the crown to accommodate a trip line which we will discuss in a later chapter. There may also be a second eye to enable tandem anchoring (two anchors in series).

Anchor with wooden stock of the English Frigate "The Crescent" which sank off Norway in 1808.
Photo ©2004 by Tomasz Sienicki.

Anchor in Horta, Azores with an iron stock.
Photo © 2010 by Daria Blackwell.

Chapter 2: A Brief History of the (Pleasure) Boat Anchor

Before describing the various anchors on the market today, we would like to give you an introduction into the evolution of small boat anchors.

Much has changed in the technology of anchoring a boat safely in recent years. So much so that any prudent mariner, either leisure or professional, would be wise to review what they have on their vessel, gain a better understanding of what an anchor actually does, and see what characteristics are important. An anchor used to be gauged by its weight, but is that still the case?

Ever since man ventured out onto the water using water craft to fish, travel, transport goods, or (in more recent times) for pleasure, the most important thing he or she had to be able to do was park the vessel. Initially, this simply meant dragging it up on a beach, but the time soon came to stop (anchor) while on the water. Looking past the development of ropes, chains, cables and other ancillary gear needed to connect the anchor to a boat, let us take a look at where it all started and where we are today.

At first there was the stone on a rope. The first innovations and improvements soon followed. Someone thought to drill a hole in the stone to make it easier to tie the rope to it. About 2,000 years ago someone else encased a stone in a wooden framework adding the first flukes to improve holding. Today we call this a killick anchor. Another innovation was drilling further holes in the stone to attach flukes directly to the stone. Of course, there were many permutations of this, but they all meant that boats were anchoring ever more securely.

It literally took millennia to move from such a rock on a rope to the admiralty pattern anchor introduced in the 19th century. In the meanwhile, the Romans developed an anchor somewhat reminiscent of it, though lacking the necessary steel forges they made the collar and stock out of lead with the shaft and flukes still being made of wood.

Hooking Gear ⚓ Anchors

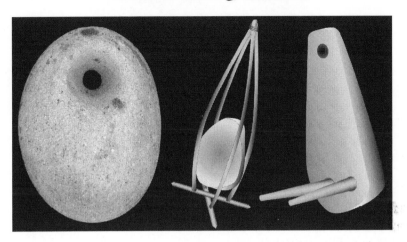

Both the Roman anchor and the later Admiralty anchor have a stock at one end of the shank that is at right angles to the pair of flukes. The stock orientates the anchor so that one of the flukes digs into the ground irrespective of how the anchor hits the bottom.

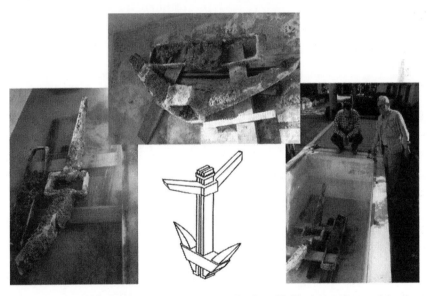

Photos by A. Yfantis, M. Likeridou, and H. Tzalas; Hellenic Institute of Ancient and Medieval Alexandrian Studies

Today the admiralty pattern (A.P.) anchor (also known as the Fisherman, Luke, etc.) graces government building lawns around the world and can be found in fancy jewelry designs. However, it is also still very much in

9

use and can be found on classic and modern cruising boats, particularly in areas with rocky coastlines.

A century later the hinged stockless fluke type anchor that is used on many large ships to this day was developed. As it had no stock, this anchor was easier to stow. Adding a hinge was a big innovation as it

allowed the paired flukes to dig into the bottom more efficiently and irrespective of which way the anchor landed on the bottom.

The next big innovation was the Coastal Quick Release anchor (CQR, also known as Clyde Quick Release), which was introduced in the 1930s by Sir Geoffrey Ingram Taylor. It is a single fluke anchor with a weighted tip based on a double-bladed agricultural plowshare. Like a plow, it is designed to dig into the substrate. The hinged shank is intended to permit directional movement without the anchor pulling out; however, the hinge is prone to wear, and once worn, will compromise the effectiveness of the anchor significantly.

Hooking Gear ⚓ Anchors

The CQR represented a major advance in anchor design and stimulated 20th century innovations for recreational anchoring. Recent studies have shown that its holding power does not compare well against newer anchor designs. Indeed, this anchor, once very popular among cruisers, has been shown in numerous sophisticated tests by independent bodies to plow through sea bottoms on more occasions than one might appreciate for a good night's sleep.

In the 1940s, Richard Danforth redesigned the ship's fluke anchor to have wide sharp triangular flukes and a stock at the crown for use on sea planes and military landing craft, which had been using the more cumbersome Northill anchor. Much lighter than the stockless fluke, his steel Danforth anchor had a high holding-to-weight ratio and soon found its way into the pleasure boat market. At about the same time the Brittany anchor was introduced in Europe. It, too, is a derivation of the ship's anchor, and has wide, flat, and pointy flukes, and no stock, though some newer versions do. Lighter versions of the Danforth followed and today the aluminum Fortress anchor is one of the more popular brands. This is a very good anchor for muddy bottoms.

Original Brittany, FOB anchor with stock, original Danforth, aluminum Fortress

The first of the claw type anchors was invented by Peter Bruce from the Isle of Man in the 1970s to secure North Sea oil rig platforms. It was

later scaled down for small boats, and copies of this very popular design abound. The claw anchor sets easily and very fast, though its holding power is not as great as the newer scoop type anchors. Claw anchors are quite popular on charter fleets as their percentage set on the first try in many bottom types is very high.

The Delta anchor was derived from the CQR. It was patented by Philip McCarron, James Stewart, and Gordon Lyall of Simpson-Lawrence Ltd in 1992. It was designed as an advance over the anchors used for floating

systems such as oil rigs. It retains the weighted tip of the CQR but has a much higher fluke area to weight ratio than its predecessor. The designers also eliminated the sometimes-troublesome hinge. This is another oft copied design

with the European Brake and Australian Sarca Excel being two of the more notable ones. Although it is a plow type anchor, it sets and holds reasonably well in hard bottoms.

With the invention of the Bügel Anker in the 1980s by German three-time circumnavigator Rolf Kaczirek, anchor design started to get really interesting. He wanted an anchor that was self-righting without necessitating a ballasted tip, so he added a roll bar. Instead of a plow share, he used a flat blade design.

As none of the innovations of this anchor were patented, it has often been copied. The copies are reportedly not always reliable.

Hooking Gear ⚓ Anchors

It was Frenchman Alain Poiraud, who changed everything with the introduction of the scoop type anchor in 1996. The scoop anchors are shaped like a shovel with a concave fluke. Remove a shovel's handle and add an anchor shank and you have a scoop type anchor. Just like a shovel is designed to dig, so it is with a scoop anchor – it digs, and if you apply more pressure, it digs deeper.

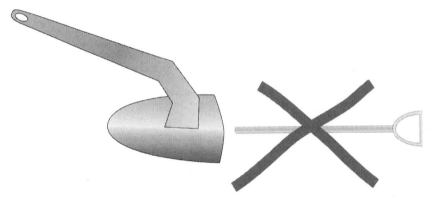

The scoop type anchors represent one of the true breakthrough design advancements in the last decades in the marine industry. The common challenge with all the scoop type anchors is that they set so well that they can be difficult to weigh. They also tend to bring up loads of sediment – both problems we are happy to live with!

So, Alain Poiraud changed the fluke from concave to convex and added a weighted tip like the Delta had. The increase in holding power was immense. He also made the shank hollow in an attempt to have the anchor land on the seabed in the correct orientation.

The Spade sets and holds well in most bottom types given sufficient scope. It can also be disassembled for easier storage.

Chapter 3: The Current Generation of Anchors

It is only in the 20th century that anchor designs took a dramatic leap forward technologically, and only in the last twenty years that drastically different designs have been introduced that bear no resemblance to the old hooks and weights of the past. This is certainly due in part to the proliferation of smaller pleasure craft. The diversity of their needs with regard to handling, weight, and other characteristics, as well as their large numbers, created the demand for new designs. It also caused experienced cruisers to apply their other-worldly skills to good use in developing new anchors to help their boats stay put where they left them.

There are many different types of anchors available today, and it seems that novel shapes and structures are being devised each year. Some appear questionably radical while others convincingly represent technologically sophisticated designs. Although some of the available anchors such as the C.Q.R.™, Danforth®, and Bruce® can hardly be considered contemporary designs, they must be taken into account in our discussion because there are so many of them in use. With the used boat market come legacy acquisitions of older anchors that continue in service for many years.

To make it easier to think about anchor designs, we have grouped the common types of small craft and yacht anchors into five main categories: the traditional ones that act like hooks, the plows, those with flukes, the claws, and the more recent scoops. There are many variations within each of these categories as well as some that fall outside these parameters. However, there are performance features that anchors within each category share that will make it easier to think about anchor selection for your particular needs.

Some types of anchors hold best in a particular type of bottom like mud, sand, shell, rock, or seaweed. A few have proven to hold in a wide variety

Hooking Gear ⚓ Anchors

Anchor types

Five major categories of anchors include the hook (Luke and Grapnel shown), plow (CQR and Delta shown), fluke (Danforth and stockless navy pattern shown), claw (Manson Ray and SuperMax shown), and scoop (Spade and Rocna shown). Some photos courtesy of the manufacturers.

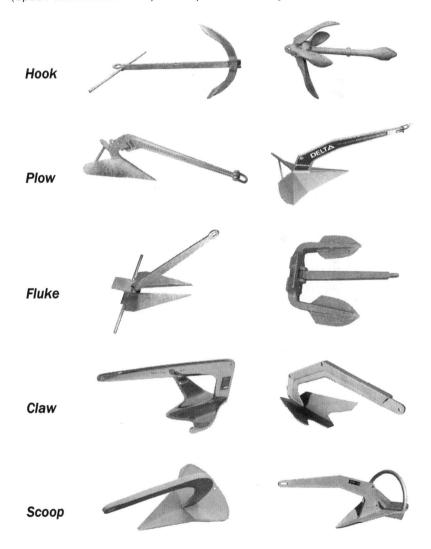

Hook

Plow

Fluke

Claw

Scoop

of bottoms. In fact, some of the newer designs challenge the traditional thinking that a vessel should carry several different types of anchors aboard, although we still like having multiple options available to us.

Some anchors offer solid construction with no moving parts; Delta, Bruce, Rocna, Vulcan, and Ultra are examples of such construction. Some anchors have moving parts; CQR, Danforth, and Fortress are examples here. Other anchors have parts that are meant to be disassembled for storage. These include the Fisherman, Fortress, Spade, Mantus, and Kobra.

Asking experienced people in your area is a good way to learn the types of anchors that people trust for your cruising territory. This can also be a great way to get a lively conversation (i.e., heated debate) going. To see what people out and about have to say about anchors, just visit the sailing discussion boards about the best anchors such as the one at www.ssca.org or www.cruisersforum.com. But remember that many cruisers have legacy acquisitions on board – anchors that came with their boat and they never replaced. So it may be that their experience is based on antiquated technology. We'll take a look at what independent evaluations have shown about the many new anchor types and try to make sense of the diverging opinions and reports.

What Makes a Good Anchor?

An anchor needs to have a few key characteristics to be worthy of trusting your boat and your life to it. We would argue that these five characteristics are important:

- ⚓ Always orients itself correctly and sets easily
- ⚓ Offers good holding power in all types of bottoms including sand, mud, hard pack, weed and rock
- ⚓ Veers readily and will not pull out with changes in wind and tide
- ⚓ Able to handle high loads on any part of its structure without damage
- ⚓ Can be retrieved and stowed readily

Hooking Gear ⚓ Anchors

That's a lot to ask of an anchor. Let's see how each of the major categories delivers.

Hook-type Anchors

The hook-type anchors come in many permutations. They include the fisherman and grapnel style anchors. The fisherman type anchor has indeed been around a long time.

Hook type anchors typically have two or more relatively narrow flukes which are intended to hook into the bottom. Hook type anchors are generally quite heavy and have relatively poor holding power. A hook-type anchor can, however, be useful for rocky bottoms and for kedging. Kedging is a technique that allows a boat to be pulled along by setting and pulling against an anchor.

A home-made hook

With the stock at right angles to the fluke, a fisherman style anchor has a natural tendency to rotate one of the flukes towards the bottom and thus presents a single-entry point. It sets fast in any type of bottom and is very stable.

With one fluke dug into the bottom, the other fluke points straight up and can easily snag the rode. This is depicted in the familiar maritime fouled anchor symbol where you see a rode wrapped around the anchor. It is much better to see that on a gold chain around your neck rather than on the anchor chain at the bottom. Because of the relatively slender flukes, the fisherman has a low drag value and thus poor holding, particularly in a softer bottom. It is

A hook type anchor can be hard to stow and deploy

also quite difficult to retrieve, stow or handle without damaging the boat. That's why small yacht anchors were made to disassemble and even to fold.

Good Features

- ⚓ Presents a single sharp point
- ⚓ Catches well on rock
- ⚓ Very stable

Things to consider

- ⚓ Upwards pointing fluke(s) can snag rode... classic 'fouled anchor'
- ⚓ Low drag or holding power value
- ⚓ Heavy weight
- ⚓ Difficult to retrieve, stow or handle

Hooking Gear ⚓ Anchors

Fisherman

Perhaps the most readily recognized of all small yacht anchors is the Fisherman, also known as the Herreshoff, Luke, Kingston, Kedge, as well as other names. This is the old traditional style descended from the Admiralty Pattern that today is most often seen on lawns in front of municipal buildings providing nautical character to the environment.

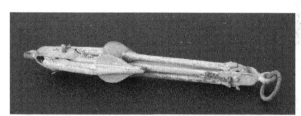

*Folding Dirigo anchor obtained from
Reynal de St. M. Thebaud, Jr.*

The 1914 Nat Herreshoff design, once the world's most popular small boat anchor, has been out-done by more modern ones but is still considered a good anchor for rocky bottoms and remains popular among the schooner fleet in Maine. There is an aesthetically lovely three-piece bronze reproduction by J.M. Reineck & Son in Massachusetts which reportedly will hold equally well in all bottoms, will not bring up loads of muck so it is easily cleaned, will not affect the compass, folds flat for storage, and will not stain because it cannot rust.

In 1999, *Young America* raced in the America's Cup carrying a 40 lb Luke three-piece storm anchor aboard to meet the requirements of the IACC Rule. They liked the fact that it could be taken apart and stowed close to the centerline.

In fact, diving down in popular and 'notoriously bad' anchorages throughout the Caribbean, we noted that they were frequently crisscrossed with furrows plowed by plow anchors dragging merrily through the bottom.

Nevertheless, the plow-type anchor is by most accounts still commonly in use on recreational vessels around the world. Newer plow anchors have significant design improvements and do often outperform older designs in independent rating tests.

Good Features
- ⚓ Single point penetration
- ⚓ Self-stabilizing
- ⚓ Sets and resets easily
- ⚓ Good performance in most hard sea bed types (hard sand, hard mud, rock, weed)

Things to consider
- ⚓ Less effective in soft muddy or sandy bottoms
- ⚓ Weight on the heavy side
- ⚓ A plow tends to plow!

The CQR™

The CQR (Coastal Quick Release also known as Clyde Quick Release) was invented in the 1930s by Sir Geoffrey Ingram Taylor, a physicist, mathematician, and specialist in fluid dynamics and wave theory. The CQR brand is now owned by Lewmar and they have changed the "CQR" acronym to mean "Secure". The CQR from Lewmar has Lloyd's Register approval as a High Holding Power anchor and is guaranteed for life against breakage.

The CQR is still a very popular anchor, although its popularity is steadily declining. Because it has been around for a long time and for many years represented a major improvement in anchor design, it has built up a substantial user base. The discussion about CQRs tends to be very lively, with some cruisers swearing by it, others suggesting that its time has passed.

The CQR was considered suitable for many sea beds and weather conditions. It offers drop-forged construction and a hinged shank designed for consistent setting and holding. The hinged shank is intended to permit directional movement without pulling out, but the hinge is prone to jamming and wear and creates a tendency for the anchor to roll out. It's swiveling head can make the CQR more difficult to stow. When the hinge is worn, the performance of the CQR is reportedly greatly reduced. Bear in mind that there are countless imitations and copies of this anchor, some of which simply do not work.

We have a large CQR, which came with our boat. We had it on board for years. We found it to work reasonably well in hard mud and sandy bottoms. It set fairly quickly and under most circumstances held reasonably well. It tended to plow through the softer substrates, and thus did not have optimal holding characteristics in soft or muddy bottoms. It reset itself after major wind shifts, but it did so after appearing to have pulled out (we could tell by the fact that our vessel was not where we would have expected it to be). The anchor has a tendency to 'snake' across the bottom, pulling out and resetting along the way. Compared with the newer anchor designs, the flukes were relatively small. Consequently, the weight required was considerably higher than other anchor types.

The CQR is still one of the most popular anchors among cruising sailors. In the Seven Seas Cruising Association ongoing online equipment survey, with more than 1300 responses as of early 2011, 32% reported using a "hinged plow" [CQR and its clones] as the primary and another 18% used the same as the secondary anchor. So, about half of SSCA members who responded relied on a CQR. By May 2017, with 2069 members weighing in, 30% still had a hinged plow on the bow, and another 19% had it as their secondary.

In a survey of the Ocean Cruising Club – among the most adventurous and experienced sailors in the world – in 2008, 87% of their members responding to a survey reported using the CQR as their primary anchor. By 2016, only 19.8% said they still carried a CQR as the primary bower anchor.

Anchor preferences seem to be evolving.

It is interesting to note that in surveys and on forums there are many verbatim mentions of the CQR as being an excellent anchor with the qualification that "in X-years of cruising, we've only dragged Y-times". In our opinion, given the performance of some of today's new anchors, dragging any number of times does not make for a great anchor or a good night's sleep. In our experience, in almost every case where a boat dragged anchor in our time cruising North America, Europe, the Caribbean and North Atlantic islands, the anchor in use was the CQR. We too dragged once – right into a mooring field. And that is why we replaced our CQR. You can pick one up relatively inexpensively at boat jumbles around the world.

Manson Plough

The Manson Plough is one of many CQR copies. Manson began manufacturing the Plough anchor in 1972. Since then it has become popular in the Australasia region as an all-purpose anchor. Manson specifies that is built tough to withstand the rigors of cruising in the Southern Ocean. The Manson Plough is certified by Lloyds Register as an HHP (High Holding Power) anchor.

Lalizas Plow Anchor CQR

Manufactured in Greece, this hot dipped galvanized CQR copy anchor is reasonably priced.

Hooking Gear ⚓ Anchors

Plastimo Soc®

Plastimo manufactures an anchor that also looks much like a CQR under the brand name Soc. It is a hinged plow anchor, available in hot dipped galvanized and in 316L stainless.

The Delta™

The Simpson-Lawrence Delta anchor, also now available from Lewmar, is another plow-style anchor which was originally developed as an advance over the anchors used for floating systems such as oil rigs. The Delta has a much higher fluke area to weight ratio than the CQR which is extremely important in delivering holding power. Once an anchor is set, it is the amount of seabed above it that determines how well it holds. So it stands to reason that a larger fluke area will deliver more holding. Also, compared to the CQR's massive shank, the Delta's much flatter shank causes less resistance when it buries into the bottom.

The Delta has a one-piece design with no hinge which delivers simplicity in function. The high-grade manganese steel used in its construction gives it maximum tensile strength. Because of the shape of the plow, its shank profile and ballasted tip, the Delta anchor is self-launching, which is a minimum requirement for any modern anchor. Once on the bottom it usually turns straight up and sets in its own length. The large throat dimension, sharp shank, and linear nature of the force on the tip allow this anchor to penetrate weeds, sand, shells and grass. Like all plow-type anchors it is less effective in soft or muddy bottoms.

The Delta is relatively easy to stow. It has no moving parts, no screws, no pins, and no structural issues. Based upon the manufacturer's information, a 22-pound Delta has the same holding power as a 45-pound CQR.

Over many years of use, our Delta shows no signs of wear or deterioration. It is guaranteed for life against breakage and recognized by Lloyd's as a High Holding Power anchor.

For storage it disassembles easily and there is even an available custom padded storage bag complete with tools to assemble and disassemble the anchor.

As it does go deep, the Fortress can be hard to free from the bottom. As a result, the flukes can be bent if force is applied in the wrong direction, as may occur if you try to free it from the bottom by powering forward – something one should never do anyway regardless of the anchor in use (except the Super SARCA and other slotted anchors). The Fortress comes with a lifetime parts replacement warranty should anything get damaged or bent. The Fortress is both American Bureau of Shipping (ABS) and DNV (Det Norske Veritas) certified as a Super High Holding Power anchor.

The Guardian is a less expensive utility version of the Fortress. Both are manufactured by Fortress Marine Anchors headquartered in Fort Lauderdale, Florida.

Other Fluke Anchors

There are countless other brand named and generic fluke anchors. The Manson Racer was designed specifically for racing sailboats and provides guidelines for matching the anchor requirements of racing rules. The stockless Britany® and the FOB, which has a stock are French versions and are quite common throughout Europe. The stockless Jambo anchor is made in Austria and has sharpened tips on its flukes for penetrating hard bottoms.

Hooking Gear ⚓ Anchors

The stockless navy style fluke anchors like the Manson Kedge are popular on mega yachts and large ships as they can be hauled up until they rest with their shank in the hawse pipe and the flukes against the hull or inside a recess in the hull.

Some additional fluke anchors without stocks

Brittany

Manson
Kedge

Jambo anchor

Some additional fluke anchors with stocks

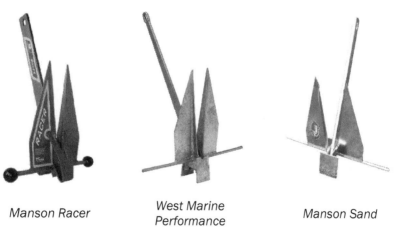

Manson Racer

West Marine
Performance

Manson Sand

and hot dip galvanized. The Super MAX is available with either a rigid or a pivoting shank, the latter enabling the angle to be changed for different bottom types.

The Super MAX fluke is said to be larger than similar sized anchors. It is an easy setting anchor and is reported to obtain "unsurpassed" holding performance. The anchor was designed to be most effective in soft ooze, mud, and sand. Super MAX anchors have a limited lifetime warranty.

Flook

Although it is virtually unknown outside of Australia, the Flook (flying hook) anchor made by Dulmison Marine in Australia is an interesting addition to the claw types. It is designed to be launched folded and will fly away from the boat through the water when you throw it forward. When you jerk the line, it unfolds and engages the bottom. It is designed to be used with an all rope rode. Our own tests have confirmed that it does actually fly away from the boat.

The Flook can be a useful anchor for kedging, for seaplanes and for small vessels wishing to remain securely set over a fixed point. It is ideal for holding a vessel off a wharf, jetty or mooring piles. It also enables the setting of a second (stern) anchor without deploying the dinghy.

Anchorlift XR and CX Anchors

Both the XR and CX from Anchorlift are claw anchors. The CX is close to the original Bruce design but the XR is a departure. It has a short claw that enables it to sit as close to the bow as possible. It has only about 60% of the weight of the Bruce and is intended for sport fishing boats which require as little weight in the bow as possible. Both have a Limited Lifetime Warranty.

Hooking Gear ⚓ Anchors

Scoop-type Anchors

The scoop anchors are a design innovation introduced in 1996 by Frenchman Alain Poiraud. His Spade anchor represents one of the true breakthrough anchor design advancements in the last decades. The scoop anchors are shaped like a shovel with a concave fluke. Remove a shovel's handle and add an anchor shank and you have a scoop type anchor. Just like a shovel is designed to dig, so it is with a scoop anchor – it digs. If you apply more pressure (pull harder), it digs deeper. They have caught on fairly quickly. In 2016, almost half of the Ocean Cruising Club members who responded to an anchoring survey reported having a scoop type anchor as their primary.

The scoop anchors are versatile and appropriate for use in many bottom types. As a group they are fast setting. Scoop anchors are designed to dig deeply into the bottom and are unlikely to roll out during a reversal. Being solidly constructed, the scoop-type anchors, as a group, are on the heavier side.

Such a deep-setting anchor must fulfill several additional criteria to ensure high holding. The anchor must be stable, must not break-free in rotation, and the shape must allow the evacuation of materials backwards as it digs deeper. If not, in certain bottom types a scoop-type anchor might conceivably become clogged and then break out by shearing out of the ground. Having used several different scoop type anchors over many years, we have not seen any of these problems. In fact, the harder the wind blows, the deeper we see them dig even with reversal of wind or current direction.

This anchor design introduces some challenges. As they set deep, they can be hard to retrieve.[1] They also tend to come up with so much muck in their fluke that they can be difficult to weigh without a windlass. A wash-down hose or multiple buckets of water are, therefore, necessary to clean it all off. Frankly, it's a price we are more than willing to pay to keep our boat secure.

Another interesting dilemma created by the exceptional holding power of these scoop type anchors are the "snatch loads" created when a boat yaws or rises and falls with the waves – a problem not experienced to the same extent with plow type anchors. Snatch loads are sudden sharp impacts on not just the anchor but the associated gear. Including deck hardware. It is thus critical to use snubbers[2] and reduce yawing as much as possible.

Good features
- Set rapidly in almost any bottom; sharp tip cuts into seabed, even weed
- Dig deep for excellent holding power
- Relatively easy to stow on bow roller

Things to consider
- Anchors set deep and may be hard to retrieve, realistically best handled with a windlass or capstan
- Anchors and rode bring up loads of seabed when retrieved

---

[1] Please see the chapter on anchor retrieval on how to easily overcome this.

[2] Please see chapter on rode selection for a discussion on snubbers.

Hooking Gear ⚓ Anchors

The Spade

The Spade anchor has been well accepted since its introduction in 1996. It is manufactured in three materials (galvanized steel, aluminum, and stainless steel). The Spade is manufactured by Sea Tech & Fun, a Tunisian company. It was

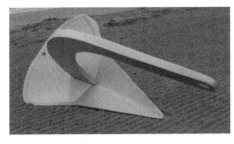

designed and developed by biomedical engineer Alain Poiraud (Hylas) who passed away in February 2011. It has a concave shape and large surface area, which together compact the substrate providing high holding power. It has a hollow shaft that is designed to orient the anchor correctly as it hits the bottom. It is a relatively easily set anchor with a highly weighted tip that digs in quickly.

The Spade has several patented design innovations. An angled ballast chamber ensures optimum penetrating angle every time and best possible weight distribution. The hollow triangular shank profile is strong without upsetting weight distribution. The concave blade (double concave form is patented) delivers 'optimum' holding power, and the 'ears' prevent blade edge penetration.

The Spade is self-launching and it fits snugly on most bow rollers, presenting a rounded forward surface. The Spade disassembles for more compact storage. It can be easily dismantled into shank and body for transport. As a result, it is

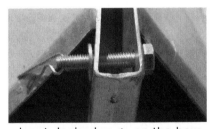

conceivably prone to coming apart when least desired, e.g., on the bow roller or while anchored. To avoid this, the manufacturer recommends replacing the self-locking nut each time it is disassembled. We recently spoke with one Spade owner who reuses the nut time and again, but we would not recommend taking such a chance.

Roll Bar Scoop-type Anchors

These anchors are similar to the above scoop-type anchors with the addition of a roll bar which helps orient the anchor so that it always lands correctly and digs in quickly. The roll bar is often credited  to Rolf Kaczirek the manufacturer of the Bügel, but it was actually patented by Peter Bruce in 1973.

Like the other scoop anchors, the roll bar scoops set quickly and easily. Given adequate scope, our experience has shown that the harder you pull on them the deeper they dig.

One caveat has been pointed out with regards to the roll bar. If the anchor lands upside down in soft mud, the roll bar may do nothing to right the anchor, and the anchor may neither set nor hold. This is something we have not yet experienced.

Good features
- Roll bar makes it orient and set readily
- Very good holding power in virtually all bottoms
- Will not roll out during reversal
- No moving parts, stow readily on bow roller

Things to consider
- Breaking out can be difficult
- Bring up loads of muck - need windlass and wash down system
- Roll-bar may interfere with bow platforms or bowsprits
- If the anchor lands upside down in soft mud the roll bar may not do anything.

Hooking Gear ⚓ Anchors

The Bügel

The Bügel was designed and
manufactured in Germany in the
1980s by three-time circumnavigator
Rolf Kaczirek. It is patented in the US
as an asymmetrical unballasted boat
anchor. The Bügel Anker was the
earliest of the modern era anchors
and is indeed still a popular anchor in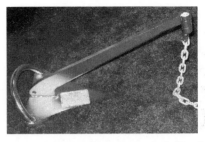
Europe. Interestingly, the Bügel was never properly commercialized
elsewhere.

The Bügel sports a simple design with no moving parts, a straight shank,
and a flat blade. Technically it is thus not really a scoop type anchor. The
flat shape of the blade is less efficient than a concave scoop shape. It
was the first of the scoop-types to adopt a roll bar (i.e., Bügel, German
for bow) in its design for proper orientation on the bottom.

Since its introduction, the Bügel has been in service worldwide and
proven to be a good all-around anchor. The ability to quickly set and hold
even in poor holding sea bottoms such as mud, clay, shale, gravel, rock
and grass is its most appreciated strong point. The ergonomics of the
compact design facilitates easy handling.

The roll bar helps it orient itself readily. The sharp point offers the quick
penetration of a plow. It has little tip weight, however, and the flat one-
piece blade does not confer maximum holding power. There is an
attachment hole in the shank for a shackle to a tandem anchor or a trip
line. Stowing it on a bow roller may at times be problematic because of
its straight shank and minimal depth between shank and fluke. The
Bügel is certified by Germanischer Lloyd as a High Holding Power (HHP)
anchor.

Bügel anchors are produced commercially by German steel
manufacturer WASI, whose version is available only in 316 stainless,
which is commensurately expensive. As the design is very simple, it is
inexpensive to manufacture and easy to copy. Most Bügel type anchors
today are built by amateurs or one-offs made by metal working shops.
Many of these are of rather dubious nature and quality varies widely.

49

Often, they are not built according to the original patent and lack skids and a reinforcing edge on the fluke. As always, beware of copies without identifiable markings.

The Spoon

A modified Bügel copy, the Spoon is manufactured by Sea Tech & Fun, who also make the Spade. Its differentiating feature is that its fluke is upturned at the crown. The shank is more curved than the Bügel, and this may result in its fitting some bow rollers better. Like the Bügel, it sets fast and holds

well. It is a reasonably priced anchor that should perform reasonably well.

Sea Tech & Fun also sells a Seablade anchor which looks remarkably like a Rocna with a curved shank like the Sword. We have no personal experience with these anchors.

The Rocna

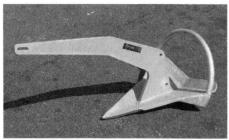

The Rocna anchor was designed by Peter Smith, founding partner of New Zealand's Cavalier Yachts, and adopted the roll bar as a distinct feature of a high-performance anchor. It was the first new scoop anchor to follow after the success of the Spade. In a relatively short period of time, the Rocna gained a favorable worldwide reputation. It is now licensed and manufactured by Canada Metal and is sold worldwide.

The Rocna has no moving parts and is solidly constructed of high strength alloy steel. The solid steel fluke or blade is folded rather than rolled to create its unique shape. This also reinforces the blade to make it highly resistant to bending. The roll bar is hollow pipe to allow weight distribution elsewhere. The shank is cut from high tensile steel which is resistant to bending or twisting. The Rocna undergoes a nine-step anticorrosion process culminating in hot dip galvanizing. It is also available in stainless steel, hand polished to create a lustrous shine.

The roll bar which helps it orient itself readily was derived from the Bügel, but that is where the similarities end. The design is well thought out. The sharp point offers quick penetration and the large concave surface area provides especially good holding power in mud and sand. It consistently sets easily and quickly and likes to go very deep in soft bottoms. It stows readily on the bow roller, although the roll bar may interfere with some bow sprits and pulpits. There are attachment holes in the shank for a shackle and a tandem anchor, as well as in the blade for a trip line.

Our experience is that the Rocna digs deep and holds very well in any type of bottom. We have often found that it does so even where cruising guides state that the holding is poor. As with all of the scoop anchors, the Rocna brings up loads of bottom substrate with it, so both a windlass and a wash-down system are realistically needed. Breaking out can be difficult at times, especially after being anchored in a prolonged blow, as it holds so well.

We have cruised extensively with the Rocna as a primary anchor. In fact, we can recall only one instance of difficulty setting the Rocna, and it was in the outer harbor of a small island well known to be choked with thick weed. In fact, we brought up bucketsful of weed with the anchor and decided to grab a mooring that day instead.

We have found the Rocna to be an extremely reliable storm anchor. We spent two days anchored off a remote island in a gale with consistent 50 knot winds, gusting much higher, with no movement of the boat. The only difficulty was retrieval of the anchor afterwards. The chain had been buried to a depth of at least 20 feet and it eventually came up loaded with mud. It took a long time to retrieve the anchor and clean up. Staying put was worth every ounce of effort. We concur with the independent test results and with the blog reports that the Rocna is one of best all-around anchor choices.[5]

---

[5] There have been some reports of the Rocna not resetting under certain conditions. Please see the appendix for more information.

In 2011, Rocna anchors suffered a setback after manufacture of the anchors was moved from New Zealand to China. Allegations surfaced that Hold Fast, the company with the manufacturing rights to the Rocna, had used steel in the fabrication of the anchors shanks that did not meet the stated manufacturing specification. Some of the photos spread around the internet were genuine photos of warranty claims while others were of dubious origin. Consumers and competitors jumped on the bandwagon to condemn Rocna. West Marine issued a 'product specification notice' and offered to refund the purchase price to any owners with concerns. Shortly afterwards, Canada Metal Pacific (CMP) acquired the rights from Hold Fast, moved the manufacturing to Canada and settled all of the only nine warranty claims for bent shanks submitted by 2012, of more than 12,000 Rocna anchors reportedly in use. The faulty anchors turned out to be early prototype anchors that were made for testing in China and somehow got out into the market. No problems have been reported since.

Recently, reports have surfaced infrequently describing situations when the Rocna could pull out and not reset. Steve Goodwin from s/v *Panope* videotaped a series of anchor tests in which the anchors were put to extreme reversal. He posted these on YouTube. When the Rocna pulled out it remained full of substrate and did not reset. Practical Sailor reported a similar result. We have never had this experience because the Rocna has never pulled out in our experience. The only time we could even speculate being in a situation where it might pull out is if the seas in the anchorage were so extreme that the vessel would be bucking dangerously enough to lift the anchor. We have thankfully not been subjected to such conditions.

RINA (Registro Italiano Navale) has awarded the Rocna a Super High Holding Power (SHHP) classification. Its facilities are RINA approved and individual anchor certification can be provided on request.

Hooking Gear ⚓ Anchors

The Manson Supreme

In many ways, the Manson Supreme, manufactured in New Zealand, appears and performs very similar to the Rocna.[6] The Manson Supreme is available in galvanized and stainless steel, and in standard sizes ranging from 5lb to 400lb with larger custom sizing available.

This anchor has two 'slots' for attachment of the shackle. The much smaller 'sand slot' is used for all bottom types except for rock and coral (not that anyone should be anchoring in live coral). The upper 'rock slot' enables the shackle to slide up the anchor to where a trip line would normally reside thereby allowing you to free the anchor if it gets caught. The 'rock slot' could be a bit of a concern where a shift in wind could result in the shackle sliding to the shank and pulling the anchor out just when you least want it to do so.[7] In our experience, it is not unusual to encounter unexpected radical wind shifts. We would, therefore, recommend against using this long slot for overnight anchoring or if leaving the boat unattended even for a short amount of time. As a slot might also weaken the shank, the Manson Supreme has a strengthened high tensile steel shank to overcome this concern.

The fixed shank and scoop fluke are intended to dig deep. The spear head and winglets help the anchor dig into hard substrates and set quickly. It is reported to engage the bottom immediately and holds well in comparative tests. Lloyd's Register EMEA has approved a Super High Holding Power (SHHP) rating for this anchor.

---

[6] See appendix for more information on the Supreme not resetting on reversal under some conditions
[7] See note on Slots and Holes below.

The Mantus

The Mantus Anchor is an interesting addition to the roll bar scoop type anchors. We found it to set and hold very well, as would be expected. It is manufactured in China from A36 carbon steel. The  nose is machined out of a solid block. It has no welds, is 3/4-inch-thick and is bolted so it can break down for easy storage. Mantus Anchors are guaranteed for life against any faults in materials or manufacturing, including galvanization. If the anchor is bent or deformed, this is not considered regular wear and tear, and the manufacturer will replace the anchor.

Perhaps the biggest difference between the Mantus and all the other roll bar scoop type anchors is that it can be disassembled into three parts for easier storage. This is a very interesting attribute that we as cruisers really appreciate. The only other disassemble-able scoop type anchor that we are aware of is the Spade. Another differentiation is that the roll bar is attached to wings (ears) that extend out laterally from the anchor blade. This gives the roll bar a wider arc, presumably to increase its righting ability. We once had our rode get caught under the 'wings' as our boat swung around in shifty light air conditions. The chiseled tip of the blade is thickened to give it a bit more weight, though the manufacturer has not gone quite as far as the Spade or Ultra with their heavily lead-weighted tips.

The only criticisms we had is that the provided nuts were not self-locking (Nyloc). That has changed since we wrote to the manufacturer; they now recommend always use locking washers, or nylon lock nuts, and tightening the nut securely. Additionally, the bolts are not drilled and pinned (see Spade experience). So, care should be given, and the bolts should be inspected prior to each use of the anchor.

Hooking Gear ⚓ Anchors

Knox Anchor

The Knox anchor recently crossed our bow. On first glance, it would appear to be a cross between a fluke type anchor and a roll-bar scoop. However, as the flukes are not hinged and the overall design is very much a scoop, we have included it here.

The Knox anchor is a very interesting looking design by the late Professor John Knox of Scotland applying over 20 years of accumulated research. Prof. Knox developed a rigorous testing method to assess anchor performance and has written many published articles on the subject.

The patented divided fluke is the key design feature responsible for the Knox Anchor's high holding power. The fluke's sharpened edges are arranged at the optimal angle to ensure rapid chisel-like engagement with the seabed. The flukes are constructed of high tensile steel, greater than 350MPa and reinforced by stiffener plates to provide high resistance to bending. The shank is made from 900 MPa steel; a very high strength rolled quenched and tempered steel. This has been used to ensure that the shank will not bend in a wind or current shift – as has been seen to happen with other anchors.

As with other roll bar type anchors, the roll bar ensures that when the anchor is lowered to the seabed it always settles with the tip of one of the half-flukes bearing on the seabed, at the right orientation for immediate engagement and burial. The flanges encourage immediate engagement and ensure that the anchor does not roll out even when forced to plough through the seabed by excessive force.

For its stated holding-power, it is on the lighter weight side and boasts a higher holding force per unit weight than any other comparable anchor design.

Some Other Anchors

XYZ Extreme® Anchors

The XYZ Extreme, developed by Dragomir Ivicevic, an industrial design architect, looks like it deserves an award from the Museum of Modern Art. In the company's own words, "The XYZ Extreme anchor has stunning appearance."

The XYZ is a departure from conventional anchor design. It has a disproportionally large fluke and a short strong shank that is affixed relatively close to the sharp saw-like tip of the fluke. It is said to break hard surfaces and set deep in a short distance.

The XYZ is reported to veer around a 360-degree arc without breaking out. It appears to perform best in soft bottoms according to a 2008 report in *Practical Sailor*. In some other comparative tests, it has not performed as well (see later section).

The XYZ enables choice of a fluke made of 316L stainless steel or of light marine grade aluminum (3/8"/10mm solid machined plate) that could be exchanged in minutes. The shank is a mirror polished 2205 stainless steel in both cases.

The 6th generation of XYZ Extreme boat anchors has a saw cutting blade that is machined with precision from an ultra-hard solid plate of a 17-4PH stainless steel. This metal is used by US Navy, NASA and in the aerospace industry for demanding applications. Very high yield strength can be achieved. The XYZ claims that the 'Cutting Edge' enables penetration through hard bottoms including slippery weeds, coral, small rocks etc. But the XYZ has a Lifetime Limited Warranty against breakage only when used in seabed such as sand, mud clay and other soft bottoms. The guarantee does not apply to use on rocks and hard sea bottoms or lack of proper assembling and is limited to repair or replacement of parts of the boat anchor or of the complete boat anchor.

Hooking Gear & Anchors

The Bulwagga

The Bulwagga was an interesting design by
Peter Mele of Crown Point, NY. It was designed
to dig into heavy weed bottoms of Lake
Champlain. It is no longer in production.

The symmetrical three fluke configuration
ensures the anchor lands in perfect
deployment position every time it reaches the bottom. Once on the
bottom the pivoting shank adjusts itself to the correct angle of pull. A
pull on the rode shifts the anchor onto the leading edges of two flukes.
This anchor surprised many in its reliability.

Box Anchor

The Box Anchor is a design from Slide
Anchor Company in Arizona. The Box
Anchor folds flat for storage then quickly
pops open into an box configuration with
four flukes on two sides and a securing
pin that holds it open. The manufacturer
claims that it requires no chain and only
a 2 to 1 scope (approximately a 45
degree rode angle). There is no skill
involved, just toss it overboard.

It is reported to set quickly into
any bottom type in one foot. If
there is a reversal of wind and
tide, the rode passing over it
pulls the anchor out, flips it
onto its other side, and resets it again. It is now sold for use on a lake or
ocean bottom and for anchoring houseboats as well as pleasure craft.
We are not aware of any independent reviews of its performance.

Summary of the Characteristics of Major Anchor Categories

	Hook	Plough	Fluke	Claw	Scoop	Rollbar-Scoop
Best for Bottom Type	Rocks	Hard sand, shell, shingle, weed	Soft Sand, Soft Mud	Soft Sand and mud, hard sand and mud	Most bottom types	Most bottom types
Examples of Brands	Fisherman, Luke, Herreshoff, Kingston, Kedge, Grapnel	C.Q.R., Delta, Hydrobubble, Brake, Sarca, Kobra, Pro Plow, Manson Plough, Cooper	Danforth, Fortress, West Marine Performance, Manson Sand, Manson Racer, Guardian, Britany	Bruce, Lewmar Claw, Manson Ray, Super Max, Pro Claw	Spade, Ultra, Vulcan, Sword, Raya, and others	Buegel, Rocna, Manson Supreme, Mantus, and others
General Behavior	Catches well on rock, Useful for kedging, Presents single point	Digs well into hard bottoms, Sets and resets easily	Digs deep into soft bottoms when set well, Light weight, High efficiency, Launches well, Stows flat	Highest percentage set on first attempt, One piece construction	Cuts and sets well in most bottoms, Digs deep for good holding, Most are easy to stowe on bow roller, Will not roll out during reversal	Rollbar orients anchor for easy set, Digs deep, Consistent holding in most bottoms
Consider-ations	May snag rode, Heavy, Low holding, Difficult to handle	Less effective in soft bottoms, Tends to plough, On the heavy side, Hinged variants suject to jamming	Slightly more difficult to set, May not reset on breakout, Hinge prone to jamming, Flukes cn be bent on retrieval	Less holding power for weight, Not effective in weed at rocky bottoms	Anchors and rode bring up loads of muck when retrieved due to deep set, Breaking out can be difficult, Need windlass and wash down system	Anchors and rode bring up loads of muck when retrieved due to deep set, Breaking out can be difficult, Need windlass and wash down system, Roll bar can interfere with bowsprits and platforms

A Note on the Cost of Anchors

Proper Anchor Value

$$pAV = BVB - BVA$$

Where:
1. *pAV - proper anchor value*
2. *BVB - boat value before hitting rocks*
3. *BVA - boat value after hitting rocks*

provided by Tomasz

You've spent a great deal of money on your boat, and when you anchor you are putting your boat and your own safety at stake as well. Shouldn't you buy the best performing anchor you can afford to protect your investment and potentially your life? Just think of your anchor as an insurance policy.

If you have an unlimited budget, you can of course go one step further and acquire the best performing and best-looking anchor for your boat. But if you are on a tight budget and need to compromise, you might forego the beauty options, such as shiny stainless versus galvanized steel. Most anchor manufacturers offer multiple options that can satisfy your budget while providing a quality product you will be able to rely upon for years. Keep in mind that stainless steel, unless of very high quality, is not always corrosion-proof. In prolonged exposure to harsh marine conditions, stainless steel can succumb to rust which may weaken the structure. Stain-less is not always stain-free. Unfortunately, the corrosion may occur in places where it is often not easy to spot.

Not all anchors that look alike are created equal

In several of the online discussions boards we have followed over the years, we have seen people balk at the price of a given anchor, opting instead for a cheaper knock-off. Quality does count and, when you think about the total value of your life, your boat, and all your gear on board, a good quality anchor is certainly worth the money you pay for it.

As the skipper of the boat, your family and your crew depend on you to make the best decisions for their comfort and safety. If you are out cruising or plan to, you'll be spending more time at anchor than sailing. Your per failure cost for a cheap anchor will far outweigh your per use cost for a great anchor. And, of course, peace of mind is priceless.

We mentioned earlier that boaters should beware of cheap imitations. We once snagged something huge (or were the victims of an anchor-eating monster of the deep) and had to cut away our trusty Fortress anchor. We replaced it with another fluke-type anchor that came with our boat. It was somewhat larger and heavier than our original Fortress. It had no markings on it so we could not identify the manufacturer or model.

For some reason, we kept having difficulty setting the anchor when we had never had problems before. We spent a whole season wondering what had happened to our anchoring skills, until we bought a new Fortress. What a difference!

The same thing applies to other anchor types as well. We had a CQR copy that never set in any type of bottom. There are countless Bruce, Spade, and Bügel knock-offs that we have heard simply do not hold.

approval and/or acceptance as a HHP anchor, satisfactory tests are to be made on various types of bottoms, and the anchor is to have a holding power at least twice that of an ordinary stockless anchor of the same weight.

Super high holding power (SHHP) anchors

A super high holding power anchor is an anchor with a holding power of at least four times that of an ordinary stockless anchor of the same mass. A super high holding power anchor does not require prior adjustment or special placement on the sea bed. The SHHP anchor mass should generally not exceed 1500 kg.

Note

Neither HHP nor SHHP is a particularly high standard. An ordinary stockless anchor is extraordinarily inefficient when compared to other types on a weight-for-weight basis. These standards are easily exceeded by most anchors on the market today regardless of whether they have classification or not. Independent tests show a number of modern anchors capable of exceeding even SHHP. That said, the designation does distinguish newer more efficient designs, such as the Spade, Rocna, Manson Supreme, and Ultra, from the older ones, such as CQR (hinged plow) and Bruce (claw), among which the latter, while HHP capable, would not meet the SHHP standard.

One additional designation, the American Bureau of Shipping (ABS) Superior Holding Power (SHP) for restricted service certification, is equal to or greater than the Super High Holding Power (SHHP) certification provided by other classification societies. ABS also provides lists of approved anchor chain and rope manufacturers, as well as rules for just about anything else manufactured for the marine market.

Chapter 6: Anchor Tests

Now that we've studied the intended characteristics of various groups of anchors, let's examine the many independent tests that have been published to compare anchor performance in recent years. It is not our intent to suggest what the best anchor is. We simply would like to help you to better understand how to interpret the published results so you can make some informed decisions about your own situation and what might work best for your boat and cruising territory.

As each boat, sailing territory and crew configuration is different, it is a small wonder that boaters have many opinions about what works best. We try to stay up to date on the latest "anchor news" because reports of anchor failure can be very important to our safety and success in anchoring. We particularly look forward to tests conducted by independent bodies such as *Practical Boat Owner*, Boat US, US Sailing, West Marine, *Practical Sailor/Powerboat Reports,* and American Bureau of Shipping.

Although they are useful in providing comparative data about how different anchors behave relative to one another, the tests cannot be entirely reflective of the true conditions boaters experience out in the real world. By their very nature, they need to be conducted in artificial circumstances to provide measurable results and to be replicable to as great an extent as possible. In fact, every test has to be weighed on its own merit. Conditions vary widely between different places, different conditions on different days, and even different sections of bottom in an anchorage. Then there are the different techniques employed in a given test. Looking closely at all these factors can help us understand why an anchor may have performed radically differently in two seemingly similar tests.

In testing and comparing the performance of anchors, there are two commonly measured and reported variables: setting and holding:

⚓ Setting capacity refers to how quickly and efficiently the anchor catches and buries into the bottom after deployment.

⚓ The holding capacity refers to how much force it takes to cause the anchor to pull out or drag along the bottom.

What is important to note, is that these two performance variables can be very different for the same anchor in different bottom types. Consequently, one anchor may perform better in soft mud, another in hard sand, and still another in rocks or kelp beds.

Because different bottoms have different characteristics, such tests should be repeated in different places with different bottom compositions to be valid. It makes sense that a hard bottom may be more difficult to grab, but once an anchor does dig in it may hold well. A muddy bottom might be easier to set in but more difficult to hold; and pretty much anything should sink into a soft muddy bottom, but will it hold? Each bottom has its own unique characteristics. Even different types of mud and sand can act differently. Mississippi mud may act differently from Long Island Sound mud or San Francisco Bay mud or Mediterranean mud. That is what makes it so interesting. So the first place to start when reviewing a new anchor test report is to look at three things:

⚓ What bottom composition are the anchors being tested in?
⚓ What variables are being considered?
⚓ What technique is being used to test the anchors?

Testing became an issue with the proliferation of new anchor designs hitting the market. The early tests were criticized as being unreliable for application to real world conditions as they were often conducted under what was effectively 100:1 scope, using a dynamometer attached via rode to an anchor and hauled by a truck on a beach.

When asked to look at and interpret the results of the early tests, the renowned anchor authority of the time Earl Hinz stated simply, "We don't know everything about anchors yet."

Fortunately, in the time since then, we have learned a great deal and the newer series of tests do much better at simulating conditions expected while boating.

Hooking Gear ⚓ Anchors

European Tests from the 1990s

A typical erroneous, and to this day commonly used, recommendation is to select an anchor solely by its weight. Because of the differing holding characteristics of anchor designs (not even taking bottom type into consideration), one cannot compare the weight of one anchor to another. It is the holding power that must be compared.

This was nicely demonstrated in two highly scientific tests under controlled conditions in the Mediterranean and in Holland conducted in the early 1990s. They were particularly useful in bringing about an understanding that the overall design of an anchor is a more important consideration than just its weight. For example, they showed that a 15 lb Fortress has greater holding power than a CQR or Bruce weighing in at over 40 lbs. The large surface area of the flukes of the Fortress anchor more than make up for its light weight.

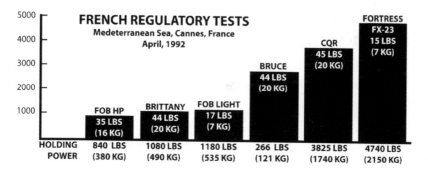

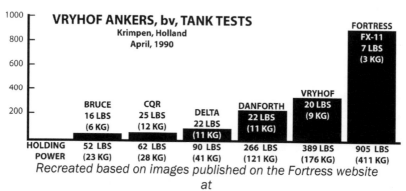

Recreated based on images published on the Fortress website
at
http://www.fortressanchors.com/AnchorTestFrenchHolland.ht

69

Alex & Daria Blackwell

US Tests from the '90s

On June 17 and 18, 1995 the Safety at Sea Committee of the Sailing Foundation conducted anchor tests on five selected sites on Puget Sound.[8] The tests were co-sponsored by West Marine Products and attended by their representative, Chuck Hawley. Also, in attendance were Portland naval architect Robert Smith, who has written about and tested anchor behavior extensively, and Andy Peabody of Creative Marine who manufactured the SuperMax anchor. Diving services and underwater video by Dwayne Montgomery of Emerald City Diving documented the results. US Sailing maintains reports of these tests on its website.

A 5:1 scope was chosen as a constant factor for all tests because it was the standard for a series of tests performed in San Francisco in 1990[9] and the most common standard used by Bob Smith in his Columbia River Tests.[10]

In these tests, two very clear things emerged.

1. The Bruce set the first time almost every time (97%); all the others set at a rate of 55-65% on the first try. The Bruce was, however, the worst ranked in holding power.

2. The Fortress had the highest consistent holding capacity among anchors tested across the range of bottom types. It was, however, among the more difficult to set.

One suggestion they made in their conclusions was that an anchor that is a little more difficult to set may actually set better thus providing better

[8] Safety at Sea Studies. 1995 Anchor Study. Puget Sound.
http://offshore.ussailing.org/Assets/Offshore/SAS+Studies/anchor+study.pdf
[9] Safety at Sea Studies. 1994 San Francisco Anchor Tests.
http://offshore.ussailing.org/Assets/Offshore/SAS+Studies/1994+anchor+test.pdf
Safety at Sea Studies. 1990 Mud Anchor Tests.
http://offshore.ussailing.org/SAS/General_Information/Safety_Studies/Safety_At_Sea_Studies_-_1990_Mud_Anchor_Tests.htm
Safety at Sea Studies. 1990 Sand Anchor Tests.
http://offshore.ussailing.org/SAS/General_Information/Safety_Studies/Safety_At_Sea_Studies_-_1990_Sand_Anchor_Test.htm
[10] Safety at Sea Studies. Portland Oregon Anchor Study. Robert A. Smith.
http://offshore.ussailing.org/SAS/General_Information/Safety_Studies/Safety_At_Sea_Studies_-_Portland__Oregon_Anchor_Study.htm

holding. One should note, however, that these tests preceded the availability of the newer scoop type anchors. Another note was that two anchors, the Luke and Davis, never set completely and, therefore, were not included in further trials of holding capacity.

It is also important to note that the Fortress and the Max sustained significant damage during these tests. Both had their flukes and shank bent. The damage was sustained under conditions that would be generated by a 56-foot boat in 63 knots of wind, conditions for which they would have been significantly undersized.

Summary of performance rank order in independent tests conducted in the 1990s

Rank	Setting+	Holding					
	5:1 Scope	SF Mud+	FL Sand+	Columbia River+	Puget Sound+	Mississippi Mud*
1	Bruce 44	Fortress FX 37	Fortress FX 37	Fortress FX 37	Fortress FX 37	Delta 35
2	Super Max 17	Danforth H33T39	Danforth H1800	Danforth H33T39	West Marine Performance 35	Super Max 17
3	West Marine Performance 35	Danforth Plow 38	CQR 45	Danforth Plow 38	CQR 45	XYZ 17
4	CQR 45	Delta 36	Bruce 44	Delta 36	Super Max 17	Bulwagga 29.5
5	Fortress FX 37	CQR 47		CQR 47	Delta 35	CQR 48
6	Delta 35	Bruce 46		Bruce 46	Bruce 44	Bruce 46.5
7	Luke 50 Slow Drag					
8	Davis 45 Never Set					
+Sailing Foundation/West Marine						
*American Bureau of Shipping Certified but conducted by Creative Marine.						

Further Tests

In tests by Creative Marine in Mississippi Mud in 2003[11] that were certified by ABS, once again the Bruce did not hold very well. But neither did the Spade, the Fortress, nor the Digger. The West Marine Performance (fluke style anchor), the Bruce and the CQR set readily but dragged readily as well. The only anchors that set and held were the Delta, the SuperMax with swivel arm, the XYZ and the Bulwagga. They

---

[11] http://www.creativemarine.com/newprodct/anchor%20test/absreport.htm
http://www.creativemarine.com/newprodct/anchor%20test/soft_mud_bottom_anchor_test.htm

did only one test per anchor, but it was done under very typical conditions with about a 5:1 scope and a vessel powering in reverse after the anchor set under drift in a light breeze.

In several different tests over time, *Practical Sailor* (and sister publication *Powerboat Reports*) rated a large selection of anchors.[12,13,14] In 2001, they compiled the results of multiple tests conducted in different places at different times to provide a "value guide"[15] for anchors, based on both setting and holding performance. In scientific circles, merging unrelated comparisons would be considered an invalid approach and certainly not statistically significant. In cruising circles, however, it is interesting how readily people will latch on to any information they can get their little muddy paws on. They also conducted an anchor reset test at 6:1 or 7:1 scope in sand with the angle of pull changed to 140°.

Not surprisingly, the *Practical Sailor* tests revealed that the Bruce sets well and resets well. The Bruce, which is no longer manufactured for the yachting market, is well known for setting faster than most other older generation anchors, which we have confirmed first hand. However, with its mediocre holding performance, *Practical Sailor* and other authorities advise going a size larger than recommended by the manufacturers of claw type anchors. The Spade, as the only representative of the newer scoop anchors, was rated number one in average holding capacity, followed by the Bulwagga and the CQR. The Spade also did not break out but aligned or veered to the new angle of pull with no movement.

The early tests by *Powerboat Reports* and *Practical Sailor* have been criticized by several anchor manufacturers. They allege that the tests are flawed because they were conducted with an anchor dropped in shallow water close to a beach, with the rode taken to shore and attached to a dynamometer on a truck, resulting in an effective 100:1 scope, not something any boater could ever practically achieve when one considers that a 5:1 scope is a realistic ratio. The mud tests were further criticized for having been conducted in Florida mud, where there is only a thin layer

---

[12] Practical Sailor, The Bruce Anchor Sets Best (Feb 1998), In mud, the CQR and Barnacle Rank at the Top of 17 Anchors (Dec 1999)

[13] Practical Sailor, In sand, the Spade and Bulwagga Rank at the Top of 15 anchors (Jan 1999),

[14] Practical Sailor, In mud, the CQR and Barnacle Rank at the Top of 17 Anchors (Dec 1999)

[15] Practical Sailor, Anchor Reset Tests (Jan 2001)

Hooking Gear ⚓ Anchors

of mud over a lime/coral base. This could explain why the Fortress, which is a true mud anchor, performed poorly.

Later tests took more practical approaches in attempting to simulate many scenarios likely to be encountered by boaters. We have summarized the top results of the *Practical Sailor* published reports in the following table.

Practical Sailor Tests:
Top results in tests conducted over the years

Set in sand[6] Feb 1998: Top 3	Bulwagga	Spade	Bruce
Holding in Sand[7] Jan 1999: Top 3 of 17	Spade	Bulwagga	CQR
Holding in Mud[8] Dec 1999: Top 3 of 17	CQR	Barnacle	Spade
Reset in sand/Mud[9] Jan 2001: Top 3	Spade	Bulwagga	CQR
Set & Hold in soft mud[16] Feb & April 2006: 2 parts Price (3:1,7:1)	XYZ >$200 Claw < $200	Bulwagga Bruce	Davis Talon Danforth/ Performance
Adjustable anchors in soft mud, Oct 2006	Fortress	SuperMax Pivoting	Spade Sword

---

[16] Practical Sailor. Soft Mud Anchors for $200 or less. Part II. April 2006

In Mud Jan 2008:[17] 2 new anchors	Ultra	XYZ Extreme	
Soft over hard sand [18] 12 anchors (Scope 4:1, 7-8:1)	Fortress Efficiency* 50	Spade 80 Efficiency 28.1	Bulwagga Efficiency 22
Extreme Conditions**[19] Nov 2008: 3 anchors	Manson Ray – Best choice	Rocna – Recommended	Manson Supreme – Budget Buy
"Real World"[20] Dec 2008: 3 anchors 1 boat	Manson Ray	Rocna	Manson Supreme
*Efficiency defined as maximum load pressure recorded divided by measured anchor weight. **Short scope (2:1) and Bad bottom (Rock over sand/gravel) also tested at 10:1 scope.			

Of interest are some of the later reports from 2008 onward when the newer generation scoop type anchors started gaining prominence. These included the Spade, the Rocna, the Ultra, and the Manson Supreme. None of those tests, however, truly compared these new anchors to each other in direct trials under normal conditions. *Practical Sailor* concluded that you can't go wrong with the newer designs, even under extreme conditions.

Perhaps the most comprehensive of the independent tests to date was conducted by West Marine in cooperation with *SAIL Magazine*,[21]

---

[17] Practical Sailor, Three new anchors throw their weight into the Practical Sailor Chronicles. January 2008.
[18] Practical Sailor.
[19] Practical Sailor, Rock and Roll. PS *takes heavy-duty roll-bar and Bruce-style anchors to the extreme.* November 2008. p 34.
[20] Practical Sailor, Hooked in the Real World. December 2008, p32
[21] Sail Magazine, Holding Power. October 2006

Hooking Gear ⚓ Anchors

Yachting Monthly,[22] and *Power & Motoryacht*[23] in 2006. It included 14 contemporary and classic anchor designs and showed that the best setting and holding characteristics are now being demonstrated by the newer anchors such as the Rocna and Manson Supreme, with the Spade, Delta and Fortress still right up there in the rankings.

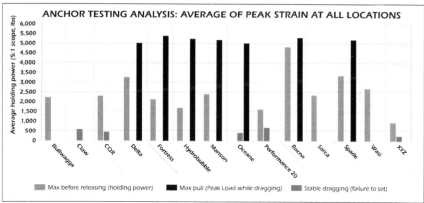

Tests conducted by West Marine produced interesting results with 14 anchors tested on a hard sand bottom. Published in Sail Magazine October 2006 and reproduced with permission.

They first tested maximum pull before an anchor released and maximum pull while dragging through the hard sand bottom. They reported stable dragging for anchors that never held.

Of the more popular anchors, the CQR and Claw did not perform well at all. Surprisingly, the XYZ did not fare any better than the CQR whereas it had been *Practical Sailor's* top pick in a test a short while earlier. The Bulwagga also performed better in the *PS* test.[24] West Marine's own Performance 20 fared poorly.

The Rocna performed best in this series. It had the highest maximum holding power (before releasing). The Manson Supreme, Hydrobubble, Spade, Fortress, and Delta all performed admirably. Although they released earlier than the Rocna, they still provided a significant peak load while dragging. The others pulled out when they released but did

---

[22] Yachting Monthly, Ultimate Holding Power. December 2006

[23] Power and Motoryacht, Anchors Aweigh February 2007

[24] This only brings us back to stressing that no tests are all encompassing or totally conclusive.

reproduced the same report in English.[27] More interesting were the results when the angle of pull changed by either 70 degrees or 180. The anchors fell into two categories: those that dug deeper when the angle changed or those that could not continue to hold when the angle changed. Newer designs generally outperformed older versions, even when the angle of pull was changed by 70 or 180 degrees. The Spade, Kobra 2, Manson, and Bügel all proved excellent choices. There was a concern expressed about the Manson slot under reversing conditions.[28] Once again, anchors that had not performed well in the West Marine trials were underperforming in the French trials as evidenced in this statement: "The CQR's results in this test were so astonishingly poor that we wondered if they sent us a faulty one."

Another German test studied 10 anchors in bottom conditions that ranged from soft sand, to sand and mud, and a cruddy combination of sand, mud, shells and weed.[29] The Kobra 2 and Manson Supreme once again proved worthy selections, while the Rocna and Bügel copy did not quite match up. The same test was reported in *Boote* in October of the same year.[30]

In Italian tests[31] of the newest generation anchors in a variety of substrates, the Brake and Spade were top performers in all types of bottoms tested. The Supreme and Rocna, though solid performers, were deemed slightly less desirable because of the roll bar. The XYZ and SARCA were poor performers in this series.

Italian Tests of the Newest Generation Anchors as reported in Vela, May 2009

Anchor	Rating
Spade	*****
Brake	*****
Rocna	****
Supreme	****
XYZ	**
Sarca	**

---

[27] *Yachting Monthly*, Which Anchor is Best? November 2009
[28] See our note Part 1 Chapter 2: Slots and attachment holes in anchors
[29] *Yacht Skippers Magazin*, Ankertest Vertrauensfrage. August 2009
[30] *Boote*, Von Grundstucken und Haltungsnoten. October 2009
[31] *Vela*, Ancore di nuova generazione. May 2009

Hooking Gear ⚓ Anchors

Practical Boat Owner published an interesting article by Professor John Knox, a physical chemist, now-retired and sailing the coast of Scotland.[32] His interest in anchor performance started with a storm he encountered while at anchor in 1988. In 1993, with the help of Dr. Kevin Scott, an electronics expert, Dr. Knox invented the Anchorwatch. It measures anchor cable tension, remembers maximum load, and sounds an alarm when a preset load value is exceeded. They sold about 50 of these gizmos before deciding the market was not sizable enough. But the device used on his own boat allowed him to collect a substantial amount of data. So armed with this scientific evidence, Dr. Knox set out to measure the Ultimate Holding Capacity (UHC), which is the metric applied to oil rig anchors and in recent magazine anchor tests, to evaluate how recent anchor types fare against more traditional designs.

Dr. Knox then devised an anchor test to measure the UHC, the force at which an anchor breaks out from the seabed, the Dynamic Holding Force (DHF) or resistance the anchor offers as it starts dragging until it pulls out, and the Static Holding Force (SHF) the tension when the anchor is static but just about to drag. Finally, he calculated the efficiency of the anchor defined as the UHC divided by the weight of the anchor. The anchors were tested in medium-hard sand in the Firth of Forth in Scotland.

Consistent with prior independent tests, the newer anchors, Spade, Rocna, and Manson Supreme, performed significantly better than the older CQR and Bruce style anchors. The Spade and Rocna had efficiency ratings of about 30 while the heavier Manson Supreme had a normalized efficiency of 21. All three anchors engaged the bottom immediately and were recommended by the author. The Delta was shown to be a reliable anchor with an efficiency of 11 for the larger models. The CQR and Bruce delivered efficiencies of between 3.5 and 9 and were hard to engage in hard sea bed.

---

[32] Anchors on Test. *Practical Boat Owner* 538 August 2011, p.81-87.

Summary table of UHC values and efficiencies of anchors Anchors from 4-22 kg weight, tested in medium-hard sand at Gosford Bay, Firth of Forth					
Anchor type and nominal weight	Actual weight (kg)	Fluke area, sq dm	UHC normalized to 120 kgf for 5.1kg Spade	Efficiency = UHC/Weight	Initial engagement with hard sand/mud
6kg Spade	5.1	4.5	120 (mean of 9 tests)	24	Excellent
15kg Spade	13.3	8.4	420	32	Excellent
9lb Delta	4.1	4.6	34	8	Moderate
15lb Delta	6.7	6.3	76 (3 tests)	11	Moderate
35lb Delta	16.3	11.4	186	11	Good
15lb CQR (dug in by hand)	6.7	4.4	68 (2 tests)	10	Dug in by hand
15lb CQR (laid on side)	6.7	4.4	44 (maximum SHF)	7	Dragged on surface
45lb CQR (laid on side)	21.5	9.6	175 (maximum SHF)	8	Poor - eventually after 2m initial drag
5kg Bruce	5.8	3.6	35	6	Dragged on surface
15kg Bruce	16.1	5.9	80	5	Not tested
5kg Atlantic (Claw)	4.9	3.3	43 (2 tests)	9	Dragged on surface
15kg Marathon (Claw)	14.2	6	50	3.5	Not tested
15lb Manson Supreme	7.3	5.3	90 (3 tests)	12	Excellent
25lb Manson Supreme	10.7	9.5	225	21	Not tested
5kg Rocna	4.1	4.6	85 (3 tests)	21	Excellent
15kg Rocna	16.2	10.3	480	30	Not tested

Anchors on Test. Practical Boat Owner August 2011.
Reproduced with permission.

Dr Knox notes, "...when the CQR anchor is forced to plow it rolls out sequentially while executing a serpentine track. This could be extremely serious in conditions when the anchor is working at the limit of its holding." This corroborates our own experience with the CQR. One can observe such serpentine tracks in many anchorages.

The same study tracked what the author calls a Static Holding Force: the 45 lb. CQR snaked and rolled, never exceeding a normalized holding of 175 kgf, while the smaller Rocna 15 (33 lb.) set and buried quickly as its holding climbed steadily toward 480 kgf. This illustrates the chief difference between the newer anchors which keep digging under load and the older plow type anchors which set and reset until they hit maximum and release.

Hooking Gear ⚓ Anchors

Distance Ploughed, meters

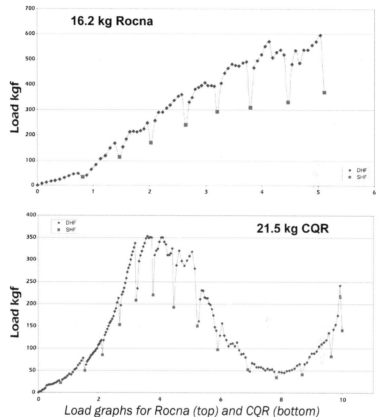

Load graphs for Rocna (top) and CQR (bottom)
The dipped points track the Static Holding Force (SHF) for each anchor: the CQR snakes and rolls unstably, never exceeding a normalized SHF of 175 kgf, while the smaller Rocna sets and buries quickly as its SHF climbs inexorably toward a normalized SHF of about 480 kgf.

Dr. Knox concluded when looking back on the original storm that prompted a lifetime of investigations, "we would have been much safer had we been able to use modern anchors. A 15-kg Spade or Rocna, or a 20-kg Manson Supreme, would have achieved the same result" [as a 15 kg Bruce and a 16 kg CQR set together].

Catamarans and snatch loads

A series of tests conducted in Australia [and subsequently published also in *Practical Sailor* (May 2012)] using a catamaran (Lightwave 10.5m – 38ft) is the only anchoring study of which we are aware that documented a catamaran's behavior at anchor. In a field study, multiple anchors were tested relative to load generated by wind in an anchorage. The maximum loads decreased with increasing scope — this we would expect. The load generally stayed below 700 pounds at the scope normally recommended for anchoring (at least 7:1). But at low scope ratios, slightly less than 3:1, maximum loads were observed which topped 1400 pounds at 23 knots.

Moreover, virtually all of the peak loads were temporary shock loads caused as the boat veered in the wind, which could potentially pull an anchor out. These peak loads were most pronounced with the newer anchors which dig deeply and tend not to move. We've noticed this jerking motion, both side to side and forward and back, on catamarans as they surge at anchor. This snatch load can have a seriously negative effect on deck hardware. As the scope increased, the peak snatch loads decreased, until at 10:1 scope they calculated that it would have almost disappeared.

It was calculated that the load of the 38-foot catamaran would be equivalent to a 45-foot production sloop and, therefore, an anchor chosen solely on the basis of boat length might be undersized for the load generated by a catamaran.

Read more at: http://www.mysailing.com.au/news/testing-the-new-generation-of-anchors

Veering tests

Interestingly, the best performing anchors in veering tests of 90 and 180 degrees have been the Ultra, Spade, and Kobra – all of which have wing-like protrusions. It is thought these winglets help to stabilize the anchor in the substrate. Our personal experience with an Ultra anchor in a 30-

knot sustained wind is that the anchor completely disappears along with the first few feet of chain. It veers without pulling out, digging deeper with increasing wind speed. In contrast, most plow anchors sit closer to the surface.

You may be aware of the excellent work of Steve Goodwin on s/v *Panope*. He has done an extensive series of anchor tests by rigging up a waterproof video camera in such a way that it allows the viewer to see exactly how an anchor sets and resets (or not) under water. He used 2.5:1 and 3.5:1 scope (rather minimal by our standards), set the anchor simulating emergency conditions, and then reversed it by 180 degrees. He has posted these videos -- many hours of testing -- on YouTube.

In one of his tests, he demonstrated that the Rocna does not reset under certain conditions, which corroborates anecdotal reports appearing on forums (see prior discussion of Rocna anchor). Only four anchors made it past this reset test without any issues: Spade, Sarca Excel, Super Sarca and Mantus. His 40-minute video #56 compiles his series of tests in one video. It is well worth watching:

https://www.youtube.com/watch?v=I59f-OjWoq0

The Australian test mentioned previously also studied veering at 90 and 180 degrees using a winch on a beach as well as a runabout in water and was conducted under controlled conditions in hard sand and soft mud. In hard sand, the best performing anchors in the 90-degree test were the Kobra, Ultra and Spade – all anchors with winglets, but they were not measurably superior to other anchors tested. In this test, the CQR, Claw, Ray, fisherman and Cooper failed to set at all.

They then tested the Kobra, Spade, Super SARCA, SARCA Excel, Supreme, Delta, Rocna and Ultra in a 180 degree turn test, using anchors set under high load and connected to two winches set in opposite directions. The convex anchors – Delta, Super SARCA, SARCA Excel and Kobra – and the concave Spade broke out of the seabed clean, somersaulted and immediately re-set.

They tested the Super SARCA without the bolt in the slot in its shank so that it could self-trip; it took longer to fully re-set in this configuration. It

Any boat, new or used, that you purchase should come with an anchor and rode. Check your anchor(s) to make sure it is the right type for the predominant bottom you are likely to encounter. What came with your boat may not be what is best for it. This also applies to new boats. We have often seen grossly inadequate anchoring tackle supplied with a new and costly vessel.

Be sure to inspect all parts of your gear closely for wear and check with the manufacturer of the anchor for their recommendation of size for your boat. Check to be certain that no part of the anchor is bent, as a bent anchor will never hold properly again. What may have been considered good enough for a lunch hook in one place may not hold you in a blow overnight somewhere else.

Anchor Sizing

You will come across many tables attempting to correlate the right anchor for your vessel. Many of these use horizontal load as a gauge. The load is the force exerted by your boat on the anchor when it is set in the sea floor.

The table produced by the American Boat and Yacht Council (ABYC) is a good starting point in finding an appropriately sized anchor for a given boat. It is cited often and refers to the load expected on lunch, working and storm anchors for sail and power vessels of various dimensions.

Using this as a guideline, for the average size boat in the 35-40-foot range you should be looking at about 1,000+ pounds load when selecting a primary anchor and twice that for a storm anchor.[33]

One note of caution about the tables – though they address load, they do not translate what this means under real life circumstances but rather apply it generally based on boat dimensions. Load must be derived from factors pertaining specifically to your boat (including

---

[33] Please review our chapter on 'Scope', as the amount of rode you let out has a direct bearing on the percentage of an anchor's holding power.

windage, draft, shape, keel type, and weight) as well as factors about the circumstances (such as wind, current, wave action, scope, cushioning effect of ground tackle, and shear).

American Boat and Yacht Council (ABYC) Recommendations for Anchor Sizes					
Boat Dimensions			Horizontal Load (lbs.)		
Length	Beam (Power)	Beam (Sail)	Lunch Hook	Working Anchor	Storm Anchor
10'	5'	4'	40	160	320
15'	6'	5'	60	250	500
20'	8'	7'	90	360	720
25'	9'	8'	125	490	980
30'	11'	9'	175	700	1,400
35'	13'	10'	225	900	1,800
40'	14'	11'	300	1,200	2,400
50'	16'	13'	400	1,600	3,200
60'	18'	15'	500	2,000	4,000

What size anchor? This is the chart produced by the ABYC. It specifies load not weight and does not take specifics of your vessel into account.
It also does not address multi-hulled sailboats.

For example, a sailboat will have more windage than an open motor boat of the same length, but that is never part of the equation in a table. A ketch with two masts will have more windage and thus exert a greater load on the ground tackle than a sloop. A cabin cruiser presents a substantial surface area and will exert a very strong load when the wind picks up. A cruising catamaran of the same length will have even more windage. Then there is all the gear on deck: dodger, bimini, furled sails, a BBQ, dinghy, engine on mount, etcetera. Weight is another important factor. Full tanks and a large amount of gear increase the total weight of the boat and this affects the load put on the anchor and associated tackle.

The load exerted on an anchor will also increase dramatically as wind increases and the sea state deteriorates. As the wind speed doubles, the holding requirement quadruples.

Remember also that the scope of the anchor rode (see chapter on Scope) affects how much load an anchor will hold. No matter how big an anchor is, if you do not let out sufficient rode, it will not hold.

It is important to understand and consider all the factors when choosing an anchor. The tables simply cannot take all the variables into account. As there is really no practical way for a non-professional person to calculate the load generated by his or her boat, and there may always be circumstances that increase the load, it is wise to err on the larger side when selecting an anchor.

> **Fact:** *Five square yards of flat surface generates 10 pounds of pressure in a 10-knot breeze. At 30 knots, the same 5 yards creates 90 pounds of force, and at 100 knots, 1,000 pounds.*
>
> *And remember as your boat yaws, the surface area increases dramatically!*

Be sure that your anchor is appropriate for your needs. A 'lunch hook' should be able to hold your boat in a 15-knot breeze. The main or 'working anchor' should hold comfortably in up to 30 knots of wind. A 'storm anchor' is typically for winds up to 45+ knots. Anything more may require multiple anchors for safety.

It should also be noted that empirical data suggests that the load a storm anchor needs to hold is considerably higher than what is recommended by the ABYC – some will argue by a factor in excess of five!

Perhaps the most outspoken advocate of big anchors is naval architect Steve Dashew. His advice is quite simple: "Look at the average size of anchors in use for boats of your type and double the size. After doing this, if you think you can swing it, add another 50 percent." His position is that if you carry one reliable anchor equivalent in size to the two you normally rely on, you will never drag and never need to set more than one anchor. Now whether you agree with this or not, it remains undisputed that the bigger the anchor of a given type, the greater the holding capacity. It is not so much the weight of the anchor but rather its sheer size.

Extreme weather and unpredictability seem to be increasing with global climate change. So, if you wish to err on the side of safety, buy the best anchor for your boat in a bigger size than recommended.

Most anchor manufacturers have similar tables to the one issued by the ABYC listing the holding power of their anchor by its corresponding weight. They may also include recommendations on which of their anchors is suitable for a given boat length and how much chain to use if selecting a rope rode. It is worth reading the fine print or footnotes to determine how they came to their recommendations. Although most manufacturers are very diligent in their delivery of highly reliable information, it pays to be careful. One manufacturer, for example, recommends a much reduced scope for their anchor without explanation and with contradiction in different documents.

If you review reports of independent sources in conjunction with the manufacturer's input and make allowance for your particular vessel, you should arrive at a reasonable conclusion.

Simple advice

- ⚓ As you are not purchasing a stone weight, always select an anchor based on its holding power and setting ability and not solely on its weight
- ⚓ A bigger anchor will always hold better than a smaller one of the same type – "bigger is better"
- ⚓ Avoid no name knockoffs – they may be cheaper, but they may also suffer from inferior quality and performance
- ⚓ If you have an older generation anchor and it is not working all that well (you experience plenty of anchorages where the holding is poor), consider upgrading to one of the newer generation designs.

Part 2: Making the Connection – The Anchor Rode

The rode (also known as anchor cable) is what connects your anchor to the boat. Without it your anchor is not going to do you a world of good. It is consequently an important part of your tackle and worthy of serious consideration.

Wave and wind action will cause the boat to move. In storm situations this movement can be quite violent. As the anchor is (hopefully) firmly embedded in the seafloor and the other end of the rode securely connected to the pitching boat, this energy must be absorbed by the rode. This energy absorption is referred to as 'dampening'.

Without adequate dampening, these forces are exerted directly on the deck hardware and on the anchor. The boat's motion might thus result in catastrophic deck hardware failure or in the anchor being pulled free from the bottom. Therefore, a rode should have good dampening characteristics.

The rode needs to have ample strength to hold your boat without breaking even under extreme loads. Squalls can and will occur and winds can suddenly go from a benign 10 knots to an uncomfortable 50 knots exerting high loads on your gear.

The rode also needs to be resistant to abrasion or chafe, as well as to UV light, or it can fail. And finally, it needs to be relatively easy to handle and store.

Chapter 1: Rope Rode

Originally all ropes were made from natural fibers such as manila, hemp, linen, cotton, coir, jute, silk, wool, hair, or sisal. Today most are made of synthetic fibers. Those used for rope-making include polypropylene, nylon, polyesters (e.g. PET, LCP, HPE, Vectran®), polyethylene (e.g. Spectra®, Dyneema®, Amsteel®), Aramids (e.g., Twaron®, Technora® and Kevlar®) and polyaramids (e.g. Dralon®, Tiptolon®). Some ropes are constructed of mixtures of several fibers or use co-polymer fibers. Rayon is a regenerated fiber used to make decorative rope. Rope can also be made out of metal, as in wire rope.

For a rope to be useful as an anchor rode, it has to satisfy the four criteria we outlined:

- ⚓ Good energy absorption
- ⚓ Withstand heavy loads
- ⚓ Good chafe & UV resistance
- ⚓ Easy handling and storage

One characteristic shared by all ropes is that their fibers are exposed to abrasion or chafe. We will be discussing how to protect against chafe in the chapter 5.

Ropes Suitable for an Anchor Rode

Nylon Rope

Nylon (polyamide), with its excellent elasticity (18 to 25%) and resistance to ultraviolet light, has for many years been the rode of choice. However, it is precisely nylon's elasticity that can be a problem. When anchored (including on a sea anchor) on an all-nylon rode, a boat may surge fore and aft like on a bungee cord in stronger conditions. Not only can this be quite uncomfortable, but it can cause serious friction within the rope. This has proven to be the cause of rode breakages as internal friction can cause its fibers to heat and melt.

Rope Rode Characteristics

An all rope rode has the advantage of being light, elastic and generally easy to handle and store. However, external abrasion or chafe, where the rode comes in contact with another object on your boat or on the sea floor, and internal abrasion of the fibers, when the rode stretches and contracts repeatedly, can significantly impact its overall strength as well as its life span.

The lack of weight in a rope rode does also have a drawback. The angle of pull directed at the anchor can be poor when the anchor is initially deployed if insufficient rode has been let out. In this case the anchor may not set, or it may hold poorly – please see the section on 'scope' for more on this.

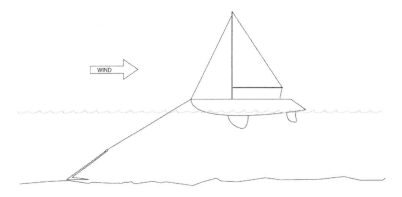

Rope Rode Characteristics

- ⚓ Light weight
- ⚓ Generally good elasticity (polyester and nylon)
- ⚓ Good UV resistance (polyester and nylon)
- ⚓ Relatively easy handling and storage

However

- ⚓ Susceptible to chafe
- ⚓ UV degradation (polypropylene)
- ⚓ Angle to anchor from boat can be less than optimal

Chapter 2: Chain

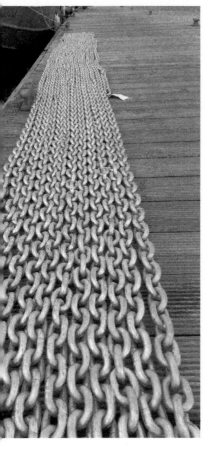

Chain has a very high tensile strength and is very resistant to chafe. Because of these characteristics alone it is used as a rode by most long-distance cruisers as well as on larger vessels. Its weight helps it easily fall into an anchor locker.

The downside, however, is that chain is heavy, and this can be very relevant with the lengths needed for an all chain rode. With an all chain rode you will most likely need a windlass. The chain rode and windlass add a lot of weight to the vessel's bow area, and so may affect performance underway. Another downside is that chain does not stretch.

Finally, chain can have a tendency to hockle if twisted. This is particularly problematic if it happens in the chain locker as it may jam while being fed out of the spurling pipe[35] (or navel pipe).

Catenary Effect

Because of its weight a chain rode will sag in light to medium winds requiring significant energy to straighten it out. This catenary effect provides excellent energy absorption. It also improves the angle at which the anchor initially addresses the bottom.

---

[35] The spurling pipe is a pipe or tube through which the anchor rode passes from the chain or anchor locker to the deck of the vessel. It is also known as the navel pipe. It is sometime incorrectly called the hawse pipe, whereas this is the through-hull opening or pipe in the stem (bow) of a vessel through which the rode passes.

provides excellent energy absorption. It also improves the angle at which the anchor initially addresses the bottom.

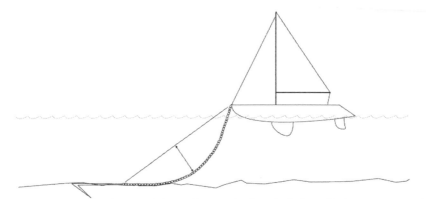

The energy required to straighten the sag in the chain is called catenary and this in turn provides excellent energy absorption in light winds (up to about 20 knots). The sag in the chain also gives the rode a good angle of pull on the anchor.

In strong wind situations, when elasticity is needed most, a chain rode will provide absolutely no energy absorption. Chain does not stretch. When the wind picks up it goes bar taut, transferring all the shock loads caused by wave and wind action directly to the anchor and deck fittings. This may cause the anchor to break out or a deck fitting to fail.

Though much touted, the catenary effect is thus actually of little consequence while a vessel is at anchor. This is particularly the case when it would me most needed; in a high wind situation.

When bar taut a chain rode has no stretch, no catenary and thus no energy absorption. It also will provide a less than optimal angle at which the anchor addresses the bottom.

Making the Connection ⚓ The Anchor Rode

Chain Characteristics

- ⚓ Strong – High Tensile Strength
- ⚓ It is resistant to chafe and UV
- ⚓ Provides significant dampening in light to medium wind
- ⚓ Provides good angle for anchor to address the bottom in light to medium wind

However

- ⚓ It is heavy: significant weight in the bow, need windlass, which adds more weight
- ⚓ Does not stretch. In stronger wind with wave action shock loads to anchor and deck hardware may cause either to fail.
- ⚓ Chain may hockle if twisted.

Chain Specifications & Terms

Working Load Limit / Safe Working Load

WLL or SWL (also rated capacity) is the maximum load that should be applied in direct tension to an undamaged straight length of chain. The chain should not be stressed beyond this.

This is typically a predefined fraction (commonly around 1/4) of the minimum breaking force of the chain. It provides a safe margin of error. It can vary and a lower ratio can be used to make a chain look better than it really is. Check against the breaking force if you are unsure.

Proof Tested

All quality chain is proof tested by the manufacturer. A load is applied to the newly produced chain as a quality control measure. It is not a performance measure.

Minimum Breaking Force

This is the minimum force the manufacturer has found under which the chain will break. Breaking force values do not guarantee that all chain segments will actually endure these loads.

Chain Sizing / Calibration

The chain and windlass wildcat[36] need to be matched (calibrated) to each other. If you already have a windlass, make sure the chain matches it precisely. Check with the windlass manufacturer and chain supplier for the correct size. The chain size (diameter) is often stamped into the base of the wildcat.

The exact link length, which is determined by the pitch and diameter, is of most importance to the windlass wildcat. Mismatched sizing in this regard will cause problems during windlass operation. An even slightly incorrectly sized chain can jam on the windlass. The internal link width can also vary widely from one standard to another.

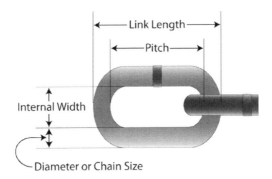

As new chain is quite expensive, our recommendation is to try before you buy. Before buying a new chain, we first purchased a 10 meter (30 foot) length and ran this through our wildcat with and without load, prior to committing to buying the full length (100 meters). This short length has come in handy for our rope rodes, so it will not go to waste.

Listed chain sizes almost always refer to the link diameter, i.e. the diameter of the rod of steel which forms the chain link. However,

---

[36] Windlass gypsy in the UK

remember that in different regions different units of measure may apply: for example: metric and imperial or standard.

A problem is that there are also long and short linked chains with the same diameter. With regards to anchor chain, only short link is generally of interest. However, there is no single standard for what comprises a short link chain.

Chain Standards

There are different standards that all have their own sizing peculiarities. This can make purchasing a new chain even more difficult.

- ⚓ North American chain may use ISO standards (international standard), which can be longer and wider.
- ⚓ In Europe, there is EN (specified by the European Committee for Standardization CEN) and DIN (from the Deutsches Institut für Normung) chain. They present the same size measurement for the diameter of the link but vary slightly in pitch and width.

Chain Grades

Of course, there are differing grades of chain. Various systems use different terminology, the most common starts with a "G" and then has a number; this is usually 1 or 2 digits, for example, G4 or G40 (these are both the same). The higher the first digit, the higher the breaking force.

So, when you select a chain for your rode, go for the higher breaking force. The most common is proof coil, G30, or BBB. It is not as strong as G40. The latter may cost a bit more, but it will be a better product for the same weight. In fact, on new builds, the better manufacturers are specifying smaller sized, higher grade chain to save weight without compromising the breaking strength they need. The saved weight can then be used for a larger sized anchor, with commensurate better holding power.

Chapter 3: Combination Rope and Chain

When one considers the characteristics of either an all chain or an all rope rode, with each one having significant positive attributes plus specific downsides, it is not hard to come to consider how a combination of the two might be beneficial. In fact, most anchor manufacturers recommend adding a length of chain to an all rope rode.

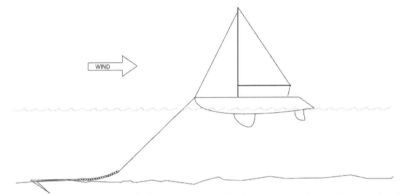

With a combination of chain and rope, chafe is avoided and the angle at which the anchor addresses the seabed is improved in lighter winds.

The chain will keep your rope rode from chafing against rocky or otherwise abrasive seabed and the weight of the chain improves the angle with which the anchor initially addresses the bottom. It may provide further dampening to reduce tugging on the anchor and deck hardware in light winds.

The exception to the rule is the fluke anchor. If you have chain attached to the anchor (or an all-chain rode) and deploy too much rode at once prior to setting the anchor (see section on setting anchor), the weight of the chain may pull the shaft down and cause the flukes to 'float' on the bottom and not dig in.

Making the Connection ⚓ The Anchor Rode

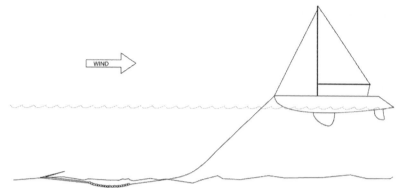

The weight of a chain may cause the anchor flukes of a fluke type anchor to float and the anchor may not set.

If the anchor is deployed correctly, adding chain to the rope rode used with a fluke anchor is still beneficial. In fact, we have anchored countless times without any problems with our Fortress fluke anchor using a heavy all chain rode.

Although each manufacturer will suggest a different length of chain for their particular anchor and some experts will state that the chain length should be the same as the boat length or a multiple thereof, we have been quite successful in adding about 20-30 feet or 7-10 meters of chain to the end of our rope rodes. (Our boat is 57 feet long.)

If you are not using a windlass, the rope rode may be tied off to the chain or to a shackle. The rope may also have an eye with a reinforcing eyelet and then be connected to the chain with a shackle. If you are using a windlass, you must splice your rope to your chain as a shackle going through your windlass gypsy will be bad news. It may be spliced to the chain in one of a number of different ways. If you have a rope to chain connection, you must inspect this regularly for wear. If you see signs of chafe at the splice or eye, you have successfully located the 'weak link' in your rode and it is important that you cut away and replace it.

Combination Rode Characteristics

- ⚓ Weight of chain improves the angle at which the anchor addresses the seabed and provides further dampening in light winds to reduce tugging on the anchor and deck hardware.
- ⚓ Most anchor manufacturers recommend some chain for a rope rode (NOTE: Some suggest less chain others more. It is best to follow their specifications.)
- ⚓ Chain provides abrasion resistance relative to the seabed protecting the rope from chafe
- ⚓ Combination results in strength and stretch

However
- ⚓ If deployed incorrectly a fluke anchor may not set if chain is used
- ⚓ A rope to chain splice may be the weak point in your rode and needs to be regularly inspected

Snubbers

As we have seen, an all chain rode has no stretch and no energy absorption when taut. With old style anchors (hooks, plows, etc.) this was less of a problem, as the anchor would move through the substrate as shock loads were applied by wave action – that is: the anchor would drag[37] and thus absorb the energy.

The problem with an all chain rode really was exacerbated with the modern scoop type and better quality fluke type anchors, which dig deep and do not drag. Now these shock loads are transferred directly to the deck hardware, shackles, swivels, and so on, as well as to the anchor. For an all chain rode, it is consequently always recommended to add something to absorb these shock loads.

---

[37] This is, of course, very undesirable!

Making the Connection ⚓ The Anchor Rode

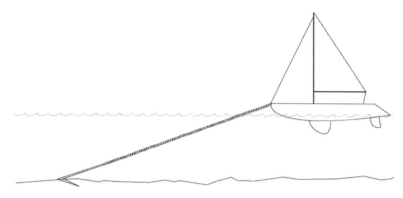

This can be accomplished with a length of stretchy rope to connect the chain to the boat. This rope provides the rode with elasticity and is called a snubber. The net result, of course is that you wind up with a rope-chain combination with all the positive characteristics it brings with it.

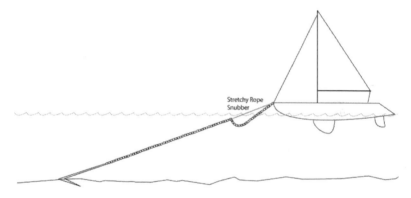

Stretchy Rope
Snubber

The snubber, nipping line, strop, bridle, or mooring compensator is most commonly hooked (or tied with a rolling hitch) to the chain and then tied off to a cleat or a Samson post on the boat. Whereas the chain is also connected to the boat, it is left loose so that the snubber may absorb the impact of any wave action. If the snubber were to fail, the chain is still there to hold the boat.

Alex & Daria Blackwell

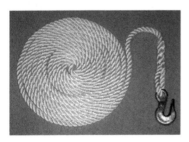

The snubbers on these boats are clearly too short to be truly effective. In addition, the chain on the upper right boat is not slack, so the shock loads are still being transferred to the deck hardware.

To be effective, the snubber should be as long as possible – the longer the rope the greater the energy absorption. If it is too short, as in the preceding pictures, it will be of little or no benefit whatsoever. The recommended length varies, but it would be wise to use at least 30 feet of 3-stranded or braided and adequately strong nylon or preferably Dacron (polyester) with a strong hook at one end.

On our boat we use a 30 foot (10 meter) double braided nylon dock line as a snubber for our all chain rode. This is strong and has a nice capacity for stretch. There are also commercially available snubbers complete with hook at most hardware and marine stores.

Making the Connection & The Anchor Rode

A Nylon or Dacron rope snubber attached to a chain rode adds stretch to absorb wave action on the rode. All three of these snubbers look to be adequately long. In addition, the chain is nicely loosened in all cases.

To attach the snubber to the chain you can either tie it on with a rolling hitch or use a chain hook. A standard galvanized chain grab hook sized for the anchor chain purchased at a local hardware store to connect the snubber to the chain rode has proven to be very adequate. And no, as long as there is tension between the rope and chain is cannot fall off.

There are, of course, commercially available hooks designed specifically for this purpose such as the chain claw or the Ultra chain grab, which can be spliced or tied to the end of the snubber.

Chain claw by Swiss Tech

*Ultra Chain Grab
by Boyut Marine*

Wichard Chain Hook

*Mantus
Chain Hook*

The snubber must also have a chafe protector where it passes through the chock, or over your bow roller. If you watch closely, even on a fairly calm day, you can see the snubber stretch and contract. Please see the chapter on chafe for more information.

Of course, if you feel there is not enough stretch in your rope rode (or dock line) there are any number of rubber or spring constructed mooring compensators that will absorb additional movement.

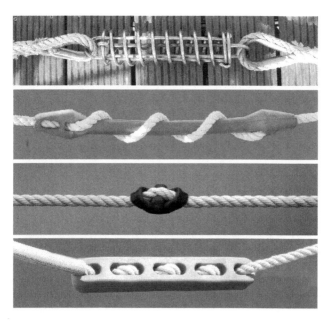

Making the Connection ⚓ The Anchor Rode

If, on the other hand, you have a rope rode and would like to reduce the movement of the rope through your chocks or over your bow roller to cut back on the chafe inducing friction, you may tie a Spectra®, Dynema® or even a chain snubber off your rope rode.

We have, for example, done this on our mooring, where we have a nylon riser or pennant. Our Spectra bridles do not stretch and thus their movement on our bow roller is minimized and any friction is greatly reduced.

Multi-hull Considerations

Catamarans and trimarans as well as some barges need special adjustments to their tackle due to their wide beam in relation to their overall length. In addition, the windlass on a catamaran is centrally located behind the trampoline or on a central beam. The bow roller is sometimes on the aluminum bar that rests between the two hulls. The aluminum bar is structurally not sufficient to handle the loads under challenging conditions. Meanwhile, the anchor locker and windlass moves the center of pivoting back away from the bow. The bows of the catamaran tend to catch the wind resulting in the boat sailing, ranging or yawing from one side to the other, gathering momentum with each swing.

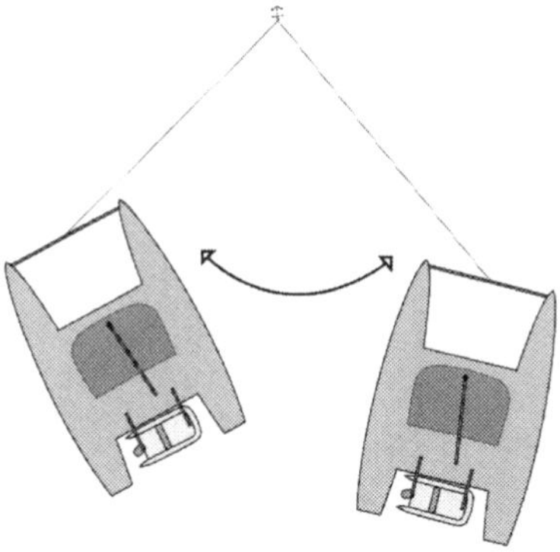

The way to counter this problem is to deploy a bridle hooked into the chain with one rope going to each of the two hulls and a retrieval line to haul the bridle back in before weighing anchor. This effectively moves the attachment point of the rode to the boat forward of the bow and will help stabilize the boat's motion. The chain can thus be left sagging in the middle.

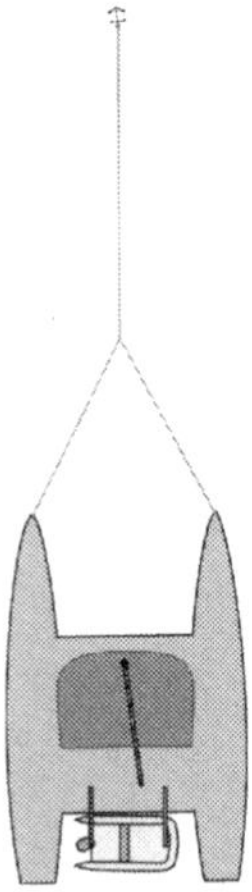

Summary

- A snubber on a chain rode effectively turns the chain rode into a rope–chain combination
- A snubber adds stretch (= dampening) to the chain rode
- A non-elastic snubber on a rope rode can reduce friction and chafe
- A bridle or pair of snubbers on a catamaran reduce erratic motion and its resultant stress on structural elements in addition to providing dampening

Chapter 4: Sizing a Rode

Just like one must select an anchor based on the load it will have to withstand, the same goes for selecting an appropriate rode.

Whereas sales people will cite the breaking strength of a given rope or chain, using this as a criterion is ill advised. Instead one should look at the working load, as this allows for factors of safety, strength loss due to knots and splices, abrasion, and aging.

For example, any time you tie a knot in a rope you effectively cut the breaking strength in half. While certain kinds of knots damage the line less than others, the 50% loss of tensile strength is a good general rule to live by. Research has shown that the figure 8 knot reduces the tensile strength by approximately 35% instead of 50% for other common knots tested.

Remember also that all rope will weaken with age and use. This can be due to UV degradation as well as wear and tear and load cycling – stretching causes internal friction and wear. Over time, ropes can thus lose 1/3 of their breaking strength.

Rode Size

When selecting an anchor rode the following rules of thumb apply:

- ⚓ 3-strand nylon rope should be 1/8" diameter for every 7' of boat length.
- ⚓ Proof coil and BBB chain should be half the line diameter (1/2" nylon line would be matched to 1/4" galvanized chain).
- ⚓ Use shackles one size larger than the chain (1/4" chain would use 5/16" shackles).

Alex & Daria Blackwell

As a general guide, for winds up to 30 knots, the following anchor line and chain diameters are recommended:

Boat LOA	Three-Strand Nylon	Chain
Up to 25'	3/8"	3/16" PC
27'-31'	7/16"	1/4" PC
32'-36'	7/16"	1/4" PC
35'-40'	9/16"	5/16" PC/BBB or 1/4" HT
38'-45'	5/8"	5/16" PC/BBB/HT
42'-54'	3/4"	3/8" PC/BBB or 5/16" HT
50'-63'	7/8"	1/2" PC or 3/8" HT
58'-72'	1"	5/8" PC or 1/2" HT

Rode Specifications

Nylon Rope Specifications
(Anchor and Mooring Rode)

Metric mm	Typical WLL (kg)*				Equiv. US approximate Inches	Typical WLL (lb)*			
	kg/m	Laid or Twisted	Double Braided	Mega Braid		lbs/1ft	Laid or Twisted	Double Braided	Mega Braid
5	0.0134	88	82		3/16	0.01	195	180	
6	0.0238	143	143		1/4	0.02	315	315	
8	0.0357	204	197		5/16	0.02	450	435	
10	0.0521	289	327		3/8	0.04	638	720	
11	0.0774		456		7/16	0.05		1005	
12	0.0937	408	544	442	1/2	0.06	900	1200	975
14	0.119	510	837	578	9/16	0.08	1125	1845	1275
16	0.143	599	891	701	5/8	0.10	1320	1965	1545
18	0.204	793	1395	912	3/4	0.14	1748	3075	2010
22	0.278	1167	1684	1436	7/8	0.19	2573	3713	3165
24	0.361	1517	2228	1694	1	0.24	3345	4913	3735
28	0.513	1885	2973	2375	1 1/8	0.34	4155	6555	5235
30	0.61	2436	4100	2790	1 1/4	0.41	5370	9038	6150
33	0.684		5052	3266	1 5/16	0.46		11138	7200
38	0.829		5277		1 1/2	0.56		11633	
41	1.033		6123		1/5/8	0.69		13500	
44	1.202		6940		1 3/4	0.81		15300	
51	1.495		8913		2	1.00		19650	
57	1.979		11335		2 1/4	1.33		24990	
76	3.392		17758		3	2.28		39150	
83	4.166		20521		3 1/4	2.80		45240	

Data Source: New England Ropes

* The working load for most kinds of rope is between 15% and 25% of the tensile strength or average breaking strength. We have used 15% in the above.

Proof Coil Chain Specifications (G30 / BBB)

Metric	Approx. weight	Typical WLL	Equiv. US approximate	Approx. weight	Typical WLL
6mm	0.85 kg/m	590 kgf	1/4"	84 lb/100'	1300 lb
8mm	1.45 kg/m	860 kgf	5/16"	120 lb/100'	1900 lb
10mm	2.2 kg/m	1200 kgf	3/8"	176 lb/100'	2650 lb
12mm	3.8 kg/m	2040 kgf	7/16"	230 lb/100'	4500 lb
16mm	6.10 kg/m	3130 kgf	5/8"	400 lb/100'	6900 lb

Medium Tensile Chain Specifications (G40 / high test)

Metric	Approx weight	Typical WLL	Equiv. US approximate	Approx weight	Typical WLL
6mm	0.85 kg/m	1180 kgf	1/4"	84 lb/100'	2600 lb
8mm	1.45 kg/m	1770 kgf	5/16"	120 lb/100'	3900 lb
10mm	2.2 kg/m	2450 kgf	3/8"	176 lb/100'	5400 lb
12mm	3.8 kg/m	4175 kgf	7/16"	230 lb/100'	9200 lb
16mm	6.10 kg/m	5215 kgf	5/8"	400 lb/100'	11500 lb

High Tensile Chain Specifications (G70 / transport)

Metric	Approx. weight	Typical WLL	Equiv. US approximate	Approx. weight	Typical WLL
8mm	1.45 kg/m	1430 kgf	5/16"	84 lb/100'	3150 lb
10mm	2.2 kg/m	2995 kgf	3/8"	176 lb/100'	6600 lb
12mm	3.8 kg/m	5125 kgf	7/16"	230 lb/100'	11300 lb

Data Source: National Association of Chain Manufacturers

Making the Connection ⚓ The Anchor Rode

Rode Length

How much rode you need really depends on where you plan to anchor. The simplest answer is "more is better", and "even more is even better".

If you are planning to anchor in a maximum of 30 feet (10 meters) of water, then your rode should be at least 300 feet or 100 meters long to allow for a 10-1 scope. This is what you would need in storm conditions – see chapter on scope.

If you are heading to Patagonia where depths are often in the 20-fathom range (120 feet or 40m) and the winds ferocious, you would need commensurately more. Given that you would be deploying a much bigger anchor in these circumstances, you might get away with as little as a 5:1 scope, but that still means you need a minimum of 600 feet or a 200-meter long rode!

It is advisable to have more than one rode; should you, for example, need to cut a rode in an emergency or wish to deploy two anchors.

We carry 100 meters of chain as our primary and have three rope rodes of the same length aboard, ready to use.

Chapter 5: Chafe

Perhaps one of the most common problems people have when anchoring, mooring, or tying up their boat is not what gear they use, but what happens when the boat moves. As your boat pitches or moves because of wave action or wind shifts, your rode or dock line will stretch and contract. It will also move from side to side.

Boats on the Rocks after a recent gale all because of chafe

The friction between a rope (rode, sheet, halyard, etc.) and another object will cause abrasion or chafe. This is a very serious issue as it significantly weakens the rope until it parts – often with catastrophic results.

During a recent Atlantic crossing I pulled out my binoculars to inspect our rigging aloft. Low and behold, I saw that our main halyard was about to part. Two weeks of light air and flogging sails had indeed taken its toll.

Chafe can occur very quickly with rope rodes. We saw a boat break its rode when a raft up suddenly was subjected to choppy seas. The wind had turned against the current and the raft-up started rapidly drifting towards a reef.

Making the Connection ⚓ The Anchor Rode

These photos were taken during a walk through a random marina.
Although these are dock lines, an anchor line can chafe through just like this
and it can happen very quickly.

In another instance with a raft up of multiple vessels of different descriptions, a catamaran tied between a sloop and a trawler started surging forward and back when the waves kicked up across a broad fetch. The opposing motions of the boats caused the connecting dock lines to rub against the chocks and cleats. The first of the ropes parted very quickly. Fortunately, the participants noticed the problem and broke up the raft before there was any further damage.

Any rope that touches edges or is exposed to objects that can rub (including other ropes) runs the risk of chafing through. Adequate protection against chafe is essential.

Chafe is caused by friction:

- Boat movement
- Rope/Rode stretch
- Rope/Rode movement

Where?

- Objects the rope may touch
- Bends around objects – even if they are smooth
- Chocks, toe rails, etc.
- Any possible points of contact

Chafe Protection is Key

With a little attention to detail and some advance planning, protecting your rode or dock line from chafe is quite easy. Look for any place your rope may potentially come in contact with something else. At these places you need to add a chafe protector.

We use reinforced plastic hose slit along its length to allow us to place the chafe guard anywhere on the rode. We want the hose to move against the opposing object and be subjected to the abrasion. We secure it to the rode with thin line that we've tied through holes at either end of the length of hose. The reason for this is that we do not want the rope to move inside the hose, as this causes friction which in turn causes heat that can melt the fibers.

After one of our lectures a very experienced seaman asked if we thought he should remove his anchor from the bow roller when he tied off to his mooring. The words barely out of his mouth, he smiled and answered his own question, "Of course!"

Making the Connection ⚓ The Anchor Rode

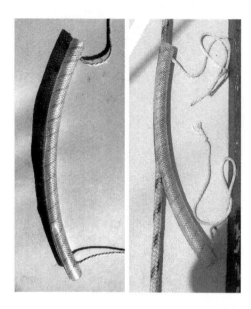

A home-made chafe protector.

Appropriately sized plastic tubing is slit along one side, and holes are drilled in either end to accommodate lanyards. The tube is then slid over the rope and secured with the lanyards.

You can, of course, also buy commercial chafe guards, usually made of similar materials or leather.

Your chafe protector should be positioned so that it protects the rode anywhere it might rub against something. Note the protector extending beyond the bow of the boat. It must also be long enough to protect the rode when it stretches under load.

An example of a dock-line that will not last much longer. Similar chafe can happen on an anchored vessel and much more quickly than you may think.

Summary

- ⚓ Chafe occurs anywhere a rope (rode, dock line, sheet, or halyard) may come in contact with anything else.
- ⚓ Chafe can cause catastrophic failure with disastrous results
- ⚓ Chafe protection is key: move or remove potential touch points and add chafe protectors to the rope
- ⚓ The chafe protector must be secured to the rope: The rope must not be able to move inside the protector.

Chapter 6: Weak Links

Please remember the old adage "The strength of the complete system is only as good as its weakest link." If there are any weak components in your setup – chafe, a poorly tied knot, a weak shackle, a rusty swivel, or an unsecured bitter end – then this is what you need to find and fix before you take off.

Any weak link can quickly leave your boat high and dry,
or broken up on the rocks

Metals Used in Anchoring Tackle

Without going into the intricacies of metallurgy, it is a good idea to take a look at what your anchoring tackle is made out of. This will give you an understanding of what you may expect or may need to look out for. It may also help you to recognize potential weak links and thus avoid them.

Mixing different metals in the various bits of anchor tackle can cause galvanic corrosion with the presence of moisture and salt in the chain locker, or in seawater which is an excellent electrolyte. Of particular note here is the problem of combining a galvanized anchor with a stainless-steel shackle or swivel (or visa-versa). Zinc (used for galvanizing) and stainless steel are far apart on the galvanic scale. Combining components of such disparate metals can lead to corrosion and potential serious problems.

Steel

Steel is the most common metal used in anchoring tackle. It comes in many different grades from regular "mild" steel (plain-carbon steel) to high tensile and tool grade steel (high-carbon steel).

Unprotected (carbon) steel rusts readily when exposed to air and moisture. This iron oxide film (the rust) is active and accelerates corrosion by forming more iron oxide. Because of the greater volume of the iron oxide, it tends to flake and fall away.

To help protect this easily oxidized (= rusted) metal, it needs a protective sacrificial anode, or a coating made out of zinc. Adding this coating is called galvanizing. There are two basic methods for doing this: electrolytic and hot-dipped. Electrolytic galvanizing applies a very thin and even coating of zinc to the steel. Hot-dipped, where the steel is literally dipped in molten zinc, applies a much thicker coating, which tends to be uneven and rough.

When selecting tackle, such as an anchor, one must take into consideration how it was manufactured. This will include whether it was drop-forged, welded, or cast. With the latter perhaps being the weakest of metal construction. Personal experience has shown cast iron to be quite brittle.

The best metal for an anchor is hot-dipped galvanized, drop-forged steel that is shaped by hammering when the metal is red hot. This can be used to construct non-welded, one-piece shanks or entire anchors. This is very different from casting, even though the anchors may look the same. The grain structure in the metal of a drop-forged anchor aligns in a manner that reduces brittleness and increases strength. Welding, if done properly, can be very strong but can also suffer from cracks that only x-rays can detect.

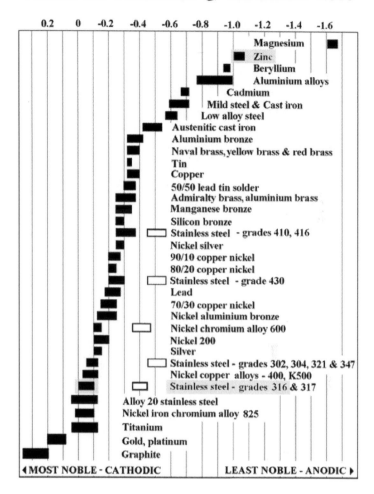

There are, of course, plastic anchors.

Stainless steel (Inox steel)

We often get questions about whether stainless steel is superior to galvanized steel when it comes to anchoring tackle. Grade 316 stainless steel is the most commonly used in marine applications – particularly those where welding is required (anchors, chain, etc. See note on welding stainless steel below).

A chief characteristic of stainless steel is that it is smooth (and shiny). Therefore, stainless steel shackles do not lock as well as galvanized and may come undone in the most unfortunate of times. Stainless steel

123

shackles in particular must thus always be seized with (Monel) wire. Stainless is also more brittle and not as strong as so called mild steel.

Stainless steel differs from carbon steel by the amount of chromium present. Stainless steels contain sufficient chromium to form a passive skin of chromium oxide, which prevents further surface corrosion by blocking oxygen diffusion to the steel surface. It theoretically also blocks corrosion from spreading into the metal's internal structure. Due to the similar size of the steel and oxide ions, they bond very strongly and remain attached to the surface.

However, this passivation occurs only if the proportion of chromium is high enough and oxygen is present. In low-oxygenated warm water (Caribbean) or mud, this skin will break down and corrosion (rust) will start. This same problem can occur in underwater keel bolts, which go through the hull and may be wetted with seawater. Rust will also occur in hidden crevasses which stay wet and or oxygen deprived. Such crevasse corrosion is particularly insidious. Stain-less is not stain-free.

Stainless steel is apparently not necessarily entirely homogenous in composition. Small specs of mild steel in it will rust over time causing pitting. This may then expand internally, weakening the overall piece of hardware. Stainless components may thus show little sign of deterioration prior to catastrophic failure. For more on this, please see the following section on swivels.

Welding Stainless Steel

Welding stainless steel can also create sites of corrosion. This is commonly known as weld decay. (See discussion on chain below.) It is brought about by the heat of the welding process causing the chromium present in stainless steel to combine with any carbon present to form chromium carbide. The steel in the vicinity of the weld is thus depleted of its chromium. This problem can be overcome by adding costly titanium to the alloy. Titanium has a greater affinity for carbon than chromium. During the welding, titanium binds the carbon to form titanium carbide and thereby leaving the chromium behind to create the passivation layer.

Aluminum

Aluminum is notably much lighter and weaker than steel. However, if correctly engineered, the tensile strength issue can be overcome. A prime example of this is the Fortress anchor. Spade also offers an aluminum version. Several anchor manufacturers have brought out aluminum versions of their anchors, which they subsequently withdrew as they were not as strong as their steel counterparts.

Of note is that aluminum is close to zinc in the galvanic table. Therefore, using a galvanized shackle with an aluminum anchor should pose no issues.

Chain

Chain links are made out of steel rod segments that are bent around a jig and then welded. Depending on the grade of the steel and the quality of the weld, this can be the location where rust sets in and degrades the chain.

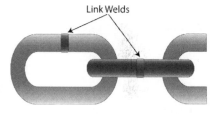

Link Welds

Most chain aboard small vessels is galvanized steel. (See chapter on Chain.) Cruisers, who want to keep their decks free of rust and have heard that chain flows more compactly into the locker without kinking if made of stainless steel, often wonder if the far more expensive option of stainless-steel chain will prove more sensible over the course of their lives.

Alex & Daria Blackwell

Copyright © Adrian Pringle s/v Lalize. Reproduced with permission.
Cracks and pitting in stainless steel chain after just 50 days of use.
Notable in his experience is the pitting / corrosion of his stainless-steel chain
– particularly at or near the welds. (See the note above on welding stainless
steel.)

Adrian Pringle shared his experience with stainless steel chain complete with photos (preceding page), which he has kindly allowed us to reproduce here. A full account of his experience can be found on the Ocean Cruising Club website in the Flying Fish Journal Issue 2007-2 under the title "The Cost of Anchoring".

He had had serious corrosion issues with a stainless-steel chain. After just three years of use it had corroded to a point where it had to be replaced. The manufacturer exchanged it. After only 50 days of use, the new chain showed signs of rust – worse yet, he found a cracked weld. Sometime later, on retrieving his anchor after a storm, he noticed severe pitting, with some links corroded by 20%.

This time the manufacturer informed him that one should not use grade 316 stainless steel for anchoring. They stated it is unsuitable in low oxygen conditions, such as warm water or in mud. Grade 318 would be better, but only if it was washed off with fresh water after use. The

126

manufacturer did replace the chain a second time – with grade 318. We look forward to the next instalment of this ongoing story.

So, what did we do when we replaced our chain? We purchased 100 meters of lovely galvanized steel chain...

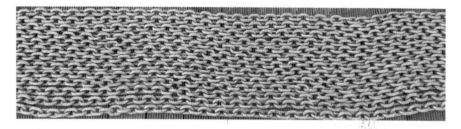

Swivels

To date we have shunned using swivels, viewing them as an unnecessary weak link in the components connecting the sea bed to our boat. Yes, we have swung at anchor for weeks at a time while cruising. Where the wind was heavy, our anchor veered as a good anchor should. In light wind situations we did note that our chain was occasionally twisted, but this always corrected itself when we weighed anchor. The twist cannot get past the toothed wildcat on our windlass, so there is no chance that the twisted chain would find its way into our chain locker. The anchor spins while coming up and any twist is straightened out.

A second reason many people opt for a swivel is that they fear that the protruding shackle pin might get stuck on the bow roller when deploying or weighing anchor. Unless the bow roller assembly has been very poorly designed or the shackle is overly wide, this should not be an issue. We have literally anchored thousands of times, sometimes two or three times in one day and have never seen this happen.

Another reason put to us recently from one fellow cruiser was that their anchor always came onto the bow roller upside down. "Open the shackle, turn the chain 180 degrees, and reconnect", was our suggestion. Guess what? It worked.

There is one place we do have a swivel – on our mooring. There is a fairly stiff tidal current where our boat is moored. Our boat thus swings a lot. As our mooring cannot veer, it is conceivable that our riser, which is part chain and part arm thick nylon, would become twisted over the course of the year. We have, therefore, incorporated a heavy galvanized swivel in the riser, which we do replace every year. So, one cannot say that we are anti-swivel.

Swivel failure

Friends with whom we were cruising in company had a beautiful, entirely stainless-steel anchoring system: stainless steel chain, stainless steel swivel and stainless-steel anchor. It was very shiny and caused anchor envy amongst friends – including us. When we arrived at our destination one evening, their crew went forward to deploy the anchor. An argument ensued briefly when the crewman asked where the anchor was. It was gone. The swivel had broken while they were underway, and the anchor had taken the plunge. They were very lucky it broke when it did and not during the night! The boatyard subsequently told them the swivel could not handle the stress of multidirectional pull as it was a unidirectional swivel (see photo).

Making the Connection ⚓ The Anchor Rode

This broken swivel was the weakest link.

Two things became evident as we looked at their problem. There was corrosion (rust) on their 'stainless steel' swivel – yes, as previously mentioned, stainless steel will rust. It is called "stain-<u>less</u>" for good reason. There was significant evidence of rust on the swivel shaft, which was hidden from view, a damp space deprived of oxygen, as is the case with many of the 'nicer' swivels on the market today.

The problem with all of these swivels is that their shaft is hidden from view. Should the shaft rust, which would seem to be likely as the space around it will remain moist, then it will no longer be as strong as it once was.

Some of these swivels have a threaded shaft with a nut welded onto it to hold the two bits together. First of all, a threaded bar (as with the one above that snapped) is inherently weaker than a solid bar of the same diameter. Then there is the issue of the welds not holding, as happened in the swivel shown here. (See above note on welding stainless steel.)

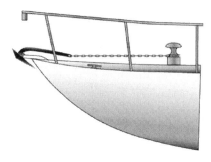

The other problem we found was that our friends were in the habit of bringing their anchor in tight to the bow roller using their windlass, as many people do – their chain was thus bar taut. They did this so that their anchor would not bounce around while underway. Given the fact that there will inevitably be movement as the boat pounds through waves, this will undoubtedly put undue strain on the swivel, any shackle, and on the windlass.

Our friends quickly purchased a new anchor and swivel and were once again the envy of the fleet. A few short weeks later, both were gone. Having reflected on what had happened, they now have a galvanized anchor and no swivel.

They also tie their anchor off to a cleat leaving their chain loose on the foredeck. We just heard that they have been successfully using this same setup for several years now.

Another reported failure of swivels occurs when the boat veers strongly to one side and then comes up short. In this instance something has to give. These lateral loads can be so great as to bend the anchor shaft. They can also cause the swivel to be bent open with the screw thread being stripped out as is shown in the photo. Alternatively, the swivel shaft may shear or, as in the example to the right, the internal retaining pin may break. Of course, this lateral load is also applied as the anchor is hauled over the bow roller – often with some gusto, so that the anchor bounces with the swivel on the roller as it rotates into the correct orientation.

Lateral Load Causing Failure

Swivel photo courtesy of
John Franklin

Pin snapped when jaw
opened

A solution to this is to position the swivel some way up the chain as is suggested by Peter Smith (http://www.petersmith.net.nz/). A short piece of chain is thus shackled to the anchor with the swivel connecting it to the rest of the chain rode. It's a good solution if you really can't do without a shackle.

The other option is to design the swivel so that it can indeed move laterally as well as twist. One such example is shown here where the manufacturer has designed in what amounts to an extra chain link. It would appear that the lateral forces would still be exerted on the jaws attaching to the anchor and on the swivel shaft – not to mention that the shaft remains hidden from view and subject to rusting.

Following the adage that simple is better, one might also consider a simple shackled-on swivel. The one we saw here could move laterally if sized correctly. Its only downside is, of course, that the shaft is still obstructed from view.

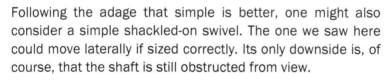

For those who truly feel they need a swivel, there is one option with which we have personal experience. It is the Ultra Flip Swivel manufactured in Turkey by Boyut Marine. It incorporates a flipping nub to assist anchor alignment, a durable Teflon-coated ball for easy rotation, and a back bridge that supports the anchor as it travels over the roller. The back bridge also looks like it would add extra strength to the already beefy swivel. This swivel also has virtually no hidden places that cannot be inspected. The connecting point is open, so that there is little chance for oxygen depletion. This swivel not only twists but will articulate to all sides reducing the danger of the lateral load. Like the beautifully styled Ultra  anchor, Boyut has produced a lovely piece of equipment machined not cast in 316 stainless steel as well. Perhaps the only drawback is that the Teflon-coating on the rotational ball may eventually wear. Even though we are still wary of swivels as part of the anchor tackle setup, the Ultra Flip Swivel may be worth looking in to.

Shackles

Once deployed, the anchor will be out of sight and you need to ensure the rode stays securely attached. Your chain should thus be attached to the anchor with a sturdy shackle. If you have a rope chain combination without a rope-to-chain splice, then you need another large shackle to tie the rope rode off to with a knot that will not move and cause chafe.

Many people opt for a shiny stainless-steel shackle. Just consider that stainless steel is, by its very nature, smooth and the pin is thus actually inclined to unscrew itself. The shackle pin also has areas at either end that will remain moist with low or no oxygen. It is here that the shackle may corrode and ultimately fail.

We would suggest using a galvanized shackle instead. As the galvanized shackle's surface is rough it tends to bind and not open easily.

Making the Connection ⚓ The Anchor Rode

Whatever you wind up using, make sure the shackle pin is secured or 'moused' with high grade Monel® wire. As opposed to stainless steel or copper, Monel is inert and will not react with the metal shackle.

Lessons Learned

The lessons learned from these experiences are in fact quite simple:

- ⚓ All stainless steel is not created equal. There is really high-quality material available – but lesser quality may not always be discernible.
- ⚓ Shackles must be sized as large as possible. Always go for at least one size bigger than the chain and seize (mouse) the shackle with Monel wire.
- ⚓ Stainless shackles have a smooth thread and open more easily than galvanized.
- ⚓ We personally find little need to have a swivel on our rode – even with an all chain rode. If you think it necessary to have one, buy only the best – one you can inspect all parts of.
- ⚓ When your anchor is on board, always secure it at the bow with lines to a cleat or other solid point and slack off the tension to the windlass. Holding the anchor with the windlass puts undue strain on the windlass, the chain, the shackle and, if you have one, the swivel.

Chapter 7: The Bitter End

We know this goes without saying but make sure the other end of the rope or chain is securely attached to a strong point of the boat before deploying an anchor. Anyone can misjudge how much rode they let out. Or what if you slip and fall on deck while letting it out? You do not want to wave good-bye to your anchor and rode. Worse would be to grab the bitter end as it whizzes past you – possibly pulling you overboard with it.

A friend was on her way home in a skiff with her two young children asleep in the cuddy cabin one fine but chilly March evening. She pulled up to a beach to say hello to friends and jumped off the boat taking the anchor ashore as there was a stiff offshore breeze. She dropped the anchor and walked up the slope while the boat drifted out – only it kept going as the rode had not been tied off. An inner voice fortunately played its hand and she turned to see the boat with her loved ones sailing merrily away. She dove into the frigid water and swam after the boat, catching up to it just in time.

"Borrowed with permission" from
Latitudes & Attitudes Seafaring magazine – now Cruising Outpost magazine

There are different schools of thought as to how to attach the bitter end. Strong and secure is the important thing to remember. For boats with an all chain rode, the conventional wisdom is to use a length of strong rope or a lashing – long enough to come out on deck so that you can cut it in an emergency.

Making the Connection ⚓ The Anchor Rode

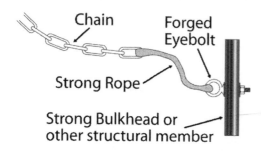

Chain

Forged Eyebolt

Strong Rope

Strong Bulkhead or other structural member

Don't forget to secure the bitter end before dropping the anchor overboard. Secure chain with rope in case you need to cut it in an emergency.

We have a spare rode on the foredeck with its bitter end tied off to the main mast. We also keep a spare rode in our aft locker, which we may use either fore or aft. As we cannot permanently attach the bitter end to a bulkhead, we have attached a small buoy in case the rode should ever wish to escape before we were able to tie it off to a cleat.

Lessons Learned

⚓ Remember to always secure the bitter end prior to deploying your anchor.

Chapter 8: Amount of Rode or Scope

We mentioned earlier that if you do not let out enough rode, and your scope is too small, your anchor will not set and will pull out. It takes an adequate amount of rope or chain for your anchor to hold properly. Scope is perhaps one of the most critical considerations in anchoring, one of the elements most often at root of problems, and one of the things that is the easiest to correct.

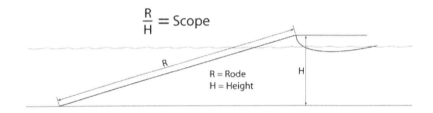

$$\frac{R}{H} = Scope$$

R = Rode
H = Height

Scope is the ratio of the length of rode (R) to the height of the bow above the bottom (H). Remember to take the tidal range into consideration.

The ratio of the length of rode to the depth of the water is called scope. The depth should be calculated to include the actual water depth at the time of anchoring, plus the height the tide will rise to at its full height, plus the height of the bow of your boat above the water line. If your boat's freeboard is five feet above the water, this can make a big difference when you are anchoring in eight feet of water.

For example:

If you arrive in an anchorage at half-tide and the overall tidal variation is 10 feet, then the tide will rise an extra 5 feet. Assuming the water depth is 15 feet when you anchor, it will be 20 feet at high tide. To this you must add your 5 feet of freeboard. So, you will have 25 feet from the deck to the bottom at high tide.

To achieve a 5:1 scope, it will take 125 feet of rode (5 x 25ft). Simple mathematics! Of course, the tide will also fall later fall to 10 ft depth, at which time you will have an 8.3:1 scope – more is better.

Making the Connection ⚓ The Anchor Rode

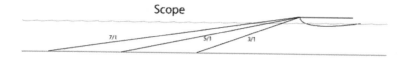

Scope

The greater the scope, the smaller the angle at which the rode addresses the bottom.

How Much Scope?

Most people consider a 5:1 ratio (scope) rode/depth to be the minimum scope for safe anchoring under moderate conditions. There are some who may suggest less with certain newer gear. With an all chain rode, you may indeed need less scope, but it is always better to err on the side of safety. We usually go for a 7:1 scope with our all chain rode, more if we are expecting stronger winds. A greater scope is better.

When calculating required scope, keep in mind that your depth sounder may be giving you the water depth under your keel, rather than from the true waterline. In this case you also need to add the difference from where it is measured to the waterline when calculating scope.

> **Example:**
>
> 8 ft measured water depth at LW
> + 5 ft freeboard from water to deck
> + 10 ft tide (18 ft of depth at HW)
> = 23 ft 'depth'
>
> ------------------------------------
>
> *To achieve a 5:1 scope:*
> 23 x 5 = <u>115 feet of rode</u>.

The calculation also does not take the motion of a boat at anchor into consideration. If a wave lifts the bow of your boat several feet, then this will also affect your scope.

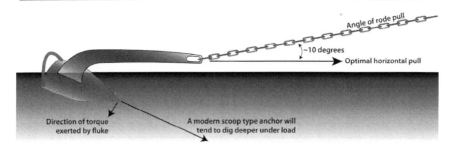

Once an anchor is set, in moderate conditions, an angulation of about 10 degrees between the rode and the anchor shank can be expected. This is caused by the torque exerted by the anchor's fluke. Taking this angulation into consideration, the anchor would be subjected to a horizontal pull at a scope of approximately 6:1. As the winds and the load subsequently increase, this angulation may decrease, and more scope (resulting in a smaller angle of pull) is needed.

In crowded anchorages, you may not be able to let out as much rode as you'd like. In this case you will need to weigh your options and see what is best for you and your vessel. If the conditions are very moderate and you are confident, they will remain so, you may choose to power set your anchor and then shorten your scope for a safe swing radius from your neighbors. It is best to set your anchor gently at greater scope and shorten the rode up after it is well set. If there is a chance that the wind might pick up and you do not cherish the idea of playing bumper boats in the middle of the night, you may consider relocating elsewhere. (See also: swing radius.)

Making the Connection ⚓ The Anchor Rode

Remember to Account for Tide

As mentioned previously, it is very important that you take the tide into consideration when working out how much rode to let out. If you anchor at low tide, or Mean Low Water (MLW), say in 8 feet of water and there is an 8-foot tidal range, it will be 16 feet at Mean High Water (MHW) and your scope will be reduced to half at high tide, with a significant reduction in holding power. Remember to plan this additional depth into the amount of rode you let out.

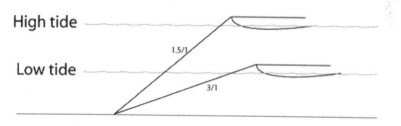

If you anchor at low tide in 8' of water with a 3:1 scope, you will be down to about a 1.5:1 scope at high tide given an 8' tidal range.

The General Rule: More scope is better

As you increase the amount of rode you let out, and the angle at which your anchor addresses the bottom decreases, the holding power of your anchor increases. Greater scope also helps the anchor dig deep into the bottom as the attack angle of the blade or fluke increases. When selecting an anchor, one must bear in mind that the stated holding power is only attained in a horizontal pull.

Effect of Scope on Angle of Anchor

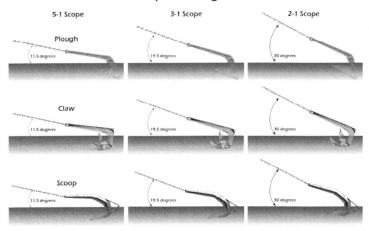

More scope => Better performance
Smaller angle, Better anchor penetration => Greater holding power
Of note is also that different types of anchors have different holding power.

If you look at what scope does to the holding power of an anchor, then the adage of "more scope is better" is even more poignant.

Estimated Percent of Maximum Holding Power as a Function of Scope

Scope Ratio	2:1	4:1	6:1	8:1	10:1	>10:1
Percentage of Maximum Holding Power	10	55	70	80	85	>85

Also, the energy absorption increases linearly with the greater scope and thus lessens the tugging on your anchor and on your deck hardware.

More scope results in better holding power

- More rode gives you more scope
- More scope gives you a smaller angle
- A smaller angle gives you better penetration
- More rode gives better energy absorption

Making the Connection ⚓ The Anchor Rode

Determining a Boat's Scope

Scope (ratio)	Angle (degrees)
1.414:1	45
2:1	30
3:1	19.5
4:1	14.5
5:1	11.5
6:1	9.6
7:1	8.2
8:1	7.2
9:1	6.4
10:1	5.74

There have been occasions when we had people tell us that they were anchoring with a 5:1 scope. They then continued stating that they determine their scope by the angle the rode enters the water – 30-35 degrees being their goal. One person even declared that he always went for a 45-degree angle.

The adjacent table illustrates just how small an angle you need to achieve to ensure that you have adequate scope out. Clearly the angles quoted above were sorely inadequate. Additionally, we would consider it difficult to accurately measure the angle at which the rode leaves the bow or enters the water for that matter.

Most people will work out how much rode they should let out based on the depth plus bow height, plus tide. To help determine the correct amount of rode to let out to attain the optimal scope, you can use a rode counter. This is done by electronically or mechanically counting the windlass turns and multiplying this by its diameter.

You can also mark your rode.

Marking the Rode

In order to easily track how much rode you have let out when anchoring, it is helpful to mark the rode at specific intervals. Whether one measures these intervals in feet, meters or fathoms is a personal choice. Bear in mind that most printed charts are now in meters and even the US NOAA charts are to be standardized in the metric system.

Any marking system should be easy to see or read at night. You can mark a rope rode using colored whipping line at regular intervals, cable ties, plastic ribbons, or colored tape. For a chain rode you can use tied on ribbons, cable ties, plastic chain markers, tape, or paint.

the rode you see to the bow height is your scope, regardless of how deep the water is!

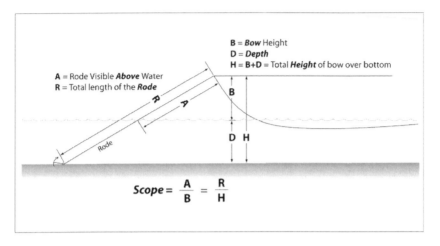

The ratio of the amount of rode you see above the water (A) to the bow height (B) is equal to the ratio of the length of rode you have let out (R) to the total height of your bow above the bottom (H) and either of these are equal to the Scope.

So, if A/B = 25'/5' = 5/1, then you indeed have a 5:1 scope!

So, finally you have a practical application for the math you were required to learn in school. Of course, this only really works with a rope rode. An all chain rode with lots of weight tends to sag unless conditions stretch it taut.

This is what a 5:1 scope looks like

Chapter 9: Kellets

An anchor kellet (sentinel, angel, chum, buddy, or rider) is frequently hailed as a means by which to increase the holding power of your anchor, reduce dragging incidents, and complement the rest of your ground tackle. As with the catenary from chain, an anchor kellet will contribute to the dampening and energy absorption **only** in light to medium winds.

Chapman Piloting, Seamanship and Small Boat Handling defines: "A sentinel (kellet) is a weight typically around 25-30lb suspended from the rode to help keep the pull on the anchor as horizontally as possible to prevent dragging in rough weather."

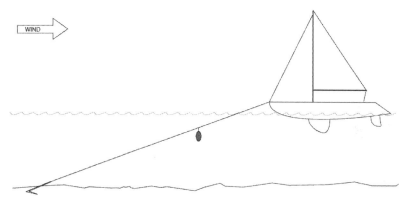

Like many subjects in boating, the benefits of using a kellet are controversial and subject of much debate. A kellet is beneficial **only in light to moderate wind conditions**. If there is a strong wind and the rode it taut, then the kellet has little or no beneficial effect. This is true irrespective of whether a rope or chain rode is used.

Kellets are essentially heavy weights you either affix to your rode or loop over your rode and lower down using a separate line. Most kellets are made out of whatever happens to be on board – diving weights or other lead objects, large iron shackles, swivels or lumps of chain may also be quite suitable. You can, of course, also buy a commercially available kellet such as the Anchor Buddy or Anchor Rider.

Getting Hooked ⚓ Anchoring Technique

Anchor Buddy in action

If an anchor does not set well or hold well and tends to drag, dated wisdom advised adding an anchor kellet. Our immediate reaction if someone mentions this scenario would be to ask the person if he or she is using an older anchor such as a CQR/hinged plow, Brittany, or FOB. If this is the case, one should first and foremost consider purchasing a good modern anchor. Any one of the modern scoop type anchors (Rocna, Supreme, Spade, Ultra, Mantus, Vulcan, etc.) sized correctly for a vessel will hold well in almost any type of bottom.

If an anchor is in any way damaged, bent or worn, or is a knockoff and poorly engineered, it simply will not hold irrespective of what you attach to it or to your rode and is thus to be considered unsafe. Remember also, that a larger anchor of the same type will hold better than a smaller one – bigger is definitely better.

Avoiding a Wrap

Perhaps the one scenario, where a (small) kellet is truly indispensable is in avoiding a wrap with a rope rode. In light air, or if you are at a location with changing currents, it is advisable to weigh down your rope rode. This will help prevent wrapping it around your keel when you swing if you have a modern fin keeled sailboat. It will also keep the rode from catching your propeller.

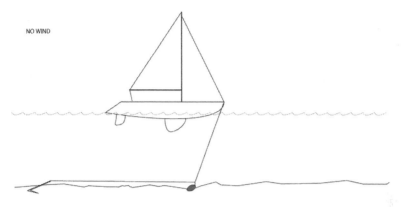

NO WIND

In a light wind situation or changing currents the kellet will keep the rode clear of the keel, rudder and propeller

We used a four pound lead weight on our rope rode, which we tied to the rode about 15-20 feet from the bow of the boat. If we then drifted over the anchor, our rode was usually safely well below our keel. Similarly, we always use a kellet to weigh down a buoyed rope, be it our trip line as discussed elsewhere, or for that matter our crab pot buoys. In this case we use an 8 oz. fishing weight.

We learned this lesson the hard way of course, having anchored without a kellet in a river with reversing current. In the morning, we had a seriously wrapped keel. We used our dinghy to tow the main boat in circles until the keel was fully unwrapped.

Potential uses for a kellet:

These pertain **only to light wind conditions**. In strong winds the rode, whether chain or rope, becomes bar taut and any benefit of a kellet is lost.

1. To improve the angle the anchor addresses the bottom
    - Positioning the kellet weighing about 25-50 pounds close to the anchor shank will pull the shank downwards and reduce the angle the anchor addresses the bottom.
2. To provide additional dampening (shock absorption)

147

⚓ Positioning a 25-50 pound kellet as close to mid-way down your rode will provide better dampening and improve the shock absorption.

3. **To prevent a wrap**
   ⚓ It can help prevent a wrap of the rode around the keel as the boat swings around in a current
   ⚓ It can contain and minimize swing radii
   ⚓ It can help dampen "sailing" at anchor

In either of the scenarios -- 1 or 2 -- above you would be better advised to deploy a heavier, or preferably a better designed, anchor than to add 25-50 pounds of lead to your tackle. Doing so will likely add less weight to your boat and will provide you with a better result.

The best way to improve the dampening of your rope rode is to increase your scope (more rode). It is usually advisable to add a length of chain to your rode, as this will help prevent chafe on the bottom, and will provide an initial improvement to the angle the anchor addresses the bottom while setting. Doubling the length of your rope rode will double the amount it will stretch and thus double the dampening. Likewise, you might double the length of your snubber to double its dampening with an all chain rode.

Part 3: 'Getting Hooked' – Anchoring Technique

"The first time I remember anchoring I took my dinghy in to a beach that I had wanted to explore. The dinghy was equipped with an anchor. I beached the dinghy, then tied the anchor to the painter, and buried the anchor a distance up the beach. I went for a leisurely walk up and over the hill to the beach on the other side of a narrow spit of land. When I returned, the tide had gone out – way out. The dinghy was now at what appeared to be about a half mile away from the water and it was going to be getting dark soon."

"Needless to say, I learned all about taking the tides into account when anchoring that day. In case you are wondering, I succeeded in dragging the dinghy, engine up, all the way out, huffing and puffing every step of the way. Since then anchoring has continued to be an 'experience';" Daria.

Years later we had a boat on Chesapeake Bay on the East coast of the US. Here anchoring seemed to be no big deal. You dropped the anchor and it stuck in the mud. There was usually little tide and even less wind during the summer months to worry about. There, it was more about finding the perfect secluded anchorage: one that wouldn't expose you to the ravages of the state bird (the mosquito), where you weren't likely to get permanently stuck in the mud on the way in, and a place that offered plenty of opportunity to secure dinner (crabbing on the river or reservations at the local crab house). It was also important that there was a nice breeze in the middle of the steamy summer months.

Each experience we have had, as well as those we have heard about, has taught us something. Each has given us an additional factor to

149

Getting Hooked & Anchoring Technique

consider when we select an anchorage and prepare to attach our boat to the bottom, where we want our hook to find a good purchase and keep us safe. Though the price you pay for your mistakes may sometimes seem high, the knowledge gained will always be valuable if you put it to good use. I am sure we will continue learning a valuable lesson each time, hopefully without damage to health or property. We will also listen to other people's experiences and advice, and merge these with our own, thereby making a greater whole.

Our 'adventures' have taught us to stay cool under pressure, work together as a team, and always be prepared with an exit strategy should we need it. Luckily, or perhaps due to good planning, our wonderful anchoring experiences far outnumber the trying ones.

Our technique has evolved into a seven-step process which we will describe in more detail on the following pages.

1. Pick a destination based on what you'd like to do when you get there, e.g., chill, go to town, visit a beach
2. Check the charts to pick a spot and select the right gear for it
3. Check the weather to make sure your chosen spot will remain protected
4. Drop your anchor and set it well
5. Allow plenty of scope while accounting for swing radius
6. Set the anchor alarm and watch schedule, if needed
7. Relax and enjoy the world around you

Chapter 1: Selecting an Anchorage

One of the more 'interesting' parts of anchoring is finding a suitable place to drop your hook. Over the years we have had our fair share of experience with things that went wrong while anchoring. These experiences have taught us to choose an anchorage with care. They have also helped us develop techniques and contingency plans that have served us well under most circumstances.

Finding a spot to anchor is not always easy in a busy harbor.

Depending on the conditions present on a given day, different areas in a particular harbor may provide the best holding ground with respect to wind direction. Some areas may provide the most comfortable place with regard to wave action. Other spots may have the most reasonable access to shore side activities. Some may even provide all three.

The cruising guides, sailing directions, and current harbor charts, though often out of date by the time they are published, will indicate where the best anchorages are and what the bottom composition is likely to be. There is not much guesswork when you are out coastal boating in developed countries with sophisticated and up-to-date charting services. In other parts of the world, especially where information on the charts is quite literally derived from buccaneer times, the selection of a place to drop your hook can necessitate a bit of trial and error.

In most anchorages, you can expect one of five main types of bottoms (or combinations of these): mud, sand, shell, weed, or rock, with soft mud being quite predominant in sheltered coves or harbors. Often anchorages are in the prevailing lee of an island or shore. Just remember that the wind and waves do not always cooperate.

Reading a Chart

Having a chart is one thing. Being able to interpret the information on it is not always that straight forward. One charting publication often overlooked by the leisure mariner, but essential when it comes to interpreting the myriad of symbols and abbreviations found on a chart, is Chart No. 1 in the US or Chart No. 5011 in the UK. These provide the key to all the symbols and abbreviations on your charts. They are invaluable in determining the difference between Rky (rocky), M (mud), S (sand), Cl (clay) or Grs (grass), s (soft), h (hard), or hS (hard Sand).

Chart No. 1 for US charts
It is available as a free download online:
https://nauticalcharts.noaa.gov/publ ications/docs/us-chart-1/ChartNo1.pdf

Chart No. 5011 for UKHO Admiralty charts.
It is available from nautical book resellers, Amazon.co.uk and directly from the UKHO
A free scanned pdf is available from: http://www.marinedocs.co.uk/chart-5011-symbols-and-abbreviations-used-on-admiralty-paper-charts-2006-edition/

Alex & Daria Blackwell

The following chart of Great Salt Pond on Block Island, RI is a good example showing many of the bottom features to look for. It tells you where to find obstructions (or better yet, where you will not find them), such as underwater cables, wrecks, as well as channels and off limit areas (preserves, 'secret' government installations, etc.). The depths on this chart are labelled in feet. In other cases, they may be in fathoms or meters so be careful to check the legend when reading your charts.

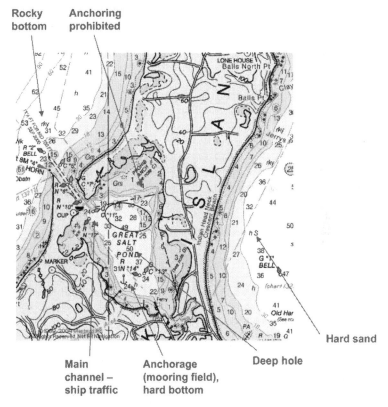

Rocky bottom
Anchoring prohibited
Hard sand
Main channel – ship traffic
Anchorage (mooring field), hard bottom
Deep hole

Charts tell you much of what you need to know about an anchorage.

Great Salt Pond on Block Island is a very popular anchorage and most newcomers try to anchor in the middle where there is usually an open spot. An astute navigator (someone who took a cursory look at the chart) would notice in advance that this is a deep hole with steeply sloping sides, where it is almost impossible to anchor.

Getting Hooked ⚓ Anchoring Technique

Anchoring Restrictions

Due to ecological and environmental concerns as well as increases in population, there are an ever-increasing number of areas where anchoring is prohibited. On the preceding chart there is an area to the north of the harbor where one may not anchor as this is a protected eelgrass area. As a general rule, and in many cases enshrined in law, one should never anchor in coral. Many more congested harbors, in places such as Florida, are extending their mooring fields and prohibiting permanent live-aboards. The reason behind this is the occasional derelict and unsightly craft left behind by an inconsiderate owner. Martinique has announced a restricted area to protect the ships sunk by the eruption of Mount Pele. Many island nations now have extensive underwater marine preserves where anchoring is not permitted.

Areas may be closed off to anchoring for good reason. In dense fog at night, friends of ours once felt their way into Karlskrona in Sweden (a naval port). They snuck out of the fairway and dropped their anchor with huge relief and turned in. They were awoken in the morning by a fishing boat informing them they had anchored in a minefield! Although they did not say so, we are assuming they missed some annotation in Swedish on their chart.

Cruising Guides

Cruising Guides and Sailing Directions provide many details about anchorages and the best approaches to them. They often give advice on anchor selection as well. However, it is worth bearing in mind that the information may well be dated, and anchorages reported as having poor holding may have been tested with older or unsuitable anchors for the bottom composition or conditions. We have often found excellent holding in harbors where a guide stated the opposite.

Picking Your Spot

There are numerous factors to take into consideration when anchoring, many of which involve common sense. Some are things to plan for, others are things to avoid. With practice it will become second nature to evaluate a situation and make a series of judgments that will lead to a peaceful night at anchor.

Try to pick a spot protected from more than one direction – a small cove or inlet can be quite ideal. Although wind is a major factor to take into account, waves are what cause the most discomfort and a strong current can contribute to the latter when least expected. Keep away from navigation or shipping channels, as well as from popular beaches. Besides creating a safety and navigational hazard, these locations will only provide annoyance to you from the other boat traffic.

Remember to also plan for tidal variation. You don't want to wake up bouncing on the bottom, or worse find your boat listing to one side and having your daughter roll out of her bunk, as happened to friends recently.

One time, we awoke to a strange motion – or rather lack of motion. We had neglected to account for the extra drop with the spring tide, during which the tidal variation is more extreme, and our keel was firmly embedded in the mud. Fortunately, we were in no hurry to go. In the end it did not take long before the incoming tide lifted us off the muddy bottom and allowed us to get underway.

Getting Hooked ⚓ Anchoring Technique

Things to take into consideration when anchoring

- ⚓ Predicted wind direction and strength
- ⚓ Height of tide at the time of anchoring
- ⚓ Depth at MLW and MHW
- ⚓ Current direction and strength
- ⚓ Swing radius
- ⚓ Access to desired activities (eg: beach walk, shore leave, fishing hole, etc.)

Things to avoid when planning to anchor

- ⚓ Stern to a lee shore
- ⚓ Proximity to mooring fields and channels
- ⚓ Sloping or grassy bottoms
- ⚓ Boats that swing differently from yours
- ⚓ Rowdy or careless neighbors
- ⚓ Areas open to a broad fetch
- ⚓ Anchoring up-wind of another vessel so you end up over their anchor
- ⚓ Anything that can foul your anchor or snag your rode

Chapter 2: Taking Weather into Account

Perhaps the most important consideration in anchoring is what the weather conditions will be while you are at anchor. Will the wind be light or strong, what direction will it come from, and will conditions change during the night? These are all factors that could interrupt your night's sleep or worse.

Weather prediction is a much-maligned science. Although one tends to remember the days the forecast was wrong, the fact is that the short-term forecast is improving all the time and more often correct than not.

Keeping a 'weather eye' open often helps.

Although the information is relatively reliable, the specific weather for a given location may differ from the larger (predicted) picture due to local variations and influences. The best approach is always to expect the unexpected. Think through what you would do if the unpredicted happens.

Of course, the most important resource for what is going to happen is using one's own eyes and senses. If there is a thunderstorm cloud or a rain squall visible, then that is what you need to plan for.

Alex and Daria Blackwell

Weather Forecasting Resources

Before even selecting an anchorage, your first task is getting a weather forecast for your local area. The weather will determine what anchorages will be safe and comfortable for the duration of your stay. Depending on where you are, there are usually several resources at your disposal.

Coastal Forecasts

If you are coastal cruising, you can avail of local radio and TV broadcasts, internet weather sites, mobile weather apps, and periodic forecasts for mariners on the VHF radio. Before setting out, you can investigate expected conditions for a week in advance via weather websites such as Windguru, Magic Seaweed, Windy, Passage Weather or any number of online and mobile services. You can also do this with your smartphone, either using the appropriate app or via the web.

In US coastal waters, NOAA (National Oceanographic and Atmospheric Administration) Weather Radio (NWR) forecasts are broadcast on VHF channels 1-7, which correspond to these seven frequencies (MHz): 162.400, 162.425, 162.450, 162.475, 162.500, 162.525, and 162.550. This forecast will specify wind direction and speed,

158

temperature and precipitation, as well as any warnings about possibly deteriorating conditions including fog, rough seas, thunderstorms, and gales.

In other countries, weather forecasts (and weather warnings in the US) or forecast notifications are broadcast on VHF Channel 16, the international hailing and distress frequency. In some places there might also be a daily weather broadcast on a local cruiser's net frequency. Channel 68 is used for this in several countries throughout the Caribbean – this is one of the things to ask about when settling in to a new harbor.

Forecasting Services

There are a number of commercial weather routing services for both commercial vessels and private yachts. Any one of these will provide fairly detailed forecasts and routing suggestions for ocean passages or coastal cruising. They will provide forecasts via email, satellite phone or via High Frequency (HF) radio. Although more relevant for planning passages, once you are subscribed you can take advantage of their services to select the best anchorage based on the longer-term forecast.

We were very fortunate on our ocean crossings to be able to avail of the service provided by Herb Hilgenberg, *Southbound II*, who has since retired. He did a personalized forecast for each yacht over SSB (Single Side Band) radio on a daily schedule. Every evening for over 30 years he worked his way around the North Atlantic advising skippers before retiring. He will be sorely missed.

Personal Education

We have taken weather courses, including a wonderful seminar by a meteorologist sailor. We also regularly attended lectures at boat shows and at Safety at Sea Seminars. The US National Weather Service provides various degrees of certification in 'weather spotting' helping civilians learn how to spot deteriorating weather conditions. They can then report on dangerous situations as they arise so that others may be warned. For example, as a trained 'weather spotter,' we can call the local weather conditions into the NOAA office. They then correlate the ground report to what they see on radar and other instruments. In essence, the weather spotter becomes the eyes and ears of the weather service on the ground. If warranted NOAA will advise the US Coast Guard to broadcast a warning on channels 16 (and 22a in the US).

One day for example, the weather service was forecasting 5-8 knots when we were facing 28-30 knots sustained. We had reefed our main and had been watching several small boats struggle with the conditions. We called it in and the weather service said they had no indication,

Lightning can be very dangerous

including from the weather buoys in our vicinity that the wind was as strong as we reported. Nevertheless, the Coast Guard issued a weather notice within minutes of our call.

On another occasion, we reported dangerous cloud-to-ground lightning and high winds to NOAA which had not been forecast but were immediately linked to radar images and broadcast via VHF to the boating community as severe weather warnings. It is possible that we may have saved some boaters from the consequences of being caught unaware out there. It always pays to obey the regulations and have one's radio tuned to VHF channel 16 while underway as well as periodically while anchored.

GRIB Files

The most basic of these are GRIB (**GRI**dded **B**inary) files. This is a mathematically concise data format commonly used in meteorology to store historical and forecast weather data. With data compiled from a myriad of sources, these form the basis for many forecasting models. The data in the file can contain wind speed, direction, barometric pressure, temperature, wave height, wave frequency, humidity, precipitation, cloud cover, and so on. Other variables that determine the scope of the data file (and its size) are the latitude and longitude range, which give you the desired coverage area, the amount of days (into the future), and the time interval between data sets.

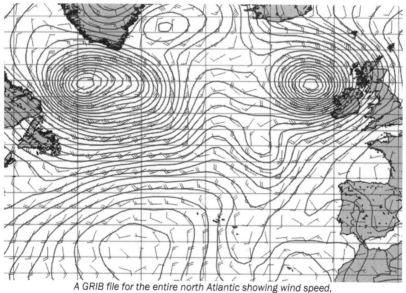

A GRIB file for the entire north Atlantic showing wind speed, direction and barometric pressure.

The more data in the file the larger it gets, which is very relevant depending on how it is downloaded. On land with broadband access, it is reasonable to download a large geographical area as in the example.

If you are using a satellite phone to download it to your boat while underway, you will be wise to select a much smaller area. My first attempt in mid-Atlantic returned a 2.5mb file, which took a long time and cost a small fortune to download. The above file, which is one part of a nine-day forecast, was over 16mb.

GRIB files can be viewed using a number of available software packages and apps. The popular zyGrib is a freeware option, as is OpenCPN grib weather file viewer which opens both Grib1 and the new Grib2 file extensions. Several PC-based charting packages will also allow you to overlay the GRIB file onto a chart. Mobile apps, such as PocketGrib, Windy, OpenCPN, Predict Wind (Ugrib) and many others provide access to GRIB files when boating within reach of mobile signal. Predict Wind also offers connectivity via SSB and satellite. Several routing programs combine a GRIB file with boat performance data to produce an optimized route. Many GRIB file services simply relay output from NWP models, usually also, but not always, the US General Forecast System (GFS) model.

Once translated and viewable on screen it is possible to track approaching weather systems and, with a little practice, come to a semblance of a personal forecast. On our ocean passages and while at anchor, we download a small GRIB file every morning and evening to give us an idea of what to expect, as well as how to avoid the worst and take advantage of the best. On land with an internet connection we download larger files to help us get a feeling for a weather window for a passage between anchorages or the best selection of an anchorage.

GRIB files can also help you relate to the forecast being given by routing services. Seeing the scenario unfolding yourself can help you partner with a weather service provider in determining the best course of action for you and your vessel. A good place to start understanding weather resources is Frank Singleton's weather pages on mailasail.com.

Selecting an Anchorage

With basic weather information in hand, you can choose your spot for maximum protection from the wind and the waves to keep your family snug and comfortable all night long.

Choose an anchorage in the protection (lee) of an island or high shore where the wind and wave action will be minimal. The longer the distance (fetch) across a body of water, the higher the likelihood of developing a chop. It is the pitching of the boat caused by this chop and the subsequent tugging at the tackle that causes anchors to drag more often than the wind strength – not to mention the discomfort you will experience. (See also Section on "Rolly Anchorage" under the chapter on Setting Two Anchors)

This ketch found the idyllic anchorage for a beautiful night. However, it would have been quite exposed if the wind had come up and swept in from the open water.

Avoid an exposed anchorage if the conditions are questionable and certainly avoid having your stern close to a shore (also referred to as the being on a lee shore). If you drag toward shore, you will have little time to react before grounding.

If there is a forecast for stronger wind, then a higher piece of land will be better, as it will protect you from the wind as well as the waves. On the other hand, if it is going to be hot, you will want to pick a spot where you will be able to scoop in some breezy relief.

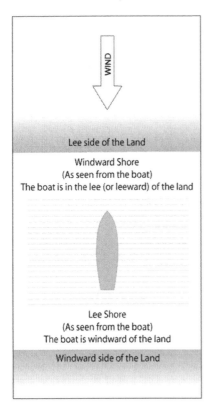

As is illustrated here, being off a lee shore is not the same as being in the lee of the land.

In most instances you will want to have the wind coming from the direction of shore. You want to be in the lee of the land.

Getting Hooked ⚓ Anchoring Technique

It is not always that you get an ideal location like this where you have a protected anchorage with plenty of room to swing while catching a light breeze.

One quiet gentle evening we were having a carefree dinner with company securely anchored in the lee of an

island. A sudden, unpredicted squall hit us. The wind gusted up to 50 knots shredding our canvas awning as it quickly shifted 180 degrees. We motored into the wind for close to an hour to reduce the load on our anchor as we feared being pushed onto the now very close lee shore. In this instance we learned how quickly conditions can change and that backup plans are helpful.

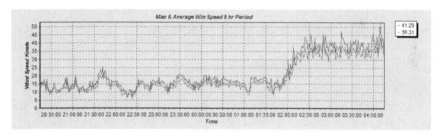

A wind chart showing the wind speed quickly going from a moderate breeze to gale force.

Localized Winds

There are of course times where the wind may do the unexpected. This is particularly likely to happen if you are in an area with high mountains.

Anabatic Winds

If you sail or anchor in the lee of a mountain, you may experience sudden reversals from the prevailing offshore to a stiff onshore breeze, placing you upwind of a lee shore. In this case you may have been subjected to an anabatic wind.

Derived from the Greek anabatos, meaning moving upward, an anabatic wind is a wind which blows up a steep slope or mountain side, driven by heating of the slope through insulation. It is also known as an upslope flow. These winds typically occur during the daytime in calm sunny weather. A hill or mountain top radiantly warmed by the sun heats the air just above it. Air over an adjacent valley, plain, or area of water does not get warmed to the same degree. The effect may be enhanced if the lower lying area is shaded by the mountain and so receives even less heat. The result is a quite stiff onshore breeze while anchored or sailing in what might have been the lee side of an island.

Katabatic Winds

Conversely, katabatic winds are down-slope winds. The term is derived from the Greek word katabatikos meaning going downhill. They are produced by the opposite effect to anabatic winds. When the air over a mountain cools at night the high-density air rushes down the slope under the force of gravity. Katabatic winds can reach hurricane speeds, but most are not that intense and may be in the order of 10 knots or less.

We have experienced these winds first hand, and, in some places, they can be quite a predictable, happening at a certain time of day. It pays to be aware and prepared to manage the situation if it deteriorates.

Chapter 3: The Rise and Fall of the Tides

A very important factor when selecting an anchorage in many parts of the world is the tide. We touch on it in other parts of this book.

In brief, tides are the changing depth of water over the course of time – usually changing more than once in a day.

The physics of tides is an immensely complicated topic, which far surpasses what a boater needs to know. We will cover only the basics that affect boating here. More detail is, of course, available in the scientific literature.

What causes the tides?

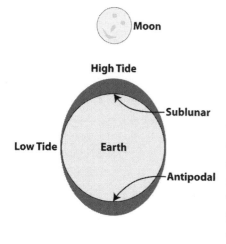

In simplified terms, tides are caused by the effect of the gravitational forces exerted by the moon and sun combined. The moon is the primary mechanism that drives tidal action and explains two equipotential tidal bulges, accounting for two daily high waters as the earth turns on its axis. The moon's gravity, for example, pulls the water on earth towards it, as in the adjacent graphic. This is how it would look if the earth were a simple, stationary ball entirely covered with water.

The earth's rotation and the land masses cause the tides to rotate in harmonic waves in circular patterns around what are called amphidromic points.

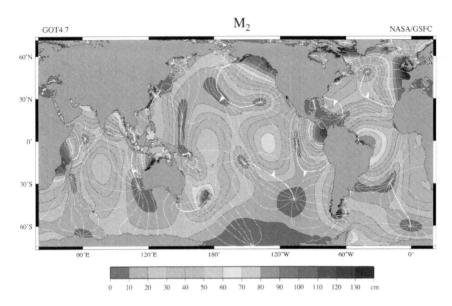

GOT4.7 M_2 NASA/GSFC

Tidal waves and variations, which can in places be quite significant.
Courtesy of Goddard Space Flight Center

These tidal waves sweep the shorelines and may or may not overlap. Where they do overlap, they may add up or cancel each other out. They may also be slightly out of phase. Some places will thus experience a semi-diurnal tide, with two nearly equal high and low tides each day. Other locations may experience a diurnal tide with only one high and low tide each day. A "mixed tide", or two uneven tides a day is also possible.

Tides are not limited to the oceans but can occur in other water bodies as well. Large lakes such as Lake Superior and Lake Erie can experience tides of 1 to 4 cm. However, that is not something most people are likely to notice.

Distribution of Tidal Phases

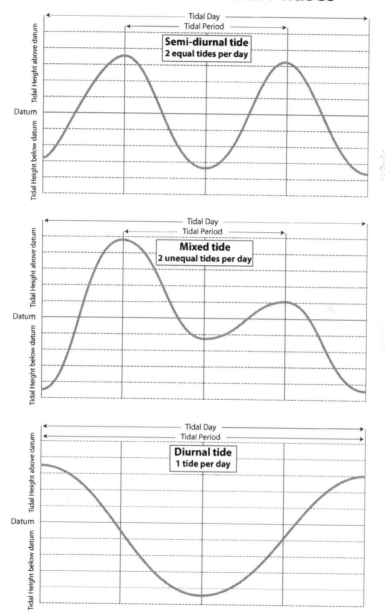

Alex and Daria Blackwell

While tides are usually the largest source of short-term sea-level fluctuations, sea levels are also subject to forces such as barometric pressure changes and wind. The latter potentially resulting in storm surges, especially in shallow seas and near coasts.

Tides also produce reversing currents known as tidal streams. The moment that the tidal current ceases is called slack water or slack tide. The tide then reverses direction and is said to be turning. Slack water usually occurs near high water and low water.

The ocean bathymetry greatly influences the tide's exact time and height at a particular coastal point. There are some extreme cases. The Bay of Fundy, on the east coast of Canada, is often stated to have the world's highest tides because of its shape, bathymetry, and its distance from the continental shelf edge. Measurements made in November 1998 at Burntcoat Head in the Bay of Fundy, Nova Scotia recorded a maximum range of 16.3 meters (53 ft.). Likewise, in the Bay of Mont-Saint-Michel in France it can also exceed 16 meters.

Tide tables list each day's high and low water heights and times. To calculate the actual water depth, add the depth on the chart (shown in MLLW) to the tide height for a given time found in the tide table. Take this tide into account when crossing shallows and when anchoring. Clearly, if there is a 10-foot tidal variation between low and high tide and you anchor close to the time of high water, you need to be certain you won't be sitting on the bottom when the tide goes out. Similarly, you need to allow adequate scope for the increasing tide if you are anchoring closer to the time of low water.

Try to avoid entering an unknown anchorage on a falling tide. If you ground on an unexpected shallow on a falling tide, you will be stuck and potentially in danger though a full tide cycle. If you enter the anchorage on a rising tide and encounter a speed bump shallow, you can wait for the tide to lift you up.

Getting Hooked ⚓ Anchoring Technique

The Rule of Twelfths

The *Rule of Twelfths* is useful for determining approximately how fast the tide will be coming in or going out. It also helps in understanding how tide driven current speeds will vary over time.

Under normal circumstances there are approximately six hours between low tide and high tide. In the first hour after low tide, the tide will rise 1/12 of the way to high tide. In the second hour, it will rise 2/12. In the third and fourth hours it will rise 3/12, in the fifth 2/12, and in the sixth, 1/12. (Totaling twelve twelfths) This same sequence of twelfths is repeated in the subsequent six hours as the tide goes back out.

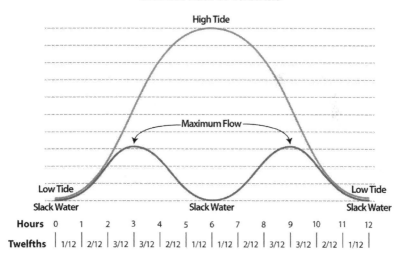

**Tidal Cycle, Water Flow
and the Rule of Twelfths**

A logical consequence of this fluctuation in the rate the tide comes in and goes out is that the water currents being driven by these tide changes will also speed up and slow down accordingly. A complication to this arises in many instances where the current change may be offset by a matter of hours from the tide change. This can involve coastal currents around headlands or in and out of bays or inlets. These currents may be quite strong when passing through narrow passages or over shallow ground. Examples of this are the Corryvreckan in Scotland, Eggemoggin reach in Maine, or the East River along Manhattan. The latter is not an actual river, but rather a connection between Long Island Sound and the Hudson River. These currents can well exceed 7 knots. Information on local currents and tidal variations can be found in the almanac covering the cruising ground in question.

Tide Heights

Another complication with tides is that their amplitudes vary with the phase of the moon and the alignment of the sun, moon and earth.

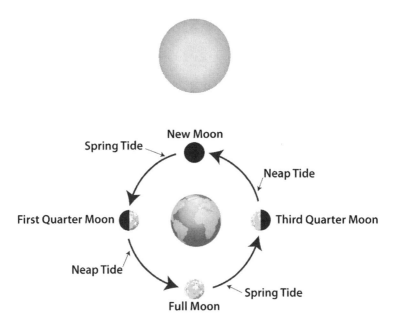

Shortly after the full and new moon, one may expect spring tides, which can be considerably higher (and lower) than the neaps following the quarter moons. During the times of the equinoxes, where the sun is aligned with our planetary system, the springs can be much higher again.

Getting Hooked ⚓ Anchoring Technique

Some definitions:

- ⚓ **Mean Higher High Water, MHHW:** The observed average of the higher high-water height of each tidal day*
- ⚓ **Mean High Water, MHW:** The observed average of all the high-water heights*
- ⚓ **Mean Low Water, MLW:** The observed average of all the low water heights*
- ⚓ **Mean Lower Low Water, MLLW:** The observed average of the lower low water height of each tidal day*
- ⚓ **Chart Datum:** The datum to which soundings on a chart are referred. It is usually the MLLW.

* The National Ocean Service adopted a 19-year period as the official time segment over which tide observations are taken and reduced to obtain mean values.

Tide Information Resources

There are many resources for determining what the tide in a given location is predicted to do. There are printed tide tables, which are handy to have for one's local cruising ground. Tide tables are also available for most locations online. WXTide32 is one of the oldest online prediction programs. The nautical almanacs contain tide tables.

There are also many electronic options today. Most GPS chart plotters have tide tables for the regions covered in the charts. There are also numerous excellent apps available for your smartphone, as well as charting apps that also include tide tables.

Keep in mind, that all tide predictions are calculated for future dates based on different models. The projections can thus vary considerably between tide information resources. The actual readings can vary based on any number of variables in nature.

Chapter 4: Dropping the Hook – How to Anchor your Boat

Anchoring can be a lovely dance in the harbor or a furiously frustrating experience, the latter providing great entertainment value to fellow boaters already hooked. A bit of preparation can make all the difference as to which outcome you have.

Anchoring is a spectator sport. It is a fact that as soon as a new boat enters a harbor, binoculars come out scanning the new arrivals and keeping a close eye on their technique. So, it pays to be prepared.

Preparation is Key

Doing it right involves a few simple steps and a bit of advance planning. If for some reason a certain spot does not feel right, then it probably is not. Be flexible and move on.

> *"If you didn't do it when you anchored,*
> *you're not going to be able to do it when it hits."*

Leon Werner from *Prism*

Getting Hooked ⚓ Anchoring Technique

A Method That Works for Us

First, choose a location that will be best suited for the conditions, including the expected wind strength and direction. The preceding chapters contain more information on anchorage selection.

Check the tide table. Determine the current state of the tide, whether it is going out or coming in, and how deep the water at your location will be at high and low water.

Judge how the tide is likely to affect the depth relative to the draft of your vessel as well as to the amount of scope you will need. You need to know the depth this location will have at both high tide and low tide.

It is advisable to cruise slowly through an anchorage to inspect it upon arrival. Note how the charted depths and features relate to the actual physical appearance. Note how other boats have anchored. If you cannot tell from what you see, don't be afraid to ask your potential neighbors how much scope they have out or any other information that might help.

> *Note: If you are towing a dinghy, make sure you pull it in and tie the painter off short prior to commencing the maneuver so as not to foul your prop! Using a floating line for the dinghy painter can help.*

Drive in a circle around the perimeter of what you expect your swing to be to make sure there aren't any obstructions, boats that could swing close, or variables in depth that may not be on your chart. Your boat will swing, sometimes completing a 360° circle.

---

* As we mentioned before, these are methods that work best for us. Every boat, every skipper, every anchor, every bottom, and every weather factor is different, so our methods may not be best for you.

Keep in mind that different boats will swing differently: sloops, catamarans, large vessels, powerboats, or flat bottom boats will all swing with very different characteristics. Some boats yaw to the extreme while others ride straight as an arrow into the wind or into the current. Take the time to observe the vessels nearby and try to anchor away from boats that move differently from yours. If there's plenty of room, there's no worry. It is when the anchorage is crowded that this becomes an issue.

1: Enter anchorage slowly

2: Circle around selected spot

3: Stop boat and drop hook

4: Back down setting anchor

Once you have surveyed the area and have chosen your spot, point into the wind and slowly head for the center of your circle. Stop the boat and let the boat drift backwards or start reversing gently. At the same time lower the anchor slowly to the bottom so that it falls with its flukes, plow, or scoop in the proper orientation. Do not deploy your anchor while the boat is moving forward, and do not just drop the anchor and entire rode off the bow as we often see people do. This is asking for trouble as the anchor and rode will fall to the bottom in a tangled mess.

Getting Hooked & Anchoring Technique

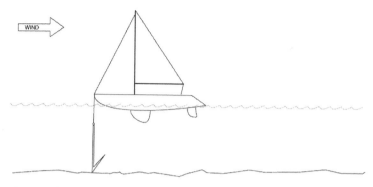

When the anchor reaches the bottom as the boat drift backwards, slowly let out more rode, leaving a little tension on the rode while doing so. This achieves two results: the anchor and chain are cleanly stretched out on the bottom in the correct orientation, and it keeps the boat pointing into the wind while starting to set the anchor.

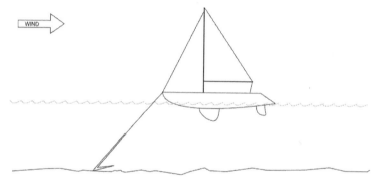

If you have a rope rode pause when it reaches about a 30 degree angle (about 2:1 scope), give it a couple of quick (gentle) tugs to set the anchor (you should feel it catch securely) while still paying out the rode as the boat moves astern. If you are paying out a chain rode, gently apply the windlass brake at this point to achieve the same result. That also helps keep the boat oriented into the wind instead of drifting sideways which so often happens. In either case, you should feel the anchor dig in and catch.

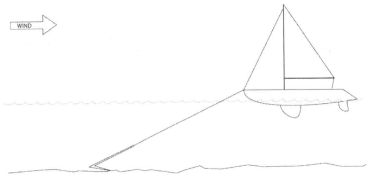

When the anchor starts to set, if the boat has drifted sideways, snub the line before letting out more rode. This will encourage your boat to straighten out so the person at the helm can continue to power gently straight backward when you let out more scope. It can be a source of consternation from bow to stern when the boat starts drifting off to one side. The bowman will often accuse the helmsperson of not steering straight when in reality the helm has no steerage at the speed of drift. Simply snubbing the line periodically and letting the boat swing to the rode can assist in keeping the dance in step. Sometimes the anchor may need to drag along the bottom for a short distance before it finds a spot it likes. The anchor may also have dropped in the wrong orientation and will need to flip itself over or turn to dig in.

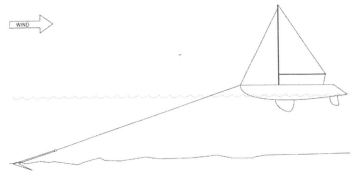

Let out some more rode and secure it on a sturdy cleat. At this point your anchor should have caught, and your boat should be swinging to it. Your next step depends on the characteristics of your anchor and on the consistency of the bottom. Sometimes, like when the bottom is particularly hard, it may take gentle tugging by the boat's movement over several hours to work the anchor into the bottom.

Now make sure the anchor is securely set by carefully backing your boat gently under power. Applying too much power may just pull the anchor out. A good anchor should go deep at this point and keep your boat securely hooked.

After setting the anchor, check to make sure your boat is not moving. This is best done with one person at the bow and one at the helm of the boat. While the helmsperson gently reverses, the other person carefully places a hand or foot on the rode stretching away from the boat. If the anchor drags, the vibration caused by the anchor bouncing along the bottom is easily felt.

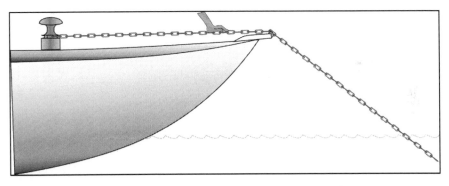

It is very easy to feel if the anchor has set or if it is dragging.

At the same time the helmsperson should take a sighting on pair of stationary, near and distant points, preferably on land, to see if the boat is moving. If the anchor is dragging, you will easily see that the two stationary points no longer align.

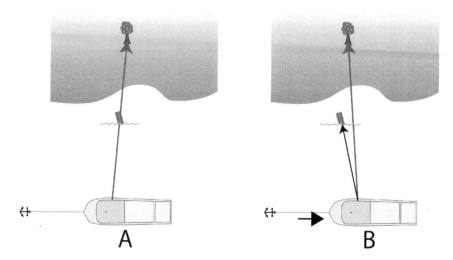

Take a bearing across two fixed objects that are a distance apart (A).
If they move relative to one another (B), then your boat has moved.

If your anchor drags, you can do one of three things:

1. Wait a little longer to see whether your anchor sets if you have enough room in the anchorage
2. Pull the anchor up and start the procedure again in a slightly different spot
3. Try a different anchor

Remember a specific type of anchor may work better in a particular bottom, and your anchor may work better in a different spot in an anchorage. There is nothing embarrassing about trying to set more than once. Conversely, it is not smart to assume your anchor is well set without checking and you wind up dragging later on.

Getting Hooked  Anchoring Technique

This skipper, intent on a selected spot pulled up several loads of weed before he relented and moved on.

Anchoring under sail

Most boaters anchor under power, the sailors having taken down and flaked the main and furled the head sail on the way in. It is not as elegant with the engine on, but it is a lot less nerve wracking, especially in a crowded anchorage.

Of course, there's the finesse of dropping anchor under sail. There are two common ways to anchor under sail. The main thing is to plan every move in advance and do everything slowly and deliberately.

Downwind

This is best done only where there is sufficient room in an anchorage. While sailing forward slowly, drop your anchor, deploy sufficient rode, and let the boat's momentum set the anchor. Quickly drop all (remaining) sails as the boat rounds up into the wind.

If you have a rope rode, it is advisable to bring your anchor aft before dropping, so that it does not foul your keel, prop, or rudder. If you have an all chain rode, you may drop the anchor from the bow.

181

Either way, try to commence the rounding up part of the maneuver before the rode snaps taut and risks damaging the finish of your hull, or the shock load is so great that it damages something.

Upwind

Furl all but one sail. Come into the anchorage with the remaining sail (main or headsail) loosely sheeted. Carefully weave your way through the anchored and moored fleet, pick your spot and point into the wind.

When your boat has stopped in the water, drop the anchor slowly, while quickly furling or dropping the remaining sail. Let the boat gently drop back with the breeze to set. At this time the helmsperson should still be steering the boat in reverse to keep the bow pointing into the wind as it goes backwards. The trick is to avoid letting the sail fill or you may start sailing forward over the anchor.

Once the anchor is set and you have paid out your rode, unfurl one of your sails and back it to power set the hook. Often this is the headsail or staysail with a cutter rig. With a ketch or yawl, it is often the mizzen that is used here.

Be aware that every eye in the anchorage is on you, whether you can actually see anyone or not! Then revel in a job well done. Actually, an anchor set under sail tends to set gently and firmly. Just be prepared to sail away if it doesn't catch.

Anchor Retrieval under Sail

Having successfully anchored under sail (whew!!), most people will succumb to using their motor for the retrieval. In stronger wind conditions, and/or when using a when using a windlass with heavy ground tackle, this is indeed wise.

However, in more benign conditions the technique is quite simple:

- ⚓ Bring your rode in until it is vertical from the bow.
- ⚓ Let the boat's motion loosen the anchor from the bottom.
- ⚓ At the same time raise a portion of your main or hoist the mizzen.

Getting Hooked ⚓ Anchoring Technique

⚓ When the anchor breaks free unfurl a portion of your headsail and sheet it in as you fall off and sail downwind. Steer well clear of other boats and their anchor rodes. The movement should raise your anchor clear of the bottom and obstructions.

⚓ When well clear of the anchorage, head up and tack without releasing the headsail sheet.

⚓ When the forward motion has more or less stopped, lash your tiller to leeward, or turn your wheel to bring the boat to windward.

⚓ Your boat is now hove-to, and you have all the time in the world to finish raising your anchor, tidy up, etc.

Safe Anchoring Technique Summary

⚓ Prepare anchor and rode
⚓ Make sure the rode is secured to the boat
⚓ Check that the anchor shackle is secured against twisting open
⚓ Turn on windlass if appropriate
⚓ Check the spot on the chart
    o Enough water for the tides
    o Shore to windward
    o No obstructions
⚓ Drive a circle around your intended spot
    o Keep eye on depth
    o Watch for obstructions and swing radius
    o Observe how other boats are anchored and how they are behaving at anchor
⚓ Drive to selected spot and stop the boat
    o Point the boat into the wind
    o Point into the current if that is stronger
    o Remember that you will be dropping back
⚓ Drop anchor slowly just until it hits bottom
⚓ If wind is strong enough, let out rode as the boat drops back naturally
⚓ If there is little wind, use idle speed to back

- 🐚 Set anchor
- 🐚 Tug on rode by hand or power back gently until you feel the anchor catch
- 🐚 Power back gently to set while checking for movement and feeling the rode for vibration
- 🐚 Let out additional rode
- 🐚 Power set properly to ensure anchor digs in
- 🐚 Secure the rode and attach a snubber

'Stern Words' About Stern Anchoring

Several years ago, *Soundings* magazine ran a pro and con feature about stern anchoring which provoked a storm of controversy. There are many reasons why one should not anchor from the stern. Most boats are designed and built to present the 'pointy' end to seas and wind. Presenting the broader stern can create more resistance to wind and seas and, thus, considerably more strain on gear. Plus, boarding seas can cause serious problems with the open cockpits, doors, and broad cabin entrances at this end, not to mention exhaust outlets which can siphon water in when pulled down below the surface. A boat anchored by the stern also has an increased risk of damage to rudders, shafts, and shaft logs.

A report in the January 2008 issue of *Seaworthy* provided a concrete example of what could happen. A 20-foot powerboat with a normal low transom was anchored by the stern off the Chesapeake Bay Bridge Tunnel while rock fishing. A large wake from a bulk cargo ship carrying coal came up on the boat sinking it in less than a minute. The fishermen were rescued but the boat sank to the bottom in the swift current.

We strongly advise against stern anchoring, unless of course you have anchors out bow and stern for special circumstances. For more on this, see the chapter on "Setting Two Anchors".

Getting Hooked ⚓ Anchoring Technique

Going Ashore and Securing Your Dinghy

At one point or another you will want to go ashore. There will most likely not always be somewhere for you to pull your dinghy in to a dock or pier. Pulling it up on a beach and tying it to a suitable rock or tree is often the best option. Or you may encounter surf and wish to anchor out past the breaking waters and swim ashore. However, there will come a time where you arrive at low or high tide and would like to ensure the dinghy is still floating or within reach when you get back.

If you arrive when the tide is out, beach your boat, drop the anchor over the side, walk a long trip line up the shore to a point above the high-water mark and tie it to a suitable stone or tree. If you want to keep your dinghy floating despite a falling tide, secure the trip line to the anchor rest the anchor on its bow and push the dinghy off into deep water. Pay out the trip line as the dinghy moves away. At the right moment give the trip line a tug. The anchor will fall into the water and secure the boat. You can now tie off the trip line and do what needs to be done ashore.

This method is also useful if there is an onshore breeze or where the beach is rocky, and you wish to avoid damaging the dink. When you want to go back out, simply pull the anchor in with the trip line and the dinghy will follow.

Place the anchor on the bow of the dinghy. Attach a long trip line to the anchor crown. Flake the trip line on the beach. Secure the anchor rode to the dinghy allowing for anticipated depth and scope.

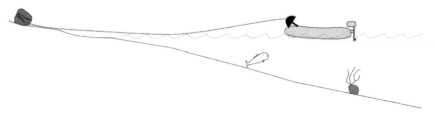

Push the dinghy out paying out the trip line

Jerk on the trip line to drop the anchor. The dinghy is now lying comfortably at anchor. Make sure its trip line is tied off to a suitable object.

Chapter 5: Setting Two Anchors

There are situations where one anchor will not suffice. The first instance that comes to mind is a storm situation, when you assess that you need more holding power. As we discussed in Part 1 of this book, your primary anchor should be sized to provide adequate holding in most conditions. If you feel your anchor is not up to the task, then you might be advised to consider upgrading it. Having said that, although we are fairly confident that our anchors are correctly sized for our boat, we do routinely set a second anchor when we know there is a big blow coming. It gives us peace of mind.

As stressed previously, in a storm situation, your best option is to seek safe harbor so as not be subjected to strong winds and rough seas.

Other times when you might consider two anchors include tight anchorages, poor holding (like very soft soupy mud), shifting currents, prevailing swell, the narrow edge of a channel, wishing to position your boat precisely over a noted fishing spot, and so on. There are many ways to deploy anchors to get yourself into the best position for safety, comfort and fun.

V-Configuration

The most commonly used method to set two anchors is in a 'V' configuration. Although this is what most people think of first in the event of strong winds, if the wind shifts or your boat yaws, your vessel will be hanging only on one anchor at any given point in time, which is not the idea behind deploying two anchors. You also run the risk of the two rodes becoming twisted and tangled leaving you with a mess to contend with when the storm abates.

To accomplish this motor as usual to windward (1), then drop and set one anchor (2). Next, motor across (3) to one side then upwind and drop

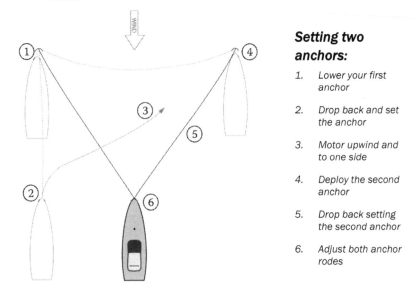

Setting two anchors:

1. Lower your first anchor
2. Drop back and set the anchor
3. Motor upwind and to one side
4. Deploy the second anchor
5. Drop back setting the second anchor
6. Adjust both anchor rodes

and set the second anchor (4 & 5). Finally drop back and balance the load between the two (6). Your goal here is an angle between the two anchors of somewhere in the range of 45 to 90 degrees.

Moitessier Mooring

If stronger winds are anticipated and you feel your primary anchor may not be adequate, you may wish to attach a second anchor to your rode in a way used by the world-famous sailor Bernard Moitessier.

You begin by deploying and setting your primary anchor in the usual way. The rode is then brought back in reducing the scope to about 2-1. A second anchor with about 30 feet (10 meters) of chain is then attached to the primary rode with a shackle and optional swivel. The second anchor is then lowered and its chain paid out. Then the main rode is let out once again.

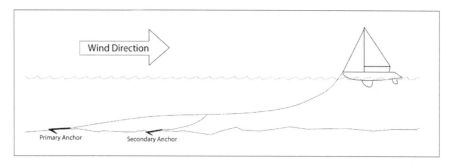

Deploy and set the primary anchor first, then bring in the rode and attach a second anchor with a short length of chain. Once the secondary anchor is deployed, let out sufficient rode.

This configuration is particularly useful if wind shifts are expected. When it does you will effectively be anchored in a Y configuration and the load is split between the two anchors. If the wind direction continues to change, the boat will hang on either or both anchors. If the wind does not shift, the secondary anchor will act like a kellet and will help reduce the extent of the boat's shear or yaw.

To retrieve this setup, bring in the chain until you get to the connection of the two chains. Then bring in the secondary rode and its anchor, while remaining anchored by the primary. Once the secondary anchor is stowed, the primary may be retrieved at leisure.

Tandem Anchoring

In extreme conditions you might wish to consider setting two anchors in series – one behind the other. This is known as tandem anchoring. U.S. Navy tests show the use of tandem anchors increases total holding power by as much as 30 percent over the same two anchors if deployed separately.

To do this, the primary anchor must have an eye or hole at the crown through which to attach the rode to the secondary anchor. The Rocna and Bügel anchors have such a dedicated attachment point, most other anchors do not. You may thus need to weld a pad eye to the crown of your anchor beforehand to be able to utilize this technique. Do not use the hole or connection point for the trip line, which most anchors have, as this may cause the primary anchor to roll and unset during a wind shift.

Attach a length of chain rode, that is at least as long as your boat (more is better), to the tandem anchor connection point with a sturdy shackle – you should only use chain for this. This connects the secondary anchor in series. To make later retrieval of the two anchors easier, attach one end of a retrieval rope to the shank of the first anchor and the other end to the shank of the second anchor. The retrieval rope should, of course, be longer than the chain connecting the two anchors. It should also be a floating line so it will suspend clear of the anchors and chain. If you do not have a floating line, then attach a couple of small fishing or other similar floats to it.

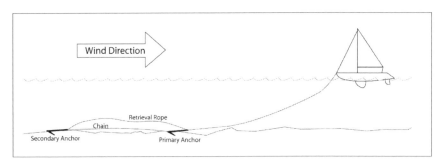

When setting two anchors in line, lower the secondary (upwind) anchor first. Reverse, pay out the rode and lower the primary anchor prior to setting either anchor. When sufficient rode for the primary anchor has been let out, cinch the rode and (at first gently) power set the anchors.

To deploy, drop the first anchor (secondary) to the bottom paying out its rode until you reach the second or primary anchor. At this point, lower the second anchor and pay out its rode without having set the first (secondary) anchor. The primary anchor will not set easily with the secondary already buried, regardless of how it is attached to the rig.

When you reach a 3:1 scope for the second (primary) anchor, cinch the rode as you usually do and set both anchors. Then let out the remaining rode. It is not critical that the secondary anchor sets at this time, as its main function is as a backup should the primary drag.

There is also a school of thought where the chain to the secondary anchor is taken from the eye of the primary rather than from its crown. When the primary anchor veers in a wind shift, it should not be encumbered by the secondary anchor hanging off its crown. Though we have yet to try this, it is interesting. This is basically a derivation of the Moitessier mooring, leaving out the length of chain, as described above.

The big advantage of deploying tandem anchors is that they are helping each other in significant ways and are thus doing more than two separate anchors on two rodes could. The primary anchor takes the primary load from the boat and along with this absorbs all the tugging and pulling from the boat's motion. It also ensures that the rode stretching to the secondary anchor is at its greatest possible scope ensuring that the secondary anchor's holding power is at its maximum. The secondary in turn keeps the primary from dragging and potentially pulling free from the bottom.

The downside of two anchors in line or in tandem is that they are both connected to one point on your boat. If the rode or the fitting fails, then you are out of luck (or need a plan 'B'). Also, if the anchors should drag or plow through the bottom, then the secondary anchor will find poor holding in the disturbed seafloor created by the primary. Using a plow type anchor for a tandem rig is thus ill advised.

Setting Opposing Anchors

If you need to keep your boat in one place, even if the wind or current changes direction, then you may need to set two or more opposing anchors. Where applicable, set the stronger/heavier anchor in the direction of the strongest flow, and the secondary in direct opposition to it.

There are two ways to accomplish this. You can set your first anchor (up-wind or up-current, whichever is stronger), then drop back letting out enough rode to equal double the scope you would normally need. Then drop the second anchor and move the boat forward bringing in the rode of the first anchor while setting the second anchor and letting out its rode. The alternative is to set the first as before, and then deploy the second with the dinghy. Of course, to accomplish this maneuver successfully, you have to have a second anchor that doesn't weigh enough to sink the dinghy!

Bahamian mooring – Two anchors from the bow

The Bahamian Moor is essentially the same as the V configuration taken to its extreme – setting the two anchors 180 degrees apart. It allows your boat to swing pointing into the wind or current – whichever exerts the greater force on your boat and wherever it comes from at a given time. It can thus be very useful in an anchorage with a strong reversing tidal flow.

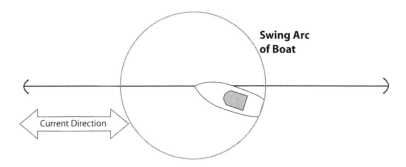

This method of anchoring also minimizes your swing radius. It is a configuration you may consider in a tight anchorage, provided, of course, that the other boats do the same. It can also be useful when anchoring close to boats on moorings where their swing radius is quite small.

However, anchoring in a mooring field is generally not recommended. You never know what is down there.

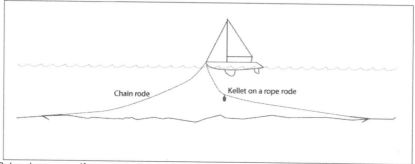

Bahamian moor – if your secondary anchor has a rope rode, remember to add a kellet to keep it away from your keel.

If one or both of your rodes are rope, and not all chain, you must ensure that you also deploy a small kellet to weigh the rope down. If you do not do so, you are liable to wrap the rode around your keel, rudder or drive shaft with obvious negative consequences. We have a four-pound lead weight aboard for this.

A tidier scenario, that avoids having two rodes coming off your bow in opposite directions, is to connect the two rodes and drop the connection point down ultimately hanging the boat on a single riser with two anchors in opposite directions. If you are using two rope rodes, you will need to weigh them down with a kellet.

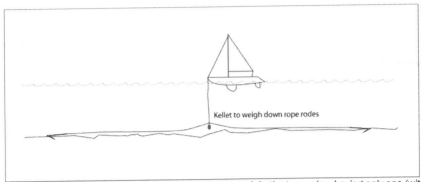

To avoid twisting the rodes as you swing around, you can join the two rodes, having only one (with a swivel) going up to the boat and weighing it down where the two join.

Connecting the rodes as described above can be quite daunting in a heavy blow. You also cannot adjust the rodes once thus connected. If you have an all chain rode for your primary and a rope rode as your secondary, you may also connect the two with a heavy-duty snatch block. This obviates the need for a kellet on the rope rode. It also makes adjusting the tension between the anchors quite simple.

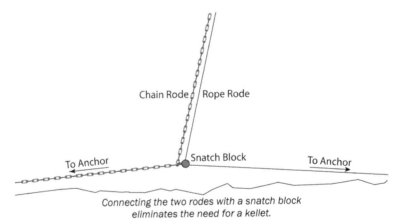

Connecting the two rodes with a snatch block eliminates the need for a kellet.

The only downside of this last method is that the two rodes will in all likelihood become twisted if and when the boat spins around with the wind and or current shifts. The extra work of undoing this is, however, outweighed by the security this system offers.

Bow and stern configuration

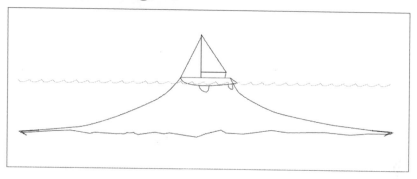

Bow and stern anchoring fixes your boat's position and is most useful in really tight situations like in a creek, or along the edge of a channel. In some places this is used to anchor close to steep cliffs. It is also very useful in a rolly anchorage.

Boat will not swing

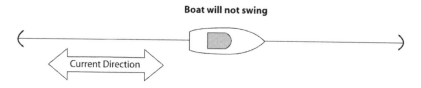

Current Direction

The bow and stern configuration maintains the position of your boat very tightly. Your boat will not swing into the wind or current. It should only be used when really needed – such as for anchoring at the very edge of a tight channel when you do not want to swing at all or anchoring off a beach when there is a swell coming in off the ocean causing your vessel to rock side to side.

There was the time a tropical storm veered off its predicted path and we took refuge in a small hurricane hole for what felt like an eternity with two anchors set in opposite directions to take into account the circular pattern of these storms. The eye passed right over us and we had about an hour of brilliant sunshine during which to check our gear before the back side of the storm hit. Our anchors thankfully held that day.

Alex and Daria Blackwell

One thing to bear in mind when anchoring (or mooring) bow and stern is that when wind and waves do come from astern it will be the same as anchoring stern-to. As we mention elsewhere, your boat is designed to ride over the waves bow first, and to repel rain and spray coming from ahead. Lower freeboard outboard motor boats are particularly vulnerable and there is a danger of being swamped and sinking.

The 'Rolly' Anchorage

There will come a time when you are securely and safely anchored but your boat keeps rolling from side to side. This is quite common in anchorages that are open on one side and where the prevailing wind comes from anywhere but from the head of the harbor. Where you have a consistent and heavy ground swell coming from a different direction than the wind, this can make for a very uncomfortable experience.

Getting Hooked & Anchoring Technique

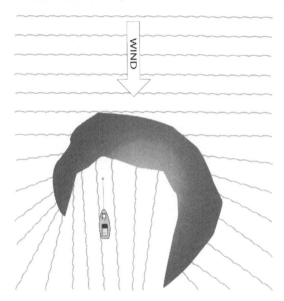

To overcome this, you can do one of three things. You can turn your boat to point into the swell by bringing a bridle to the aft quarter of your boat as in this illustration. With some adjustment, your boat will ride more easily, and you will be much more comfortable. You must, however, bear in mind that this will significantly increase the load on your anchor and is really only advisable in moderate conditions.

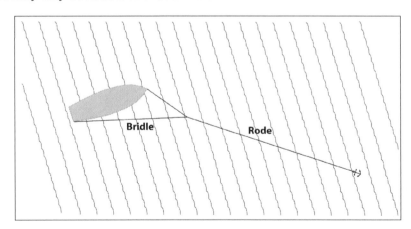

Alternatively, you can turn your boat into the waves by deploying bow and stern anchors. Though more work than the above bridle configuration, we have found that this is far more tenable as an overnight or longer-term solution for our boat.

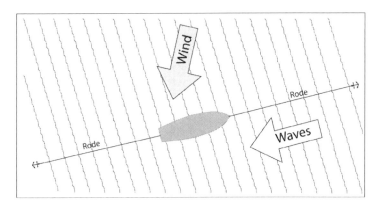

Deploying the two anchors is much the same as with any of the other bow and stern configurations. The principle difference being that you need to angle your boat to the wind. You will first set one to windward as you normally would. You may then either let out sufficient extra rode so that you can drop the second anchor, or simply deploy the second anchor using your dinghy. In light winds you can use the dinghy to pull your stern to the correct angle. Remember to allow for extra rode in this instance, as you will pull some back in again to set the anchor and turn the stern to the correct angle. This is where a lightweight Fortress or other aluminum anchor comes in quite useful.

Getting Hooked ⚓ Anchoring Technique

In this picture from the 1800s of St. Pierre in Martinique the ships are all anchored bow and stern facing into the prevailing swell.

Today the yachts off St. Pierre today are almost all anchored by the bow only and parallel to the shore – and they complain about the rolly anchorage!

A third option is to deploy a so-called flopper stopper. There are many versions of this and they basically all work on the same principal. If the boat tries to rock to one side, the stopper on the other closes up and inhibits the boat from rolling and visa-versa.

199

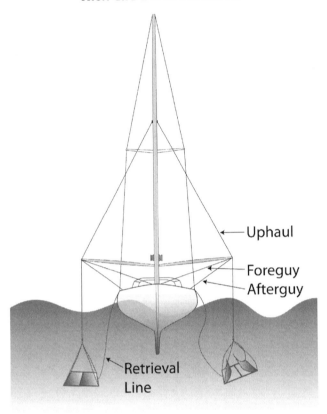

Of course, this will put a lot of strain on the rigging and it may need to be beefed up accordingly before deploying the flopper stopper.

Med mooring

In European marinas and many other places docking involves anchoring. Many marinas or docks require stern or bow to tie-ups to save space. The so-called Med mooring is basically a variation on the bow and stern configuration.

Getting Hooked ⚓ Anchoring Technique

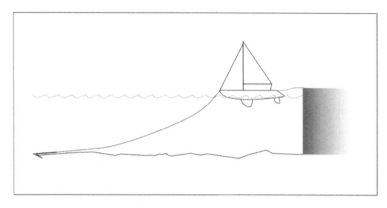

Med mooring uses an anchor to hold one end of the boat while the other is secured to the shore, a dock or a bulkhead, or a mangrove tree.

Some of the newer marinas provide permanent moorings that allow Med mooring without dropping your own anchor, but many still do not. Med mooring usually involves dropping an anchor, then bringing either the bow or stern in to secure to a dock.

Having picked up the permanent mooring ropes, they may be heavily fouled

Either way, it is advisable to do a drive by prior to attempting to go into the dock. Usually there are very able dock hands waiting to assist you

201

with the ropes. They will sometimes even have a boat to help push your's into the right position. We have often preceded our attempt with a dinghy ride in to the marina to get the lay of the land.

First and foremost, it is important to be prepared.

You will need dock lines aft (or forward if going bow in). Make sure these are tied off (remember the bitter end). We were helping a beautiful classic yacht one day and they tossed their dock lines ashore to us – in their entirety without being secured to the boat, so we had to throw them back.

Spring lines amidships and at the bow should be readied as well. You will also need to deploy fenders all around. You are likely to be "playing bumper boats" and protection for your boat and, of course, for your soon to be neighbors is critical.

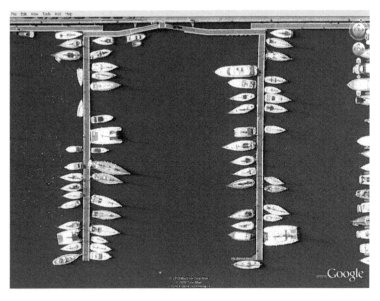

Satellite view (©Google Earth) of the marina at Alcantara near Lisbon, Portugal. Note that the boats are <u>not</u> all nicely perpendicular to the docks.

As you motor past the dock during your initial drive-by, keep an eye on the depth, so you can determine how far out you should place your anchor. Review the available slots or the slot you have been assigned, and get a feel for where the other boats have dropped their anchors, as you will need to try to avoid crossing their rodes. If there are only a few boats at the dock, it is considered good manners to come in alongside one of the boats already there. This way the available space at the dock is filled more efficiently (without gaps).

Finally, try hailing the boats you will be coming alongside. Getting your boat in safely is in both your and their best interests – besides the fact that having some willing line handlers will make things much easier for you.

1. *Prior to entering harbor*
   - *Set fenders*
   - *Set dock lines*
2. *Motor past dock*
   - *Check space*
   - *Check depth*
   - *Speak with your new neighbors*
3. *Stop boat in line with available slot*
   - *Allow for prop walk*
   - *Avoid other anchors*
   - *Allow for adequate scope*
4. *Drop anchor*
5. *Reverse into slot*
   - *Pass windward lines ashore first*
   - *Secure vessel*
   - *Add spring lines*

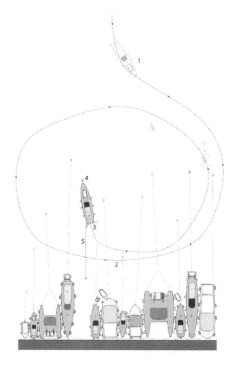

Come back around and stop your boat in line with your goal. Remember to allow for prop walk (most boats do this), and also allow for the wind or current to potentially push you to one side. Try to position your anchor location a bit upwind to help stabilize your approach. Then drop your anchor, and back into the slip or slot while letting out your rode. You may also deploy a stern anchor and go in bow first.

As you come in to the dock pass your lines ashore, or preferably to your new neighbors to bring ashore while steering you in. Once the anchor and dock lines are deployed, firm up on the anchor rode and deploy spring lines to keep the boat aligned fore and aft. It is usually also advisable to tie off to your neighbors to minimize movement between your vessels.

This same technique is useful in situations where you may wish to tuck in to the edge of a canal or creek alongside other vessels. We learned the swamp anchoring technique in Southwest Florida, which is not much different from med mooring. It kept our stern securely tied off to the mangroves while our anchor rested in the channel. We were perfectly snug while other boats on moorings and in the marina strained and pranced like broncos all night in a strong blow. One boat even dragged its anchor and ended up snuggling up to a very upscale residence's dock without the boat's owner realizing it.

Anchoring in a creek may require dropping an anchor in a channel, then securing the stern to the trees with a dinghy's help.

Getting Hooked ⚓ Anchoring Technique

As before, preparation is important. First, launch your dinghy, as you will need this to bring your stern line ashore where you will secure it to the mangroves. Drive to mid-channel and drop your anchor slightly upwind or up current. Then motor back slowly toward the mangrove setting the anchor. Drive the dinghy into the mangrove and secure a rope from the mother ship to a sturdy limb or trunk in the mangroves (chances are you will find traces of many prior lines left behind to guide you). Just be careful approaching the mangroves as they tend to have sharp spear-like branches above and below water pointing outwards. These seem to be clearly designed to puncture inflatable dinghies and poke at eyes. As the person in the dinghy ties a line, the crew on board adjusts the anchor and stern rodes to provide a tight fore and aft rode configuration.

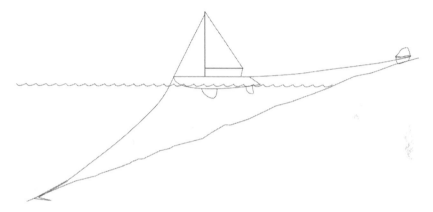

You may also use this same technique for anchorages where the depth increases rapidly relatively close to shore. Here you would drop your anchor and dinghy or swim the stern line ashore. You are thus pulling the anchor uphill for good holding. The alternative being that the anchor would slide down the slope and your boat will drift out to sea.

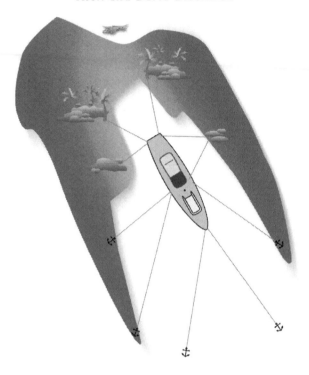

A variation of this is also a favored storm tie-up. Find as many fixed places on shore to tie to as possible and then deploy anchors to help keep your boat from moving. This is akin to deploying a spider web of rodes in a narrow channel.

Anchoring in a River

Dropping an anchor in rivers and streams can present its own set of challenges. Currents can be quite strong. If the wind blows opposing the current, the waves can become very uncomfortable if not downright treacherous. If the river is tidal, the current may reverse direction and it is usually advisable to set two anchors as in the Bahamian moor, one set in either direction of the current so that one will come into play with the shift in current.

In a river it is usually advisable to find a spot that is away from the main channel where the current will be lightest, and the boat traffic will be minimal. Bends and wide areas are ideal, as these are where you will most likely find areas of reduced currents.

There are some places we just would not anchor like on the lower Hudson River, New York. You never know what you will pull up from a river bed with this much 'history.' On such busy rivers you can also face a strong wash from the boat traffic. Not only do you have the wind, the current, but also the ferries traversing and tankers going up and down throughout the night. You are constantly subjected to their wakes squaring off and bouncing from shore to shore which can make for a very uncomfortable stay. When the need arises for us to stop in such a busy place, even we will preferentially pick up a mooring or pull into a slip.

Alex and Daria Blackwell

Comfortably at anchor on the Connecticut River

In contrast, other rivers have almost no commercial traffic at all after nightfall. Near their mouths the rivers will be tidal, but farther upstream they have a consistent downstream flow. Here a night on the river can be mesmerizing, with the water flowing past you in a constant stream without a wave disturbing its rhythm. Magic! We always wonder what secret stories the river has brought from upstream and where their travels will ultimately bring them.

Many rivers also have coves and streams that feed into them that are off the beaten path. Checking into one of those and anchoring as well as tying off to trees or rocks on shore can be a very pleasant experience if there is enough depth. You'll have the protection of the trees against the wind. Be careful not to damage the trees by tying off to vulnerable branches or against delicate bark without chafe protection. You want to be able to preserve the natural beauty for another visit.

Getting Hooked ⚓ Anchoring Technique

Stopping for a swim in the river on a hot summer day

Chapter 7: Allowing for Room

Swing Room

Boats will always move around while at anchor. This is called shear or yaw. Catamarans, mono-hulled sailboats, large vessels, powerboats, or flat bottom boats will all swing with very different characteristics. Some fin keeled boats yaw to the extreme while older, full keeled boats, may ride straight as an arrow into the wind or into the current. Take the time to observe the vessels nearby and try to anchor away from boats that move differently from yours. If there's plenty of room, there's no worry. It's when the anchorage is crowded that this becomes an issue and boats can get closer together than one might like.

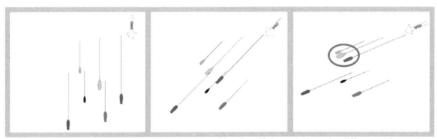

As the wind shifts, the boats in an anchorage will swing. If the rode lengths differ then it can be inevitable that boats will come too close together.

If the wind shifts, which it commonly does, then all the boats in the harbor will swing in the same direction, albeit with their own particular idiosyncrasies. Consequently, it is also good to know and match the other boats' lengths of rode. If not, what appears to be a very orderly anchorage as in the illustration below, can rapidly become a tangled mess. This usually happens in the middle of the night in deteriorating conditions.

Note also that boats on moorings have considerably less scope than anchored boats. They will swing in a much smaller arc. So, anchoring near a mooring field is ill-advised. In addition, in and near a mooring field, there will inevitably be legacy moorings and other junk littering the bottom.

Controlling Shear or Yaw

If you have been at anchor or on a mooring, you will have noticed that every boat tends to move back and forth to some degree. This is called shear or yaw.

One might think that an anchored boat would simply point into the wind. However, the topsides act like a sail and the wind will push the boat to one side. Fighting this, the rode tension pulls the bow back into the wind, exposing the other side of the boat. This is aggravated when your rode goes through a chock which is positioned to one side of the bow, enabling the wind to catch the boat on one side. Once the boat starts to move in this manner, the hull and the keel exert lift and drag forces. As these forces keep varying, an equilibrium cannot be reached.

This can make for an uncomfortable night at anchor. It can cause your anchor to twist back and forth and perhaps pull free. It can also cause your rode to chafe by moving back and forth and in and out through the chock or over the bow roller

Light boats with high freeboard and little longitudinal underwater surface area (fin keels) are particularly susceptible – powerboats, catamarans and some fin keeled sailboats are examples of boats prone to yaw. Full keeled boats tend to yaw less. On catamarans the side to side motions can be significantly reduced with a nylon bridle tied to both bows and increased scope. (See earlier report of Australian anchor tests with a catamaran.)

Yawing dramatically increases the boat's windage when the boat veers sideways to the wind. Swinging back and forth constantly changes the direction of pull on the anchor, which can loosen its hold on the bottom. When combined with the violent jolts caused by the snatch loads or wave action, a boat may drag anchor or break something - even in wind conditions that might otherwise be considered benign.

Powerboats: Usually have high forward freeboard but small surface area under the water line. They will generally show ample yawing motion.

Modern sailboats: Usually have relatively high forward freeboard and narrow deep keels. They will generally yaw considerably, because the lift force of the keel and the rudder blade favors "tacking".

Classic sailboats: Tend to be heavier and have high inertia, moderate freeboard, and long keels. They will usually yaw much less.

Catamarans: Are naturally prone to yawing and surging back and forth. (See illustration under "Multihull Considerations")

Getting Hooked ⚓ Anchoring Technique

Things that can help mitigate yaw

A traditional riding sail

To reduce yaw, move the anchor line to the very tip of the bow or in a bridle configuration – important for catamarans and other wide boats. You should center your rudder. Tying it to one side, as many people like to do, only aggravates the problem. Also center your windage amidships and aft. Sailboats and trawlers can hoist a small riding sail aft. Riding sails are fastened at the stern of the boat to force it to ride with the bow pointing into the wind, instead of swinging in an uncontrolled way when anchored.

Banner Bay produces a three-dimensional delta-shaped sail. Research has shown that as soon as the boat swings even a few degrees the forward fin cuts off the air flow to the delta wing on one side while directing it to the delta wing on the other. A correcting force is initiated immediately. This combination of the fin and

Banner Bay FinDelta™ riding sail

the twin delta wings work to center the boat, providing for a marked improvement in swing reduction.

Alex and Daria Blackwell

With a ketch or a yawl, the mizzen sail can be used to good effect.

The downside of any riding sail is that you are introducing increased windage and thus increased load on your anchor. This is something you will need to take into consideration.

You can also drop a weighted drogue or small sea anchor off the stern but remember to retrieve it before starting the engine. We bought a tiny cargo parachute from a military supply house for $10 for just this purpose.

To minimize shear or yaw:

- ⚓ Center the anchor rode at the bow
- ⚓ Reduce windage at bow
- ⚓ Add a riding sail on backstay
- ⚓ Add a drogue or small sea anchor at stern
- ⚓ Secure rudder amidships

Chapter 8: Once you are anchored

The COLREGS (Collision Regulations) dictate that you display an all-around white anchor light at night while anchored anywhere except in a designated anchorage or mooring field. As they do not dictate where the light should be, we have moved our anchor light down from our mast-top to

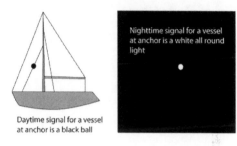

Daytime signal for a vessel at anchor is a black ball

Nighttime signal for a vessel at anchor is a white all round light

Use an anchor light at night or the day mark black ball to satisfy COLREGS.

above deck level. Our reasoning is that the skipper of a boat in proximity to ours will not be able to see a small light some 20 meters (60 feet) above but will readily see one closer to eye level. Similarly, we usually deploy a light forward and one aft to make our boat even more visible.

The COLREGS also state that a black ball must be displayed while at anchor during daylight hours. Although few boats that are not professionally skippered practice this, in the case of an accident, the question will arise. It is best to be covered for insurance purposes. A fishing trawler once accidentally drove straight into our boat in the middle of the day, while it was at anchor. The first question asked by our insurers was whether we had an anchor ball up. "Yes, then there is no problem, you are fully covered."

Alex and Daria Blackwell

Shore Leave: Prepare to Find Your Boat

Finding your boat can be dicey in the dark...or if fog sets in

Perhaps the best part of coastal boating and anchoring is what you do when you get settled in – quiet cocktails and dinner aboard or shore leave? This is the big decision of the day. Shore leave can be lots of fun but getting back to your boat late at night or, worse, in the fog or deteriorating weather can be a little challenging. Finding your boat after shore leave, when conditions have changed, darkness has fallen, or the anchorage has had many additions to its visiting fleet, can be difficult.

For some reason we tend to learn things the hard way. On one occasion fog set in while we were on shore for a delightful dinner. With no GPS or compass on board our dinghy, we guessed at the direction back to our boat across an open two-mile-wide inlet, picked out a star that we could see over the fog that corresponded with the direction we thought was right, and then set out to sea in our little dink. We thankfully guessed right that time. It taught us to be better prepared the next time.

Getting Hooked ⚓ Anchoring Technique

We now carry our handheld GPS with us on shore leave having marked the position of our boat prior to leaving. We also take along our handheld VHF, having once had engine trouble and no oars.

We have a rule for things to bring along when going ashore: engine and fuel tank sufficiently full, oars a must, life jackets for everyone, flashlights, handheld GPS with coordinates for the trip home, a handheld VHF for emergency calling, and of course a dinghy anchor with rode. Being somewhat paranoid after all this 'cumulative experience', we also usually carry a mobile phone or two. These also have charting software, charts and internal GPS. 'Back-ups-R-Us'.

We have recently installed reflective tape on our masts and we also like to leave one or two characteristic cabin lights on to distinguish our boat from the others. As a result, we have reduced our incidence of adventure significantly over the years. Consequently, we have fewer stories to tell than we used to.

Tips for finding your anchored boat:

- ⚓ Anchor light at night, black ball during the day
- ⚓ Take along a handheld GPS as well as VHF
- ⚓ Leave a characteristic light pattern on inside

Alex and Daria Blackwell

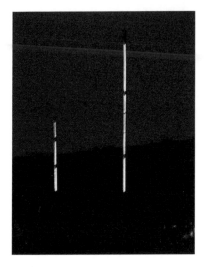

We applied some 3M SOLAS Reflective Tape to our masts to help us find (and other people see) our boat at night. This is a picture of our boat illuminated by a small flashlight on a dark night from over 100 meters away.

What to Do with Your Dinghy

With the dinghy is the largest and most important accessory to your boat. Without it one cannot readily get ashore. It is therefore worth briefly discussing what to do with it when it is not in use at anchor.

The first concern is protecting it from theft while at anchor. The simplest solution is to raise it out of the water. Boats with davits have it easy, but so does most every sailboat with a spare halyard. If you have a mizzen mast you can use it as a derrick.

Raising the dinghy adds a layer of complication to theft and is therefore a strong deterrent. We have a heavy locking cable for when we go ashore, which we also use to lock our tender to our boat at night.

As a dinghy left in the water for prolonged periods of time is subject to fouling. Raising it out of the water when not in use keeps this from happening and provides an additional significant benefit.

While towing a dinghy while underway is not an issue, we have on occasion, when we went on a day sail with friends to view the beautiful classics racing in Antigua for example, had to leave dinghies behind. There were just too many to tow. In this case, we deployed a spare anchor, which served as a mooring for the dinghy raft. Of course, this also secured 'our' spot in the anchorage for our return.

Anchor Watch

Once securely anchored, it is good practice to dive down on the anchor to inspect that it is set properly. You should also monitor that everything is in order on an ongoing basis. If there is a radical wind shift, your anchor may break free or may drag. If you have an anchor alarm on your GPS or chart plotter system, it is advisable to set it so it will keep watch for you overnight. Adjust the alarm settings to something a little greater than your maximum swing which is two times the amount of rode you let out:

Your rode is the radius of your swing circle. Double that is the furthest your boat can travel, provided your anchor does not drag.

Do also make a note of your latitude and longitude coordinates to remove any doubt should you think you are dragging. Such reassurance is helpful as you may be a mite fuzzy headed waking up from a deep sleep. If conditions are questionable or deteriorating, you should assign anchor watch to members of your crew. If you are shorthanded, you may have to take turns sleeping and watching when conditions warrant it.

We happened to be fortunate to have a nocturnal crew member, who spent the night prowling the deck – and yes, Onyx (our cat) did come to get us when there was a change she did not like. She could be very insistent. We learned to listen to her and check our situation when she sounded the alarm.

Onyx on watch duty

Even with a nocturnal crew member, it is a good idea to go topsides periodically throughout the night to check things out. You will also see how beautiful it is out there at night! We check on deck periodically if we notice any wind shifts or a change in the boat's motion. The more we anchor the more attuned we are to subtle changes in conditions. Our subconscious tends to stay somewhat aware.

If things do change, be prepared for whatever circumstances come your way.

Chapter 9: Anchors A'Weigh

When I was a child, I always thought the well-known Navy song was all about dropping anchor: "Anchors Away" as in the ad to the left. But no, it was and still is all about weighing anchor – hauling in the anchor and setting sail for far off lands. Although we do love it when our boat swings gently on her hook, after a while we do yearn to be off again to explore new destinations.

If you have a good anchor, getting it back on deck can be quite heavy work, particularly if you have set it well. Weighing anchor is best done with two people – one forward and the other at the helm. Even so, it is not complicated and need not strain your back or your tackle.

Using your engine, power forward gently at near idle speed. Follow the line back in the direction you set the anchor, pulling in the rode as your boat advances. The anchor hauler is forward giving hand signals indicating in which direction the rode lies.

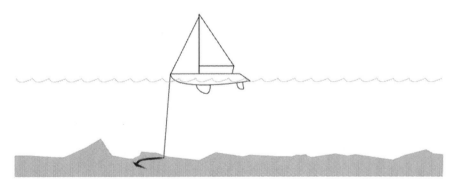

221

When you reach the point where your rode goes straight down, stop the boat and secure the line on a cleat or stop the windlass. Do not power forward to free the anchor, as you might damage it by doing this. No anchor is designed to take a strong vertical load when set horizontally.

Always let the boat do the work!

If you now simply wait for a moment, the motion of the boat bobbing on the surface will almost certainly free the anchor.

1. As the bow dips with the wave action pull in a little rode and stop.
2. As the bow rises, it will tug the anchor loosening it.
3. Repeat until the anchor is freed.

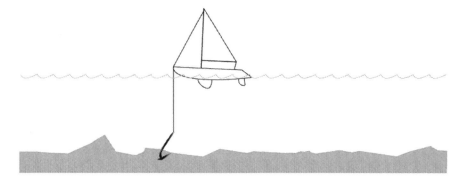

Alternatively, just power gently in reverse to help the boat do the work of freeing the anchor from the bottom. Once the anchor rolls out of the bottom, stop the boat and pull up the anchor. If manually retrieving the anchor over the side, do so slowly to avoid banging the anchor against the hull.

Getting Hooked ⚓ Anchoring Technique

Weighing anchor with bucket ready to rinse off the debris. (By the way, he just doesn't understand why he has to keep weighing the anchor when he knows how much it weighs already.)

Once you have the anchor up, wash it (and your deck) off. If you have a wash-down hose, you have it made. Otherwise keep a bucket and brush handy. The bucket should have a line attached, so you can drop it overboard to fill it and then pull it back in.

To do this effectively, you need to develop a technique such as this:

- ⚓ Tie a loop on one end of the rope. Tie the other to the bucket.
- ⚓ Firmly hold one end of the rope in one hand. Hold the bucket and a couple of loops of rope in the other hand (same as a throwing line).
- ⚓ With the other hand toss the bucket forward – in the direction of travel, assuming the boat is moving forward very slowly. While tossing it, give it a twist so that it lands upside down in the water.
- ⚓ As the bucket comes back towards you, it should sink into the water filling up.
- ⚓ Just before it reaches you pull the bucket up, out of the water – even if it is not yet quite full. If you fail to do this, the bucket will drag behind you acting like a sea anchor. This may either pull the rope out of your hands or rip the handle from the bucket. In the

worst case, it will pull you overboard, so NEVER tie the bucket to your wrist.

Weighing (Retrieving) Multiple Anchors

The worry of retrieving multiple anchors may deter some from setting more than one in the first place. This need not be so. It works the same way as retrieving a single anchor, but it just takes a little longer

If you have two anchors in a 'V' off the bow, retrieve the first one as described above. You may need to let some rode out for the other anchor if they are set far apart. Likewise, in a bow and stern configuration, slack off the upwind or up-current rode while you retrieve the opposing anchor and then pick up the other. If your windward rode is not long enough to slack off enough to retrieve the leeward anchor, you may have to deploy the dinghy to pull it out using its trip line. Alternatively, you may choose to buoy one of the anchors and drop its rode. Pick up the other anchor and then come back to the buoy for the first.

With the series or tandem anchors, bring in the primary first. Unhook the retrieval line and bring it back to your windlass and then pull in the secondary anchor. You can deal with the chain connecting the two anchors at your leisure having pulled it up onto the foredeck.

Retrieving a Fishing Anchor

Fishermen will often retrieve their anchor using the boat's forward motion and a buoy that slides down the anchor rode. The buoy lifts the anchor because of the drag caused by it submerging as in the following series of illustrations.

Getting Hooked ⚓ Anchoring Technique

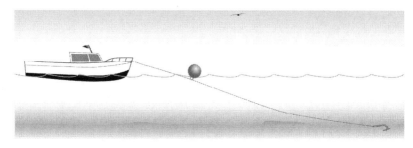

Boat riding at anchor with the buoy on the surface

As the boat moves forward and over the anchor the buoy starts to slide along the rode

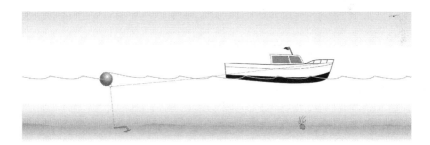

When the rode below the buoy goes vertical the buoy is pulled under water by the conflicting forces of the forward moving boat and anchor below. The further the buoy sinks, the greater the upward pull on the anchor.

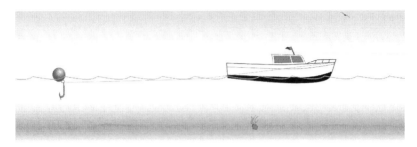

The anchor breaks free and rises up to the buoy. With the reduced downward pull, the buoy rises back above the surface and follows the boat. The anchor rode and anchor may now be retrieved.

With an all rope rode, a cam device is put on the rope and attached to the buoy. The cam is set to move only in the one direction along the rope. When it reaches the anchor, the boat may stop without the anchor going back down to the bottom. At this time the rode is retrieved, and the anchor brought aboard.

Another option works with a rope chain combination:

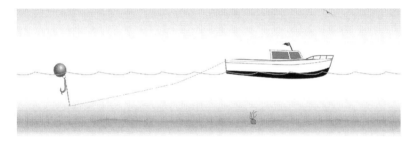

As the anchor breaks free, the chain is pulled through the ring. The chain then acts as a counter weight, keeping the anchor up by the buoy. The anchor rode and anchor may now be retrieved.

Getting Hooked ⚓ Anchoring Technique

Some available cam devices

AnchorLift	AnchorLift Pro	EZ Puller

Some available anchor lifting rings

Anchor Ring
from Ironwood Pacific

Anka Yanka
from Anchor Retrieval Solutions

The one caveat we might add to this method might be if the anchor were stuck. Motoring forward could result in a dangerous situation when the rode suddenly became taut and exerted a sudden strain on the bow cleat.

The Anchor Wanker - a solution to the chain piling problem

A common problem with an all-chain rode is the chain piling up in a pyramid (A) in the chain locker. On some boats this pyramid can extend up to the navel pipe, blocking it. This can result in the chain jamming on the windlass wildcat. A perhaps worse problem is when the pyramid

227

collapses when underway. This may cause the chain to get seriously tangled. If that happens, it can be virtually impossible to bring the chain up and out of the navel pipe when next deploying the anchor. This may all be exacerbated with the common practice of having the navel pipe off-center.

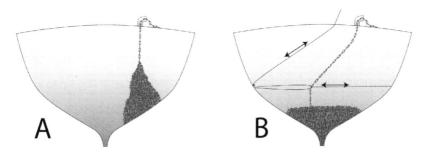

A solution to this (B) was given to us by John Franklin. He calls it the *Anchor Wanker*. A line is attached to one side of the anchor locker. It is looped around the descending chain and pulled through a pad-eye or pulley attached to the same side of the hull. From there it is brought out on deck – i.e. through the anchor hatch, if you have one. An elastic cord (bungee) is then attached to the opposite side of the anchor locker. The other end is tied off to a ring that the line has been passed through. These attachment points all need to be in the same horizontal plane.

When the free end of the line is pulled rapidly up, the shock cord extends, and the bight of the line is pulled across the anchor locker. This displaces the top part of the chain pile and causes the growing pyramid to collapse. Of course, you must stop hauling in the chain before you do this, as otherwise you run the risk of getting the line entangled in the chain. How often one needs to pull the line is a matter of practice. John's suggestion is to do this at 30 m and again at 20 m, then every 5 m thereafter. When there is chain to displace one can feel it and also hear the pile collapsing.

Getting Hooked ⚓ Anchoring Technique

Weighing Weighty Tackle: A Need for a Windlass

If you have an all chain rode, or you have a heavier/larger boat, then you either already have a windlass or you want one. Manually hauling in heavy ground tackle is not going to make cruising and anchoring something to look forward to.

Technically speaking, the term 'windlass' refers only to horizontal winches. Vertical designs are called capstans. Yacht windlasses and capstans often have two drums, a smooth one with flanges for hauling rope, and another with recesses that are matched with your chain. The latter is known as the wildcat (US) or Gypsy (UK). It is also sometimes called a chainwheel. As stated in the chapter about chain it must be noted, that chain and wildcat must be very well matched, as otherwise the chain may bind on it with disastrous results.

The two basic types or styles of "windlasses", vertical (capstan) and horizontal (windlass), are differentiated by how the drive shaft is oriented. Vertical capstan windlasses, which make up the majority of windlass sales for yachts, have the rope and/or chain wildcat above deck and the motor and gearbox below deck. Horizontal windlasses are often mounted completely above the deck with rope and chain gypsy/wildcat located to either side. Deck thickness and under deck space are the two of the considerations when deciding on which of the two types to fit.

The chain wrap on a capstan is a little over 180° which means that the load the chain links are carrying on the chain gypsy/wildcat is distributed over more than half of the available link-carrying, chain wheel pockets. In a horizontal windlass the wrap is reduced to only 90°. Therefore, the load carrying pockets are reduced to less than a third. The more chain on the capstan, the more the load will be distributed.

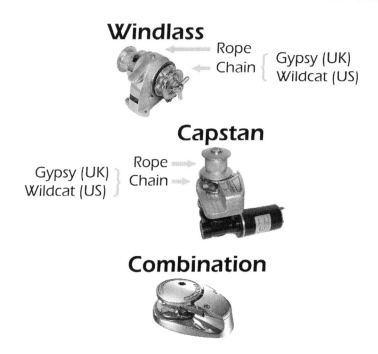

Windlass

Rope
Chain { Gypsy (UK)
Wildcat (US)

Capstan

Gypsy (UK)
Wildcat (US) } Rope
Chain

Combination

For chain rodes, most popular on cruising boats as well as larger sail and motor yachts, and rope rodes, either a windlass or capstan can be used.

There are also combination capstans and windlasses for use with a rope/chain combination rode. The dividing walls of the chain pockets have a groove to accommodate the rope. A combination rope/chain rode can also be used on a two-barrel capstan system. At the rope/chain join, it is usually not too difficult to drop the rode from the rope barrel down to the chain gypsy/wildcat.

Combination systems are very popular on boats up to 15m (50 feet), where rope/chain combination rodes are more prevalent. The advantage of the combination system for the smaller boats is that it is more compact and adds less weight on the bow. However, the weakest part of such a combined rode is the splice between the rope and chain. Going through a combination windlass on a regular basis causes a lot of wear on the splice and it needs to be inspected or renewed on a regular basis.

Using a Windlass

It is prudent to power forward gently against the wind when weighing anchor to take the strain off the motor as the rode is brought in, especially with a heavier boat or in windy conditions. Not doing so puts unnecessary strain on the windlass, which is only designed to pull an anchor up.

It is always recommended to have your engine running while operating the windlass – even without taking the above into consideration. The windlass is powered by a strong electric motor. This motor draws a lot of electricity and may deplete your battery. The windlass is often wired into the engine-start battery, so it would be doubly bad if that were to be drained.

As already mentioned, do not try to haul your well-set anchor out of the bottom with the windlass. Let the boat do the work. As soon as the anchor is loose, it should pull up quite easily.

When selecting a windlass, two things to consider are the maximum pull capability and the working load of the windlass. Maximum pull, sometimes referred to as stall load, is the maximum short term or instantaneous pull of the windlass. Working load is generally rated at about one third of the maximum pull. This is considered to be the load that the windlass needs to lift once the anchor is off the bottom. So, if you are anchored in 30 feet (10 meters) of water, this would be the weight of 35 feet of chain (depth plus bow height) plus the weight of the anchor, plus the weight of the muck on the anchor. High latitude sailors will often need to anchor in much deeper water. Their windlass must thus be sized accordingly.

Chapter 10: Trip Line or Anchor Buoy

A few years ago, we chartered a boat in the Bahamas and gunk holed through the Abaco Islands. One morning, having anchored in the lee of an island for the night, we had a 'bit' of trouble weighing anchor. Although we had more than adequate rode out, the island was a 'bit' further away than we remembered. We had an all chain rode with a CQR and a powerful windlass. After a while we pulled up an arm-thick cable. Our anchor had dragged, and the cable had been holding us all night. The cable that saved us was not marked on the charts we had been given.

As we had no way of lifting the anchor other than with the windlass, we had to drop it down again and then dive to free it. Had we had a trip line, this would have been no trouble at all.

If your anchor is caught on something like a rock, someone else's chain or even a cable, all you need to do is pull on the trip line to free your hook thereby releasing its hold on the bottom. In most cases the trip line will be deployed with a small buoy attached to it.

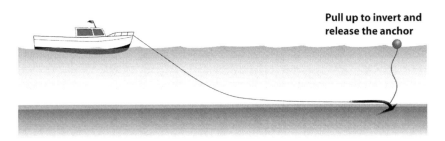

Pull up to invert and release the anchor

A trip line is attached to the anchor crown and its buoy floats on the surface.

There are commercially available trip lines. Swiss Tech America has a spring-loaded reel inside the buoy which deploys enough line to reach the anchor, keeping the line away from where an errant propeller may snag it.

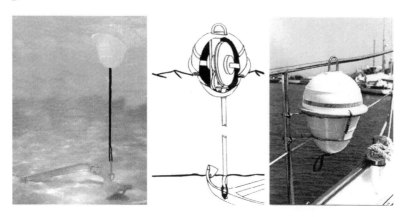

Retractable trip line from Swiss Tech

Another one, the AnchorBuoy, also has an internal spring loaded reel. This one is attached to the anchor and self deploys and retrieves. It also has a solar powered light.

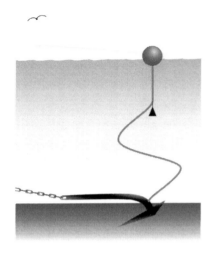

A weight prevents the trip line from floating on the surface where unsuspecting boaters can snag it with their props.

Buoyed trip lines can be home made. Our trip line is very simple. It is made from a small buoy and a length of nylon rope which we tie off to the anchor at a length appropriate to the depth at high water and allowing for the anchor to dig into the bottom a few feet.

We do advise adding a weight to the rope a few feet below the buoy to ensure the rope does not float and that nobody catches it in their propeller. We use a nylon rope as this will sink without the need for a weight. We also mark the buoy with our boat name to keep boaters from

mistaking it for a mooring.

Naturally, the trip line buoy will also mark the location of your anchor. We like this as we tend to use a bit more scope than other boaters. We have found this feature so beneficial, that we almost never drop our hook without a trip line attached. We have heard people complain about our buoy indicating that was where they had wanted to drop their hook.

The one time that we recently didn't attach our anchor buoy in a lovely deserted anchorage, another boat promptly came and anchored directly upwind of ours. The problem was they were friends of ours and very experienced cruisers. Next morning when we weighed anchor and had to pull our anchor out from underneath their boat, they quietly got the message and we learned another lesson: Always deploy an anchor buoy / trip line.

In case you need to abandon your anchor in an emergency, the trip line or anchor buoy will also help you recover it at a later time.

In a very crowded anchorage where space is a premium, it may be inconsiderate to deploy a trip line with a buoy. A simple alternative option is to add a length of floating rope (such as polypropylene) extending from the anchor crown to a point up the anchor rode. This line should, of course be longer than the maximum water depth. With this one can haul up the anchor by its crown should the anchor become stuck.

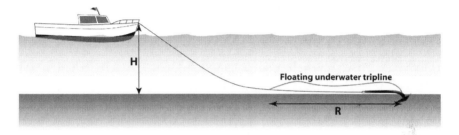

The trip line should be tied off to the rode at a distance from the anchor (R) that is greater than the height of the deck over the bottom (H).

Trip Line Alternatives

There are commercial anchor retrieval systems that replace the trip line altogether, examples are Anchor Witch and Anchor Rescue. Both of these work on a similar principal, where a cable or chain is affixed to the anchor crown and a retrieval system is lowered down the rode. The latter then connects to the chain or cable enabling the user to pull up the anchor by its crown, without disconnecting the rode from the anchor shank.

Alex and Daria Blackwell

AnchorRescue

Another useful product is the AnchorRescue made by Scanmar International. It has a chain that connects the anchor crown to a collar that rides on the anchor rode. If the anchor is caught, you can send a messenger with a rope attached down the rode. This then connects with the collar making it possible to lift the anchor by its crown.

If your anchor is caught....

You slide the AnchorRescue down the rode, bringing a trip line with it.

Getting Hooked ⚓ Anchoring Technique

This connects with the collar. You then pull up on the trip line while easing the tension on the rode.

The vertical pull is transferred from the anchor shank to the crown, enabling the user to reverse out the anchor.

Once the anchor is freed, the anchor can be retrieved normally using the rode.

Alex and Daria Blackwell

A Trip Line After the Fact

So, you dropped your hook, and like us you didn't attach a trip line at the outset. When it comes time to weigh anchor, you find it is really stuck and will not budge. This happened to us the one time we did not attach a trip line, we snagged something huge. We managed to drag it all around the harbor, but we could neither shake it loose nor lift it (like this sailor has done) without a windlass. That day we ended up cutting away our favorite hook as we did not yet know about a simple trick.

If your anchor is not buried deep in the mud or irretrievably snagged on some underwater object like a massive chain, all is not lost. All you need is a short-looped length of chain, or something to weigh a rope down sufficiently, and with a bit of jiggling you can work this down to the crown of the anchor and pull it free.

The following illustrations show just how easy it can be to rescue your favorite hook from the anchor eating monster of the deep if you are lucky.

Shorten up your rode until it goes nearly straight down.

Getting Hooked ⚓ Anchoring Technique

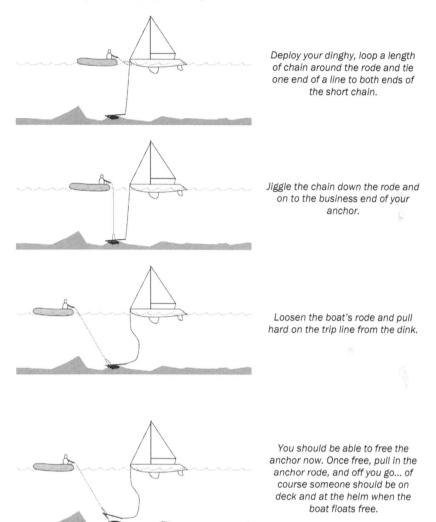

Deploy your dinghy, loop a length of chain around the rode and tie one end of a line to both ends of the short chain.

Jiggle the chain down the rode and on to the business end of your anchor.

Loosen the boat's rode and pull hard on the trip line from the dink.

You should be able to free the anchor now. Once free, pull in the anchor rode, and off you go... of course someone should be on deck and at the helm when the boat floats free.

And then there is plan B

Unfortunately, there are times when these techniques may not work. We assisted in two rescue operations several weeks apart. In one case, a boat had anchored in a mooring field; in the second case, a boat had anchored close to a dock. In both cases, their anchors happened to catch mooring chain running along the bottom in such a way that the pointy tips of their anchors lodged in the massive chain links. In both cases, it took a diver and heavy effort to release the anchors.

If you are in a situation where your anchor is really stuck and you cannot free it without taking a risk, then it is time to cut it away, as we have had to do. That is naturally more difficult with chain rode. If you can tie off a buoy and mark the anchor's location with GPS coordinates, you can always try to retrieve it later. Tying it off the stern to pull it free as some football stars did to their demise or tying it off the bow and gunning the engine, can quickly result in your boat capsizing and sinking. It is better to lose your hook and live to anchor safely another day.

Bottom line: it is best to avoid potentially problematic spots such as in or adjacent to mooring fields.

Anchor retrieval methods we do not like

Anchor Release Systems

There is a school of thought that suggests securing the rode itself to the anchor crown instead of a trip line. It is then attached to the eye of the anchor in such a way that it will break free if the rode is jerked or pulled hard enough.

Getting Hooked & Anchoring Technique

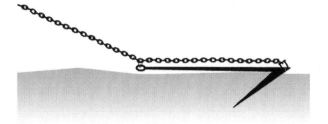

The rode is attached to the anchor crown. There is a weak connection to the anchor eye, which is intended to break if pulled hard.

Under normal circumstances, the anchor is set, pulled, and retrieved in the proper direction. If the anchor is stuck, sufficient vertical force can be exerted on the rode to break the connection to the eye. The rode becomes the trip line, and the anchor can be pulled out. In some groups, advice is given to readers to attach the rode to the eye in the anchor shank with a heavy cable tie.

There are also commercial products that accomplish this, such as the Anchor Saver® depicted here. The Anchor Saver has a sheer pin that breaks at a predetermined load calibrated for the type of anchor and size of boat it is used on.

We have reservations about using such a system. If the anchor were subjected to strong lateral loads, which might occur when the boat yaws or veers in stormy conditions – when anchor holding is most critical, it could pull out. Another potentially problematic scenario would be in a sudden reversal, as in a changing current or a squall with the anchor well stuck in the seabed. This too might cause the connection point at the shank to break.

With the anchor rode no longer attached to the anchor's shank the anchor can no longer hold. In the above scenarios the result would be catastrophic.

241

Slots and Attachment Holes in Anchors

Some anchors incorporate a slot along the length of the shank. The intention is for the user to power over and past where the anchor is set to pull the shackle from the end of the shank up to the crown. The rode thus becomes the trip line and makes anchor retrieval very easy.

Some anchors with slots

| Super Sarca | Supreme | Boss |

Wind shifts are quite normal; in fact, sudden wind direction reversals in a squall must be expected. We were once anchored in the lee of an island in a gentle 10 knot breeze, when the wind unexpectedly clocked 180 degrees and freshened to 45 knots. We were now with our stern close to a lee shore and our anchor pivoted and held well. If we had had an anchor with a slot, it is very likely that our anchor would have pulled out and that we would have wound up on the rocks.

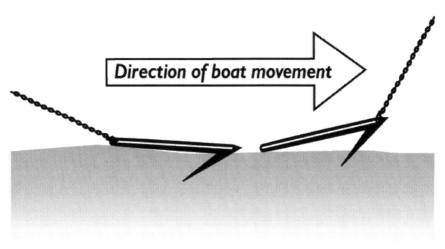

Direction of boat movement

Getting Hooked & Anchoring Technique

*Using an anchor with a slot may cause the anchor to trip out
when the wind reverses direction*

As there are many other options for anchor retrieval if it becomes stuck, we would avoid using the slot option entirely except when anchoring in rocky bottoms for short periods such as when fishing or on a dive boat. We would recommend never using a slot overnight or when leaving the boat unattended.

Chapter 11: Heaving To – Alternative to Anchoring

There will come a time when you either want or need to stop and park your boat in a place or under circumstances where you either cannot or do not wish to deploy an anchor. This can be out at sea where the water is too deep to anchor or near shore when you simply want to stop your boat for a while. You can do it by heaving to.

Heaving-to is first and foremost a very viable storm tactic. It is used by knowledgeable offshore sailors. When the wind and the seas become unmanageable, it is an excellent way to park your boat and wait out bad weather or make repairs. The fact is that after struggling to sail on in a storm, the act of heaving to has an almost immediate positive effect on crew. The boat's motion eases, the fury of the wind seems to abate, and the stress on gear, sails and the crew's morale quickly dissipates. It is truly a quieter and calmer situation that lets your crew prepare a meal, eat in peace, and get much needed rest. It also gives you an opportunity to calmly assess your situation, survey for damage, and affect repairs.

> *"Being hove to in a long gale is the most boring way of being terrified I know."*
>
> ### Donald Hamilton

Heaving to need not solely be a storm tactic. Stopping the boat at any time, to navigate, make repairs, or simply have a quiet lunch or dinner, is an option often overlooked. If you are not in a hurry, then stopping for a while can be a real pleasure. We used to practice heaving to in good weather just so we could perfect our technique (not that there is much to it). If we wanted to sit down for lunch while out sailing, we would just park her for a while and put up the table.

Getting Hooked ⚓ Anchoring Technique

Heaving to allows you to 'park' your boat while underway

When heaving to in storm conditions, you first reduce your sail area down to a manageable amount (storm jib and heavily reefed main, trysail or mizzen). To heave to you simply tack your boat without releasing the headsail sheet. It is a good idea to make this tack very slowly. Head into the wind until your speed has really come down before finishing the tack. At this point your headsail is backed and your main is trimmed for a close reach or a beat. This is where practicing is important so you can determine what works best for your boat – every boat responds a little differently.

Once you have come about, you bring the helm back over, steering the boat to windward. Fix the helm there. When your main fills, your boat will make way. It will steer to windward, towards the oncoming waves. As the boat rounds up, the main loses power. At the same time the backed headsail is pushing the boat to lee and fighting its forward movement. Your heading is a squiggly course to windward while the actual course made good is downwind, drifting sideways at perhaps a knot or two. With its sideways motion, the boat is disturbing the water and creating a significant upwind slick, flattening any chop that might otherwise be there. With your boat pointing to windward it is at the same time riding up and over the oncoming swell at an optimal angle.

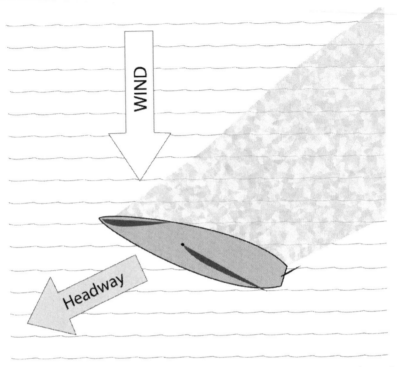

When hove to, your headsail is sheeted to windward, your main is loosely sheeted to leeward and you steer to windward

Each boat reacts differently. So, practice this before you need it. Some boats heave to better trailing a drogue off the stern or even abeam. Practical Boat Owner in the UK published one of the best overviews of how different boats behave when hove to in 2011.

Contrary to what you may hear elsewhere, heaving to works very well on catamarans, and why not? Friends of ours who own a catamaran and were told it would not work, let us talk them into trying it as we wanted to know about their first-hand experience. It worked. Since then, they have hove-to many times in all sorts of weather – and loved it. Like with mono-hulls, there is no set way to heave to on catamarans. Our friends did it just like we do with the reefed jib backed, a deeply reefed main, and the helm steering the boat to windward. Other cats like it better when the headsail is dropped altogether, and the dagger boards pulled half way up. If you have a system that works well for you, let us know.

The slick that forms behind the boat when heaving to (on a calm day).

In modern masthead sloops of moderate to light displacement, another method of heaving to in heavy weather is under storm jib alone. To heave to, trim the storm jib to windward, force the bow off the wind and then tie the helm down to maintain a slightly upwind bearing.

In a split-rigged boat, you can accomplish the same with a storm jib and reefed mizzen or trysail. On our ketch rigged boat, we have to sheet the mizzen in very flat.

In all cases, the boat will ideally seek an angle approximately 60 degrees off the wind and will then proceed forward at one to two knots. The course will be erratic as the boat rides over large swells and falls off again in the gusts at the top of the wave. The boat will occasionally take a breaking wave on the forward windward quarter that will shove the hull

247

to leeward. Your boat's progress will be a diagonal vector at about 130 degrees from the true direction of the wind, as you will be going forward at about two knots and going sideways at about one knot.

In our first crossing of the North Atlantic, we encountered six gales. We sailed through four of them and hove to in two others when the conditions became too rough. For 36 hours each time, we ended up reading, baking cookies (truly – peanut butter and they were great), and otherwise passing the time. We even had our first glass of wine at sea - our boat is dry while underway. We alternated between being terrified by the massive seas when going on deck to check our status and being hugely frustrated and bored below, while waiting for the time to pass. We also hove-to a third time in 30-foot confused seas to effect a repair on the Monitor wind vane self-steering. We couldn't have dealt with it otherwise.

Having tried a number of man overboard procedures, when we are sailing our ketch short-handed, we have come to the conclusion that our only viable option for dealing with a MOB situation, is to immediately heave to. It stops the boat quickly and safely. We can then deal with the next steps without panic.

It was interesting how many people asked us where we would be stopping at night on several transatlantic crossings. A few actually asked about anchoring mid-ocean. Now we tell them gently about heaving to – the alternative to anchoring.

To heave to in a sailboat

- Sheet in the main sail. Reef first in heavy weather. (Or drop the main and use the mizzen on a ketch or yawl.)
- Tack the boat but do not release the head sail sheet.
- When you finish the tack, your main has switched sides (normal) but your headsail is now set against the wind with its clew to windward instead of leeward as usual.

Getting Hooked & Anchoring Technique

⚓ Once the boat has settled, turn your steering wheel all the way to windward or push your tiller to leeward and secure it.

When you are ready to resume your normal course...

⚓ Unlock your wheel or unlash your tiller

⚓ Turn it all the way to the other side – falling off from the wind, jibe the main or mizzen and sail off on the original tack

Or:

⚓ Complete the tack you started when you initiated the heaving to process by releasing the headsail sheet and bringing it in on the leeward side.

Some other ideas for use of this technique

⚓ Heaving to can be useful for reefing (or dropping) the main, especially if you don't have an autopilot.

⚓ When you want to have lunch in more peaceful conditions, heaving to can be very pleasant and it lets the helmsman enjoy the meal as well.

⚓ It can be used when rendezvousing with a dinghy (if you sail in to pick up crew who were ashore). It makes getting the crew back on board from the dinghy a reasonable proposition. For this you obviously have to have enough sea room and the conditions need to be fairly well settled!

⚓ It is a viable MOB maneuver that should be practiced before it is needed.

Heaving-to in a Powerboat

When the boat feels unsafe running down sea in a gale – most powerboats are vulnerable to broaching and boarding seas on this course, heaving to may be the best tactic. Heaving to in a powerboat means pointing your bow at a 60-degree angle to the waves and applying just enough throttle to maintain headway. The best actual angle will depend on your vessel. If windage forward is forcing the bow too far off or hindering the vessel's maneuverability, a drogue might help.

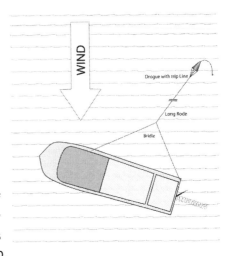

Just like a sailboat, the powerboat should gently ride over the waves at an angle of about 60 degrees. It too should be slipping to lee while motoring forward creating a calm slick to windward.

As before, this is something that should be practiced before storm conditions are encountered at sea.

Lying A-Hull vs. Heaving to

There are some people who might choose to lie a-hull instead of heaving-to. When lying a-hull the sails are (usually) taken down and the boat is turned beam to the seas. The vessel is allowed to take whatever course it pleases. One of the boats in "The Perfect Storm" did this with dire results for the crew, though the boat survived.

In theory, a sinusoidal wave, no matter how large, will not capsize a boat. However, this is not reflected in reality. In a storm there are always breaking waves. When hit beam on, a breaking wave has only to be higher than the width of the beam of the boat to capsize it. In a storm where waves will easily exceed 30 feet, it would seem fairly obvious that lying a-hull is not a desirable choice.

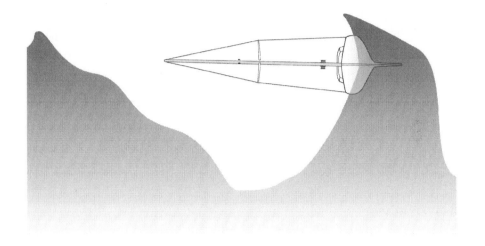

This is what lying a-hull in a storm might look like.
Not a situation we would like to be in.

Chapter 12: Sea Anchors & Drogues

The use of drag devices such as sea anchors and drogues is subject to some debate. There are those who swear by them and those who adamantly oppose their use. Having sailed through numerous gales while crossing oceans we have never had the need to use either, but that is us, on our boat. We did once consider a drogue when our steering failed, and we have used one to hinder our boat from yawing while at anchor.

Perhaps we should repeat that each boat is indeed different, and the combination of boat and circumstance will ultimately dictate what is best for your particular situation.

Sea Anchors

A sea anchor is something one might deploy from a sail or power vessel to be able to 'anchor' the boat in mid ocean. A sea anchor can also be used closer to shore for fishing or other activities. Sea anchors are deployed off the bow and are intended to keep the boat pointed into the prevailing wind and waves.

Sea anchors are either of a conical shape or are a big parachute anchor. Either is designed to trap sea water which provides the drag needed to hold the bow of the boat into the wind.

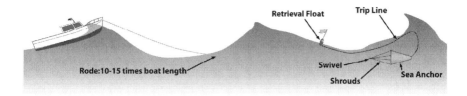

Deploying the parachute type sea anchors can be difficult. The wind may catch the cloth making deployment into the water tricky. It can also take time to open and fill once in the water.

Getting Hooked & Anchoring Technique

Sea anchors tend to spin, so a good and heavy swivel at the crown is an important component. The rode also needs adequate chafe protection at the bow of the vessel.

The rode should be long enough to place the anchor at least two wave crests to windward. Out in the ocean this may equate to about 10-15 boat lengths. Its length should be adjusted to account for changes in the wave patterns.

As the rode will be subjected to huge loads alternating with slackness, it should be made of polyester and not nylon. It has been shown that nylon sea anchor rodes may break midway at about 20% of their rated breaking strain due to internal chafe.

The danger in lying to a sea anchor or parachute anchor occurs when the boat slides backwards as a breaking sea rolls under the bow of the boat. As the hull slips back on the wave, the entire weight of the hull will fall onto the rudder. The pressure can easily bend the rudder post or shear off the pins.

As the sea anchor is usually only deployed during rough conditions, its subsequent retrieval can be quite challenging. It is essential that it has a trip line and retrieval buoy as part of the rig. Be mindful of fouling the rode during the retrieval.

Drogues and Warps

Drogues and warps are generally towed off the stern of a boat. They help you limit the speed of your vessel so you can ride the waves more safely without constantly speeding up and slowing down, falling off the waves into the troughs, or getting swamped by following seas. They can also be used to steer a boat in the event of rudder failure.

Uses for Drogues

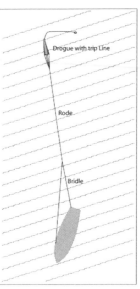

- 🐎 They can be deployed off the stern in strong following seas to increase vessel stability.
- 🐎 Towed off the stern with a bridle a drogue can be used as an emergency steering device.
- 🐎 They can be deployed off the stern of a vessel being towed. This can provide better control for the towing vessel.
- 🐎 They can be deployed to windward while the vessel is hove-to, to slow its forward motion down and give it better control.

Drogues come in many configurations, with the common characteristic that they create resistance while being dragged through the water. They are not intended to stop the movement of the vessel. A drogue can be a hank of rope (warp) or an anchor (or both together). It can be a cone-shaped device (smaller than a sea anchor), a series of many small conical devices (Jordan series drogue), parabolic webbing (GaleRider), or anything else one might deploy.

Jordan Series Drogue

Most are attached to the boat with a bridle attached to two secure points on the boat and a length of rode. At the other end they will usually have a weight to keep them submerged in the water. They may also have a retrieval line.

The bridle allows you to adjust the angle from which the waves arrive at the boat. This permits selecting a course which is more pleasant or is closer to where you want to head.

Getting Hooked & Anchoring Technique

For some boats, a drogue is also very useful to assist in heaving to in severe storm situations. In this case the bridles are adjusted so that the drogue is somewhere abaft of the beam.

There is a Caveat...

The pull exerted by a drogue is relatively small, to allow for a continued forward motion of the boat. If the waves get so big that the boat's speed suddenly increases dramatically, it may overcome the resistance of the drogue and broach, capsize and/or pitch pole.

The legendary Moitessier dragged warps with weights approaching Cape Horn until he had a revelation that made him go on deck and cut them away. Every boat likes a different configuration and his Joshua didn't happen to like warps in a monstrous sea. Instead, he learned to surf at an angle down the waves.

Part 4: 'Long-term Hooking' – Moorings

At first, we thought that moorings should really not be part of a book on anchoring. Then again, what is a mooring if it isn't a permanently installed, large anchor that you leave behind with all its gear rather than taking it along? Fact is, we migrate old anchors from our big boat to mooring anchors for our little boats.

A mooring is in essence a large, heavy anchor. Often this is a concrete or stone block, a large mushroom anchor, or a device bored into underlying rock or mud. The 'rode' is usually made up of a length of heavy chain, which is connected to the mooring line or riser by a heavy-duty swivel.

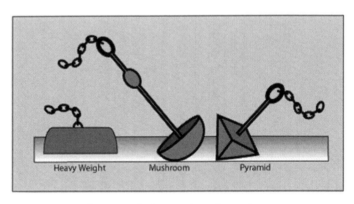

Some standard types of mooring anchors

A mooring ball (buoy) is connected to the riser. The length of line from the ball to the boat is called a pennant or bridle. Often a small pickup buoy is attached to the pennant near its outer end to make it easier for someone on the boat to reach the pennant when the boat returns to the mooring.

256

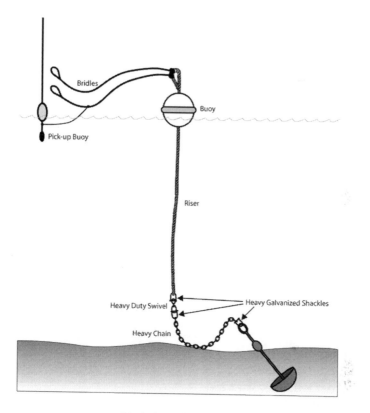

A typical mooring system

A typical mooring system deployed in a mooring field consists of an anchor connected with a heavy galvanized shackle to a heavy bottom chain which is usually about 1.5 times the maximum depth of water. A swivel with a shackle on either end will normally connect the bottom chain to riser whose length will be approximately equal the maximum depth of water – giving you a total minimum scope of 2.5:1.

The riser is either a heavy nylon rope or a chain. It will typically either go through the mooring buoy in such a way that it cannot move inside it (chafe) or the buoy is tied off to the riser. A rope pennant or bridle will go from riser to the boat's mooring cleat. A pickup buoy will often be tied into the pennant for easy retrieval when returning to the mooring. As scope has a direct relationship to the holding power of a mooring system – just like any other anchoring setup, extending the riser and pennant will improve performance where space allows.

If the mooring is solitary or the conditions are more extreme, then the mooring system can be beefed up considerably. On ours we have deployed a large deadweight concrete block. To this we have attached three significantly oversized scoop type anchors; each on ten meters (30ft) of approximately 1" (25mm) chain. The anchors are arranged at angles of 120° from each other. With this arrangement we effectively have a gigantic kellet providing a horizontal pull to whichever anchors happen to be upwind. The kellet itself is large enough to hold our boat in all but the most extreme situation.

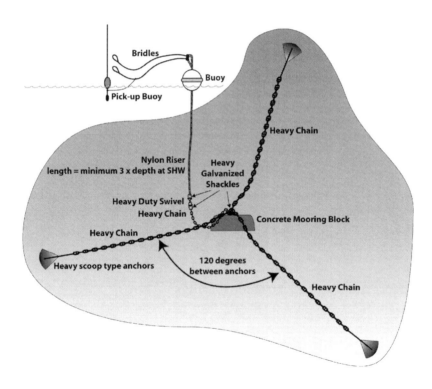

Alex and Daria Blackwell

No mooring system is complete without a safety pennant otherwise called a lazy bridle. Some harbors require safety or secondary pennants. This extra line is inexpensive compared to the cost of your insurance policy deductible. The safety pennant should be of equal size (diameter and strength) and 25%, or three feet longer (whichever is less) than the primary pennant. The theory is that the safety pennant will be in "perfect" condition when/if the primary fails. The safety pennant should also preferably be tied off to something other than the deck cleats in case these were to fail. It is often suggested that the mast is the best place to do this.

Note the two bridles coming over the bow roller either side of the head stay. In the middle is the safety pennant or lazy bridle. All three bridles have permanently attached chafe protection.

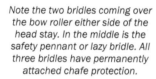

Chapter 1: Some Typical Mooring Anchors

Deadweight Anchors

Deadweight anchors work on the principle of being heavy. Whether the anchor is a block of stone, concrete, or iron, its holding power is provided by its weight. Once the weight is on the bottom for an extended period, it may become partially embedded in the sediment and a suction effect may increase its resistance to being lifted. Deadweight anchors provide reasonable reliability. If they are dragged, they will resist with constant force. Dead weights are a good choice for rock, gravel or coarse sand bottoms. In mud they will sink and hold well, though they are then more difficult to inspect. A dead weight anchor is a bit awkward to handle as it is very heavy, but once it is in position, it should not move. In calculating the size of a deadweight anchor, the type of material of the anchor must be considered.

Some typical concrete dead weight anchors

Harbors commonly regulate the size of the deadweight required, but not the material, even though there is a significant difference in densities. In seawater, concrete loses over one-half its weight, granite loses about one-third, and iron loses only an eighth. This is significant. If a mooring is designed to withstand a 4000-lb. pull, one needs at least 8000 lbs. of concrete, 6000 lbs. of granite, or 4500 lbs. of iron. At a minimum, over one ton is needed for even a small 25' yacht. To handle weights of this magnitude, a barge crane is needed. As long as this equipment is used to place the anchor, one might as well err on the side of excessive weight when placing it.

Mushrooms

Mushroom anchors are a very popular mooring anchor. These anchors work on the principle of surface area and suction effect. Cohesion of the bottom material is very important. Rocks, gravel or coarse sand lack good cohesive properties, allowing the anchor to pull free. Mushroom anchors in sand will not bury completely. They will only sink to displace an equal weight of sand. Their large round dish design is not well-suited to penetrating the bottom. They work best in a silt or mud bottom. A rocky or coarse sand bottom is not a good place for mushroom-type anchors.

Mushroom anchors, not embedded in the bottom, will get 'spun out' and lose what little holding power they have when partially buried. This can happen if the anchor is set in a particular direction and a storm blows from the opposite direction. In this case the mushroom can get spun around 180° and then can roll out of the bottom losing all its holding power.

All too often, mushroom moorings are pulled for the winter, or for inspection and maintenance of worn components. When replaced in the spring, they are often just dropped and then pulled to make sure they are not standing upright. The problem is that in doing so, the mushroom doesn't get a chance to bury itself in the bottom.

When the mushroom is not buried in the bottom and/or standing up, the chain will often wrap around the anchor, consuming valuable scope (see image of a mooring hockle below under A Cautionary Note). This commonly occurs with the vessel following the tide, pulls the chain from one side to the other of the mooring; wrapping it around the stock in the process.

To correct this situation, mushroom anchors should be dropped into position early in the season, well before they are going to be in use, and allowed to set. Inspection and maintenance should be done in the water. If the mooring is pulled, the anchor should ideally be jetted into the bottom using a stream of water to blow a hole in the sea bed for the anchor.

Dor-Mor (www.dor-mor.com) anchors are a redesign of the traditional mushroom anchor. Dor-Mor anchors are a cast iron 'pyramid' with a short shank at the base to attach the ground tackle. The pyramid design is to allow easy penetration of the anchor into the bottom. The short shank reduces the 'spinout' effect of the long shank found on traditional mushrooms.

Oversized Anchors

In the understanding that a mooring is essentially a greatly over specified anchor system, some contractors opt for the use of significantly oversized anchors, which are then connected to traditional mooring tackle. As opposed to the potential spin-out described above for the mushroom anchor, these should reset on reversal like their much smaller brethren – provided they are correctly designed and have adequate scope.

Three examples of oversized anchors used by contractors.

Shown are claw and scoop copies, as well as a mooring anchor as used on fish farms.

If designed well, the copies should reset readily on reversal. However, the fish farm anchor will not reset if flipped over.

Embedded Mooring Systems

Helical Piles (www.helixmooring.com) or sea screws are not common but are exceptionally effective. These are long shafts of high tensile steel with an attachment eye at the top and large threads at the lower end. These 'screw anchors' are screwed into  the bottom. 8 feet is a common length. The threads at the bottom are 10 to 14 inches in diameter. When embedded into the bottom with the top eye flush or into the bottom soil attached to traditional ground tackle, their holding power is very high. Recent tests have shown that their holding power is vastly greater than any traditional mooring system of mushroom or dead weight anchors. These anchors have been used by the offshore oil industry for more than 20 years and are quickly appearing in the yachting market.

Long Term Hooking & Moorings

Similarly, there are embedded systems like the Manta Ray where the anchor is pounded into the bottom with a jack hammer and then unfolded much like a wall anchor. These anchors have been deployed on land for a wide variety of uses and are now also coming into the yachting market.

In two tests conducted by *Practical Sailor* in 2009, the embedment-type anchors clearly showed greater holding power than those that relied mostly on weight and mass for resistance. The need for a diver and/or specialized equipment for proper installation however raises the price. They also suffer in soft mud. Another concern is that if the embedment anchor pulls out, there is no hope of it resetting itself or even slowing the boat's drag. Both Helix and Manta say that anchors installed more than a decade ago are still going strong.

Chapter 2: Other Considerations

Mooring Loads

Following are the estimated normal mooring loads based on Table 1 "Design Loads for Sizing Deck Hardware," in section H-40, "Anchoring, Mooring and Strong Points," of the ABYC's Standards and Technical Reports. Chain working load limits are based on data from chain maker Acco. The right chain size can vary greatly depending on the boat, harbor, and other factors.

Boat Length	20 feet	30 feet	40 feet
Mooring's Top Chain	3/8 inch	3/8 inch	½ inch
Estimated Permanent Mooring Loads	1080 lbs	2100 lbs	3600 lbs
Working Load Limit (Acco Grade 30 Proof Coil)	2650 lbs	2650 lbs	4500 lbs

Mooring Grids

Where there is a need to provide moorings for a larger number of smaller vessels, mooring grids are often employed. A grid system uses two or more extra-large anchors, connected by a ground line with multiple moorings taken off different points. This minimizes the need for deploying a separate anchor for each mooring. Usually large ships' anchors or very large concrete blocks will be set, interconnected by a large diameter, heavy chain. The traditional ground tackle is attached to the ground chain, rising to mooring buoys. Patterns and layout can vary greatly, from a two-anchor 'string' of moorings, or a three-anchor triangular pattern, to a square grid using four or more anchors.

Long Term Hooking & Moorings

Moorings arranged in a grid

The downside of such a grid is, of course, should the anchors at the ends start to move, the moored boats will bunch up and move together.

Servicing Moorings

Moorings need to be serviced on a regular basis. At the very least they should be inspected annually. Without that, worn or rusted parts, chafed ropes, hockles, and other problems will not be found.

Typical workboat for mooring inspection & servicing

Connecting shackles and swivels as well as the chain used in a mooring will corrode and/or wear and need to be inspected on a regular basis.

266

Lifting the tackle is the best way to see what is happening, but it is also possible to dive and inspect. Any worn components should be replaced.

Fouling on moorings can be considerable and the ropes buoys and chains need to be cleaned; mussels and other marine creatures grown into the rope fibers can cause serious abrasion. Often the easiest approach to cleaning the fouling is to sink the mooring riser (and chain) into the mud for the winter. Any growth will die off. To do this we remove the mooring buoy and tie off a thinner rope with a small buoy at its end. We then tie some old large shackles to the riser and drop it to the bottom. In the spring time we reverse the process and the riser is clean. Every few years we remove the riser altogether and soak it in fresh water before hanging it up to dry.

A Cautionary Note

Do you know what is down there? This hockle was pulled up from a busy harbor. Can you see the other anchor permanently wedged into this mess?

For those who think moorings are much safer to pick up than anchoring, we always ask, "How often do you check to see what is down there holding your precious boat in the night?" The answer invariably is, "Never, why should I? The outfit renting the mooring is a responsible one."

Then we show them the picture of the mooring removed from the harbor of a well-respected yacht club where the individuals who owned the moorings were responsible for their maintenance. The hockle that came up was a permanently tangled mess of rope, chain, mooring mushroom, someone else's anchor mixed in, and all kinds of other debris. The owner had complained that the water was getting deeper due to climate change and he was having difficulty getting his mooring bridle up on deck. In reality the mooring lines were so shortened by the hockle that the bridle was actually pulling the bow of the boat down. This mooring was occasionally rented to visiting yachts.

Chapter 3: Picking up a Mooring

Picking up a mooring, if you know how, is in many ways easier than dropping an anchor, but it does have its potential drawbacks, as we discussed in the previous chapter.

Moorings are usually arranged in patterns with a name or code marked on the buoys. Yacht clubs and commercial harbors often keep several spare moorings labelled "guest" or "transient" along the perimeter of their mooring fields. Hailing the marina or club on their designated frequency will alert them to your arrival. They will then direct you to your designated mooring. Often, they will send out their launch to assist you. The launch may also collect the mooring fee or take you ashore to register and pay for the rental.

Almost every harbor has its own distinct mooring setup, which always makes picking up moorings in new places interesting. When approaching an unknown mooring, it is a good idea to have a boat hook extended and ready to deploy if necessary. Often as not, you will need to fish the bridle ropes out of the water. We also keep spare dock lines on deck. Sometimes the provided bridles have been too dirty for us to want to use on deck, sometimes they have been too short for our deck hardware, and frequently there were no bridles at all.

It is always good to make a point of asking questions when making a reservation, as well as when arriving on site. Elements to bring up are length, beam, weight, and draft of the vessel. This way you can usually ensure that there will be sufficient swing room and draft, and that the mooring is big enough to hold your boat. It is also prudent to inquire about the mooring itself – are bridles included, etc.

There will be instances when a mooring is inadequate. One time, we were so close to a neighboring boat that swinging in a slightly different direction would have put us in direct side-by-side contact. Another time, we had to prove to the launch driver that the mooring they put us on was not sufficient by dragging their mooring several feet when applying gentle engine speed in reverse. The summer staff may not always be experienced enough to know better.

Picking up a mooring with skipper and crew:

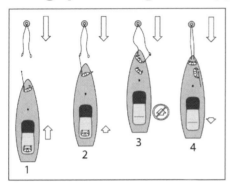

With two or more people on board, picking up a mooring is usually a simple task. Position one person at the bow and the other at the helm. Make sure your dinghy is on a very short tether or you may foul your prop on its painter.

1. Motor slowly into the wind and/or current aiming directly at the mooring. Crew is forward with a boat hook at the ready.

2. The crew signals to stop the boat when the bridle is within reach.

3. Having stopped the boat. Skipper goes forward to lend a hand if needed. Crew has cleated off first bridle.

4. The second bridle is cleated, and it is time to relax.

Note: If you are towing a dinghy, make sure you pull it in and tie the painter off short prior to commencing the maneuver so as not to foul your prop!

Scope out your assigned mooring and its environs. Drive past the mooring for a quick visual inspection to see how it has been equipped, what boats are near it, how deep the water is and what the wind and current are doing – much like preparing to deploy an anchor.

We have simple hand signals we use to let the helmsman know the situation at the bow. Right, left, slow, stop, reverse, as well as go back around are common. A set of hand-held radios can also be of benefit. (See chapter on communication.)

At this point the helmsperson may come forward to render assistance with the second bridle, attaching chafe protection, and any other tasks that may come up. Finally, it is time for all to relax.

Alex and Daria Blackwell

Once tied up we tend to power gently in reverse to make sure we won't drag the mooring in a blow. If possible, we also dive down on it to check its condition. This is a bit easier in places like the Bahamas and Fiji where it is warm, and you can actually see through the water.

Picking up a mooring short-handed

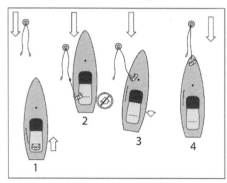

1. Motor slowly into the wind and/or current, leaving the mooring to one side. Boat hook is at the ready.

2. The skipper stops the boat and picks up the nearest bridle from the aft quarter.

3. Without needing to rush, the skipper walks the bridle forward while the boat drifts back slowly.

4. The bridle is cleated off and the skipper can now leisurely deal with the second one.

What if you are alone and want to pick up a mooring? There is nothing that says you have to pick it up from the bow. In fact, it is much easier to see the buoy if you slowly pull up alongside it. Put your engine in neutral as the boat approaches the mooring buoy so you don't foul your propeller. Don't reverse. Instead let the boat drift forward gently as you walk forward toward it. Grab the mooring bridle and walk forward with the gear, making sure you bring the lines around the outside of the shrouds on a sailboat. Then secure the lines as you would with assistance.

Some places have moorings with only one line coming off them. This could induce yaw and cause your boat to sail back and forth all night of you are not able to center the pennant at the bow. In these places we add a second dock line to the mooring and run this through the other chock (or bow roller) on the boat to balance the boat. It also gives us more comfort to know there are two lines attaching us to the mooring.

Long Term Hooking & Moorings

Other places only have an eye on a mooring ball, and you have to deploy your own bridle ropes. There are two ways to attach your boat to the ball. Pull the ball (or just the eye) up on deck using a boat hook through the eye or reach down to the ball by lying on the deck. This may be most easily done from amidships.

It may help to bring the mooring amidships on a vessel where the freeboard at the bow is higher.

This is not easy when you have high freeboard. Chances are that you will need someone down below at the mooring ball to help you attach your lines. Sailing short-handed, as we tend to do, will on occasion thus leave us with a dilemma. We resolve this by sending one person out as the advance guard in the dinghy, while the other brings the big boat in slowly. The person in the dinghy ties the lines off to the mooring ball and hands them up to the big boat when it gets there. The helmsman comes forward and grabs the lines and secures at least one to a cleat.

In places like the Caribbean you may be swarmed by 'boat boys' offering their assistance in connecting your boat to 'their' mooring. Once connected, the rest can be tended to slowly. As always, the key is to take your time. If you do things without rushing everything tends to happen more gently – and there is far less chance of something going wrong.

Part 5: 'Hooking Up With Friends!' – Tying Up & Rafting

One of the joys of cruising is getting away from the hustle and spending some quality time with your partner, spouse or friends. In all likelihood, there will come a time when out of desire or sheer necessity you will want to raft up with another boat. There is nothing wrong with being sociable.

Rafting up is a term used to describe when one boat anchors and another ties off to the 'anchor boat.' A raft-up can of course have several boats in it. The technique is more akin to docking than anchoring for all vessels but the first. The lines are deployed from one vessel to another as they would be from a boat to a dock.

Our first experience rafting up with our new sloop took place one beautiful evening. We had had a really busy work week. We motored a short distance up the coast and dropped our hook. We had to get away to 'our world' as fast as possible. The sun was slowly sinking, and we had brought out our cushions, reading material and cocktails, and had happy thoughts of another beautiful sunset in paradise in our minds.

As we settled in, we saw another boat approaching. We laughed about the 'magnet effect' as it seemed to be making a beeline right to where we were. We got back to our books and relaxed. Then someone started shouting our boat name. Startled out of our reverie, we looked out and there it was looming on the water right next to us – the other boat.

The owners of the other boat were a pair of seasoned sailors we knew and respected. Could they raft up with us they asked? With trepidation in our hearts for what might happen to our precious new boat during this maneuver, we said, "Sure!" We need not have worried as out came

273

Hooking Up With Friends! ⚓ Tying Up & Rafting

fenders and dock lines, and within minutes they had expertly and without fuss tied their able craft off the side of ours. What ensued then was a pot luck dinner, followed by a wonderful evening, and the kindling of a lifelong friendship.

Their maneuvering and deployment of gear taught us a thing or two and caused us to remember the many 'issues' we had witnessed in similar circumstances. As with all other aspects of anchoring, a little advance planning is a good thing. Prepare a few things – fenders, dock lines, and a VHF radio being a good starting point – and let's see what else it will take.

Chapter 1: Hull Shape and Fender Positioning

The first thing to take into consideration when approaching another boat (or a dock for that matter) is your hull shape and how it compares with the shape of the vessel with which you will be rafting up. The shape affects where you will need to position fenders and ropes for best protection and maximum comfort.

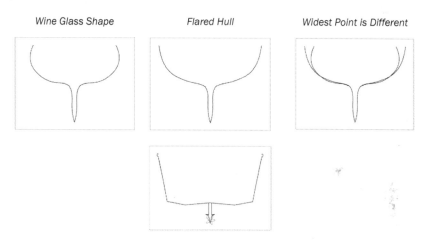

Differently shaped hulls require different fender placement

If you do this at the outset, you will be able to position your fenders in such a way that your boat will be protected. It is easier to visualize what we mean by showing how it looks alongside a dock, but you can easily see how it translates to rafting with another boat. The shape of your hull and its freeboard will determine how far down you need to position your fenders.

Fender placement and effectiveness varies with hull shape as shown here against a dock or bulkhead.

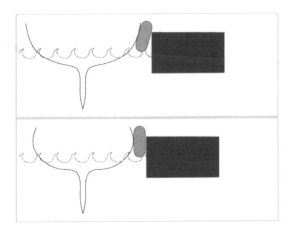

Taking this the logical step further, this same principal applies when positioning your fenders prior to rafting with another boat. The fender is positioned to keep the boats from hitting or rubbing against each other.

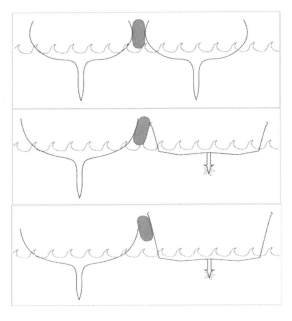

The consideration changes a little when both boats have flared hulls. In such a case, you may wish to consider deploying your fenders horizontally.

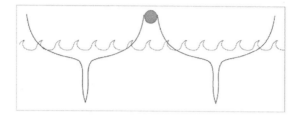

Chapter 2: Line Positioning

Just like having your fenders ready to keep your boat from bumping into whatever you are tying up to, you also need to have your lines ready. Just go to any busy dock and you will see why we feel we need to stress that advance planning and preparation is key. A frightening number of people, even some you might have thought to be experienced skippers will come alongside to dock with nary a dock line or fender in sight. The result is a mad dash at the approach, or even after the landing, to secure the craft before it either floats away or does some damage.

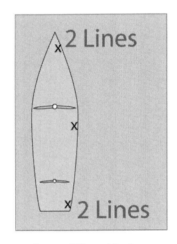

Prepare 2 lines at the bow, 2 lines at the stern and one amidships.

No matter what kind of boat you are skippering, you should have two lines at the ready fore and two lines aft. These lines should be secured to sturdy cleats and brought out through the chocks, or under the life lines in such a way to ensure that they don't get hung up when you toss them to the person ashore or bring it ashore yourself. Also ensure that the rope bend and chafe will be minimized when the boat is secured.

We like to advise having a line amidships at the ready as well.

Bring the ropes out under the lifelines or out through the chocks. Then bring them back in over the life lines or over the railing and make sure it is neatly coiled and ready to throw.

The four lines are necessary as two of the bow and stern lines will keep your vessel from moving away from the other boat or dock, and the others (springs) suppress the fore and aft movement. Make sure your springs won't get hung up on stanchions and other deck elements when led fore and aft.

The middle line (mid-ship spring) is often the most useful initially when coming in to a dock. With that one alone, the helper ashore can maneuver your boat, or secure the boat tightly to a nearby cleat, leaving you time to deploy the other lines at your leisure.

The next step is to add fenders at the widest part of your boat. If possible, tie them off to the toe rail, the bottom of your stanchions, or a solid railing. Try to avoid tying the fenders to the lifelines themselves. The movement of your boat against a dock or another boat can be quite strong and the pull on the lifelines exerted by the force on the fenders will inevitably damage the stanchions.

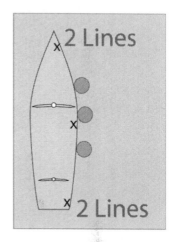

Arrange three fenders at the widest point of your boat

Chapter 3: Throwing a Rope

Let us digress to briefly review a technique for throwing a rope. This is a skill well worth perfecting for many boating (and other) applications. Like anything else, it does require some practice (and preparation) to actually get the rope to the intended destination. It is one of the things we do with new crew members aboard our boat. If done right, coming into a dock or rafting up with another boat is much simpler.

The first essential step in which the rope is coiled neatly is most often omitted or ignored. Without it the rope will bunch up when you throw it and never reach its intended destination. So, take the time to coil the rope neatly into one hand as shown. Do not coil the rope from palm to elbow as often seen. This causes the rope to twist or get tangled.

Next, split your coil into two parts. One for your throwing arm and the other (with the bitter end) held loosely in your other hand. If the end is tied off to a cleat, leave some slack for your movement. If not, make sure you hold onto it in the following step!

Now throw the coil gently but firmly underhanded, aiming just above and beyond the recipient. You will be amazed at how straight the rope will fly, uncoiling as it goes as well as paying out from what you have in your other hand at the same time! Just make sure you hang on to the bitter end.

Alex and Daria Blackwell

Coil neatly   *Hold correctly*   *Throw confidently*

Practicing off the boat will give you the skill and confidence to always get the rope to the intended recipient. This is a great skill to teach children. They will spend loads of time practicing and will acquire a skill they will use lifelong.

The Monkey's Fist

If you want to throw a rope to a person at a greater distance, you will want to use a lighter line with a weight at the end tied off to the actual rope you wish to pass to the other person. The best option here is to use a 'Monkey's Fist'.

A Monkey's Fist is made by wrapping a lump of lead with line using a 'Running Turk's Head' knot. This is in turn attached to the throwing line.

Using the same technique as above, a throwing line with a Monkey's Fist enables you to accurately throw a line over quite a distance. Make sure you don't use a lump of lead that can cause damage if you miss your intended target.

A 'Monkey's Fist' spliced to a length of line

Chapter 4: Rafting up Technique

This well-found boat is prepared for another boat to come and raft up.

Putting all of the principles into practice, the rest is actually quite easy – whether you are rafting up or coming into a dock. When rafting, it is better to designate the larger or heavier displacement vessel as the primary or 'anchor boat'. Skippers should agree as to which boat will deploy fenders and dock lines, though both vessels should be prepared in case something goes amiss. Most important, the skippers must agree as to which side of the anchor boat the rafting vessel will tie up to. If it is to the port side of the anchor vessel, then all fenders and lines will be set on the starboard side of the rafting vessel. Simple, right?

A peaceful evening among friends enjoying a potluck dinner together.

If either one or both boats have a dinghy in the water, make sure these are out of the way prior to commencing any maneuver. On the vessel coming in (to a dock or to a raft-up) be sure you have shortened the dinghy's painter to a point where it cannot get near the propeller should you need to reverse for any reason. Needless to

283

say, it is far preferable to tie the tender off to the side of your vessel which will be away from whatever you are tying up to.

The primary vessel should be securely anchored bow to the wind with all crew on deck to receive or throw lines as the case may be. The line configuration is the same as when tying up to a dock: bow and stern lines, two springs, and one amidships just in case. Deploy three fenders at the widest part of the boat, and a spare ready just in case.

A temporary raft up to exchange gear and personnel without tying up the dock.

Let us assume that the anchor boat has its fenders deployed at its widest point and that you are supplying the ropes. When coming in to raft up, approach the primary vessel slowly from astern – stopping when alongside. If you are well prepared, there is no need to rush. Throw and secure the lines in the same sequence as when docking:

> Start with the mid-ship spring line if the wind is blowing away from the anchor boat or dock. Have this line pulled in good and tight to the other boat or dock. With this line secured, your boat is not going anywhere. It can also provide leverage to pivot your vessel back into alignment should that be needed.

1. Throw the bowline first. Have the crew on the other boat secure this – but not too tightly.
2. Throw the aft spring line next. Ideally, you will have brought this forward with you. Have the crew on the anchor boat tie this off as far forward as possible. Notice that this already holds your boat in position parallel to the other vessel.

3. Throw stern line and secure at the stern of the anchor boat.
4. Then finally throw the forward spring.
5. Both boats should check for any gear that might get caught up when the boats roll or pitch (e.g., fishing gear, BBQs, super structures). Sailboats need to make sure that their masts are not lined up right next to each other to avoid the spreaders locking and causing damage as the boats roll.

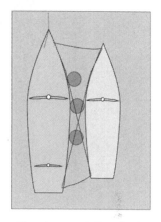

Though secured, these boats must adjust their positioning as the masts should not be lined up!

6. Release the mid-ship spring and adjust the relative positions of boats with the spring lines and tighten them there. Then relax tension on bow and stern lines. This allows the boats to separate a little, often resulting in both boats riding more peacefully.
7. Finally, adjust the fenders for optimal placement. You want the center fender positioned where the boats are the closest. The other two fenders should come into action as the two boats sway a little. Don't forget to add chafe protection to the lines!

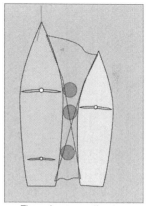

These boats are lined up correctly – their spreaders should not touch when the boats roll.

A recipe for trouble – the masts of these boats are lined up next to each other where they could interlock and cause damage to the rigging.

These masts are staggered, and all looks well!

Many times, more than one vessel will join a raft. Once the anchor is set by the first boat – preferably the largest, heaviest vessel in the fleet – other boats tie up in alternating sequence port and starboard, so the anchor boat stays in the middle. For larger rafts, it is a good idea to drop another anchor every third boat from the primary anchor vessel to spread the load out on more than one anchor and rode. Subsequent anchor boats will drop their anchors upwind and a little to one side of the raft. They will then back down alongside the other boats and tie up.

Remember that a large raft with multiple anchors does not swing the same as when only one anchor is deployed. This can cause problems if there is a major wind shift, or if conditions deteriorate, so it should only be considered for settled conditions.

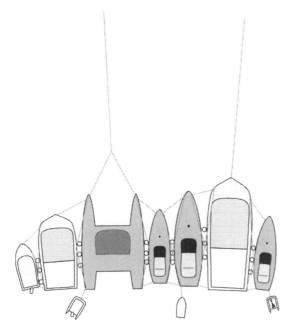

In a multi boat raft-up at least every third boat should deploy an anchor.

Hooking Up With Friends! ⚓ Tying Up & Rafting

Multiple sailboats rafted together

Sail and power rafted side-by-side on a hot summer day gives kids lots to do with friends under parents' close supervision.

Chapter 5: Rafting Safety

Swing Radius

When anchoring and rafting up near other boats, please remember that rafted boats swing differently. Allow for extra room and don't forget to take the dinghies into consideration.

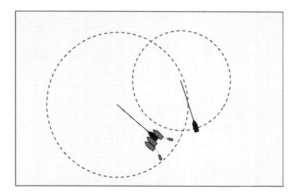

When rafting remember to take your swing radius and raft behavior into consideration.

Overnight Rafting

It is always wise to break up the raft before nightfall (or after dinner) and have everyone re-anchor safely on their own. Circumstances can and will change and weather forecasting is at best a prediction.

The anchor boat's gear is presumably sized for its own needs. Sudden strong winds pushing the large surface are of multiple boats will unduly strain the anchor and rode. If a lovely and calm anchorage suddenly gets choppy, chafe becomes an instant issue.

Please bear in mind that a raft whose anchor has broken out is not maneuverable at all. If connecting lines are broken and boats are twisted in the dark the situation can rapidly become confusing and very dangerous. The middle of the night in the storm is not a good time to safely break up a raft.

Chapter 6: Tying to a Dock

Tying alongside to a dock is pretty much the same as rafting up with another boat (see rafting up technique). Coming in to the dock may be challenging depending on where the wind is coming from, but the lines needed are all the same.

When docking up to pilings, you may choose to use fender boards. Place two fenders equidistant from the piling lowering them down to the widest point of your boat's hull. Place the fender board between the fenders and the piling to keep your boat safe. You may, of course, substitute this with a horizontal fender, but be aware that it will often get lodged to one side of a piling leaving your hull exposed with no protection.

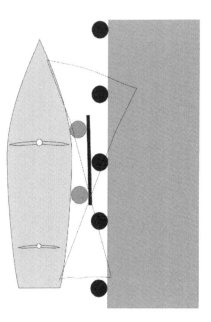

Lateral Anchor

When you are tied to a dock with an onshore breeze, or if there is a surge in the harbor, it may be advisable to deploy a lateral anchor. This is particularly useful in situations where undue pressure is subjected to your fenders, or where the boat is constantly moving, and you cannot tie a line off to a dock or object opposite from your berth.

Alex and Daria Blackwell

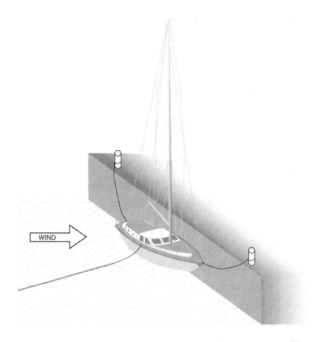

A lateral anchor can help keep your boat off a dock or seawall if there is a surge or an onshore breeze.

Once tied to the dock or seawall, bring your anchor out perpendicular to the boat using a dinghy and deploy. A good attachment point on board may be a winch or a mid-ship cleat. Tension the rode from on board your boat to pull it away from the dock. Often it is advisable to use a pair of bridles to attach the rode to the boat. This can help fine-tuning the boat's angle to the dock.

Rafting Up at a Dock

Rafting up at a dock is a common practice as it makes better use of the available dock space. The technique is the same as rafting under anchor, though the inside boats may wish to double up their lines as there is clearly going to be a lot of force exerted on them if the wind blows up. The largest boat should be positioned on the inside and the smallest on the outside if at all possible.

If a raft gets this deep, you may wish to drop two lateral anchors veering away from the dock at the bow and stern of the outside vessel. This will not only stabilize the raft but also reduce the force exerted on the inside vessel's deck hardware. The outside vessel should also run fore and aft lines, back to the dock.

Rafting Etiquette

Rafting up at a dock makes good use of available space.

For situations like a raft up with multiple boats, a note about courtesy is in order. The crew from the outer boats will invariably have to cross over other boats. When owners or crew of these boats are in evidence, asking permission prior to crossing is good form. When there is nobody on deck, crossing forward and not through the cockpit is the polite convention.

Often it is the inside boat that will need to leave before the others, who may have arrived later and will be staying on longer. In this case it is best to speak with the outer boats well in advance and arrange a time for the maneuver. It is extremely bad form to be late in leaving once these arrangements have been made.

Chapter 7: The Sunflower Raft

The 'ultimate' in raft-ups:
The Sunflower Raft American Yacht Club Annual Cruise 2005
Photo copyright © Rlaerials.com. Reproduced with permission.

The sunflower raft is taking rafting to its pinnacle. It is tremendous fun to do and something no participant will readily forget. You do, however, want to do this with experienced boaters as there are many potential pitfalls. The assembly, when done right, is akin to a ballet of yachts. Perhaps the most important aspect is having one person in charge and several lieutenants standing by, plus a few people in dinghies ready to assist.

⚓ Assign someone primary responsibility to plan it out and give orders, preferably someone who has seen it done before. Select a VHF channel without competing traffic for communication with the fleet.

Hooking Up With Friends! ⚓ Tying Up & Rafting

⚓ Pick a sheltered location with good holding and little current on a calm day.

⚓ Have the largest vessel in the fleet anchor first.

⚓ Make sure each boat is ready with dock lines and fenders on either side before approaching.

⚓ Choose a nimble vessel that backs well and can set a sturdy anchor in the opposite direction (i.e., anchor from the bow but stern toward the first vessel and the wind). Pass a nylon line between the sterns of the two primary vessels to keep them in line along the diameter of the circle. Estimate the diameter of the circle given the fleet size and adjust as boats are added.

⚓ Choose the next largest vessels and have them join the first anchored boat on either side. Have each of them set their anchors. They can do this by setting their anchors first then dropping back to raft up, or they can raft up and someone in a dinghy can deploy their anchors for them. The three big anchors to windward should hold the raft.

⚓ Continue to add vessels either side and setting anchors about every third boat. As you add boats, make sure each newly rafted boat drops back just a bit and keeps the bow looser than the stern or you will have a straight line rather than a circle. Set spring lines as well as bow and stern lines and instruct everyone to watch their spreaders.

⚓ As the circle closes, adjust the length of nylon line between the first two boats.

⚓ Keep the smallest most nimble vessels for last. They will have to back into the closing circle. When the last vessel is in, tighten up the nylon line bisecting the raft up as you adjust the primary anchor rode for the boats on the downwind side.

⚓ Arrange in advance for a helicopter to fly over when complete – you will want pictures.

Alex and Daria Blackwell

Once rafted up the fun can begin.

Go swimming in the middle, go visiting around the circle, or enjoy a gathering on the host vessel's deck. Remind everyone, as a courtesy, the bow is where one crosses over rafted up boats so as not to disturb activities in the cockpit.

Break up well before nightfall and have everyone re-anchor for a safe night.

Part 6:
When Life gets 'Interesting'
– Tips & Techniques

Chapter 1: Maneuvering in tight spaces

It's getting narrow up there. Would you be able to turn your boat around in her own length? This is the entrance to a delightful, protected anchorage in Scotland, which is not much wider than the entrance.

296

Alex and Daria Blackwell

We were just getting ready to spend a little time in marinas, which is always a source of consternation for us. We have a 40-year-old, 57-foot classic ketch with no bow thruster. She's got a modified fin keel (an almost full keel) and heavy displacement. In other words, *Aleria* doesn't maneuver very well in tight spaces. She is meant to be crossing oceans. That's one of the reasons we really like to anchor out. But in reality, everyone needs to get to a dock for fuel, water, or overnight in the absence of a safe anchorage at some point.

Our boat doesn't do very well in reverse. *Aleria's* rudder is quite small in comparison to the almost full keel. When motoring forward the wash from the propeller is deflected by the rudder and she steers well. In reverse the wash goes down either side of the keel and the rudder is quite ineffectual. Any wind that might be present exerts more force than the rudder might.

In the past, however, she did kick out left (to port) quite nicely when we first start reversing. This is due to propeller walk. It means that we could indeed turn our boat in a narrow channel or in a marina. Unfortunately, we recently had to get a new propeller. In their questionable 'wisdom', the manufacturer somehow designed their new propellers in a way that the no longer have propeller walk.

Propeller Walk

With a single screw boat, you may have noticed that your boat will kick out to one side or the other when reversing and also initially when moving forward. This is known as propeller walk, or prop walk. (*Some newer propellers are designed to not have prop walk!*) It is more pronounced when reversing as the rudder is initially less effective, but it also happens when moving forward.

As the propeller turns, the blades move from deeper water to shallower water and then back to deeper water. At the top of its rotation, in the shallow water, the blades provide less propulsion than in the deeper water. The blade is angled so that the turning propeller will propel the boat forward or in reverse, depending on which way it is turned. However, in its rotation the blade will also push out to the sides, with the top pushing one way and the bottom the other way. The direction of the rotation of the bottom blades determine which direction the stern of the boat will be pushed.

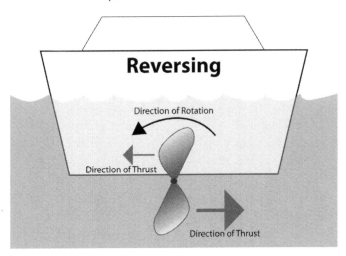

Propeller Types

Right orientated (right-handed - most common)

When reversing the stern tends to kick out to the left (port), as in the above illustration

When moving forward, tends to push the stern to the right (starboard)
=> the boat will turn left

If your prop is right handed, when you reverse, the prop walk will cause your stern to kick to port and your bow to starboard. In ahead propulsion with the rudder centered the prop will rotate clockwise (to the right) causing the stern to walk to the right or to starboard and causing the bow to turn slightly to port or left. It is more pronounced in reverse than in forward gear. Most, but not all, single propeller boats like mono-hull sailboats have right handed props.

Left orientated (left-handed – quite rare)

When reversing the stern tends to kick out to the right (starboard)

When moving forward, tends to push the stern to the left (port)
=> the boat will turn right

Left-hand propellers rotate counter-clockwise to provide forward thrust. When in reverse, they will kick the stern to the right (starboard), and when in forward the stern will be pushed to the left (port) and the boat will turn to the right.

Left-hand propellers are primarily used on twin engine boats to cancel the steering torque that results if both propellers spin in the same direction. Left handed propellers are also sometimes used on lobster fishing boats where the wheelhouse is aft and starboard. Kicking to starboard while reversing makes docking easier for these boats. We have also seen left handed props on the occasional classic sailboat.

How to tell which type of propeller you have

To see what type of prop you have, you can stand behind your boat (at the stern) and look at her propeller. Have someone shift into idle ahead propulsion and note the direction of rotation. If the propeller rotates clockwise in forward propulsion, you have a right-hand propeller. If it rotates counter-clockwise in forward propulsion, you have a left-handed propeller.

There are several other ways to tell if your prop is left- or right-handed. If you look at your propeller from the side, the leading edge of a right-handed propeller will run from bottom left to top right. On a left handed propeller, the leading edge will run from top left to bottom right.

When Life Gets 'Interesting' ⚓ Tips & Techniques

Right Handed Prop   Left Handed Prop

You can also determine which yours is by holding it in the palm of your hand. If your thumb fits comfortably on the blade when held in your right hand, it is a right-hand propeller. If your thumb lies comfortably on the blade when held in your left hand, it is a left-handed propeller.

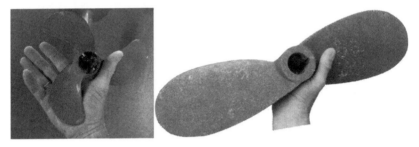

A right-handed prop blade fits comfortably in the right hand with the right thumb on the blade.

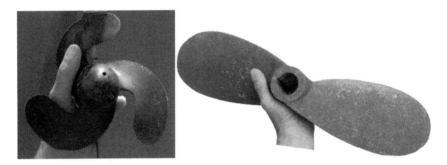

A left-handed prop blade fits comfortably in the left hand with the left thumb on the blade.

300

When a boat turns, it is actually the stern of the boat being steered, because the rudder is positioned aft. When a boat is moving forward, it pivots around a point about a third of the distance from the bow, roughly at the mast. When turning in tight quarters, therefore, it is important to watch your stern, so it doesn't kick out into an obstruction. When motoring astern, the pivot

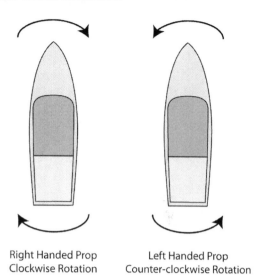

Right Handed Prop
Clockwise Rotation

Left Handed Prop
Counter-clockwise Rotation

point moves to a point one-third from the stern. Add in prop walk and these turning characteristics can be compounded.

Using prop walk to your advantage

Docking

Prop walk is a very useful asset for docking. If you have a right-handed prop and know your boat's stern kicks to port, then coming in to a dock port-side-to can make you look like a real pro. Just come gently alongside with your bow angled towards the dock. When you are within a couple of feet of the dock, put it into reverse and briefly gun the engine at about half throttle. Your forward motion should stop, and your stern will kick to port, towards the dock. When done right, you will have executed a perfect parallel parking maneuver. Your crew will be able to step off the boat to secure the dock lines with ease.

When Life Gets 'Interesting' ⚓ Tips & Techniques

Turning a boat with little room

We were cruising out of Long Island Sound in the US one year when a tropical storm warning was issued. We decided to take refuge in a marina, but the only available space meant that we had to come in, turn our boat 180 degrees in a narrow channel, and then come alongside.

We went directly into the lagoon that was hardly wider than the length of our boat. We steered very close to the port-hand side and initiated a turn hard to starboard. We then put her into reverse and gunned the engine. Her stern kicked out to port which we knew she did. As we approached the port side of the channel (almost immediately), we put it into forward and revved the engine at about half throttle. Her bow swung gently but obediently to starboard. As soon as she approached the opposite side, we put her back into reverse, and so on. Throughout the whole procedure our position had hardly changed – just the direction we were facing. After several reversals, we were facing in the opposite direction, perfectly aligned with the dock.

The proper name for this maneuver is "Back and Fill". It is also called a "Pivot Turn". One of the best places to watch how <u>not</u> to do it is Ego Alley in Annapolis Maryland. This is a relatively narrow channel that terminates with a turning area at its end. When arriving in Annapolis, most boats will motor down this channel to see and be seen. We were, of course, not the exception and did it also.

Most boats will come down the channel hugging the right side, as in the following illustration. They will then turn left into the space provided (1). Next, they will back down. As they have a right-handed prop, their stern will kick out to port (2) – irrespective of how their helm is set, as the space is tight. They will then go forward, and their boat will initially turn right before the rudder bites (3) – bringing them closer to the end of the channel. Another reverse and another forward, and they are usually tight up against the wall. The boat hook comes out and there is much shouting and consternation. If they have a bow thruster, they may save face, but it is undignified to do so.

It is quite rare for a boat to come in hugging the left-hand side as in the second illustration below. Once the initial turn has been made (1), backing down (2) pulls the stern to port achieving a better angle for an exit. It might take a few back and forths to get there but the end result (3) is quite easily attained.

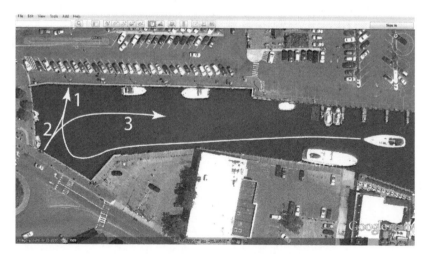

When Life Gets 'Interesting' ⚓ Tips & Techniques

Practice this maneuver in open areas before you get into a confined space. Learn how your boat reacts under different conditions of wind and current. That way, once you find that you need to pivot in a confined space, you will be well prepared to execute your maneuver with confidence.

Reducing the turn radius

Our boat has a rather wide turn radius. To pick up our mooring, which is at the confluence of a small inlet and a wider bay, we have to come in (usually with westerly winds behind us) turn around clockwise into the wind and come up on the mooring. The problem is that her mooring is in a relatively small hole in a wide-open area. It is quite shallow almost immediately

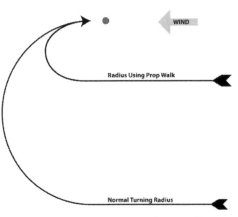

outside the swing radius of her mooring. To reduce the turning radius, we once again make use of her prop walk.

Any sharp turn is a challenge for our boat, particularly serious is a sharp turn to port. On an occasion where we wanted to get into a slip to port in a narrow channel with a current coming towards us, we opted for a 270 degree right turn again using her prop walk.

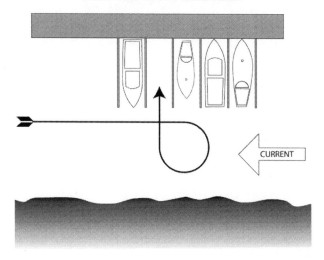

We started the maneuver by overshooting the berth and then initiating the right-hand turn. At the end of the turn we were lined up with the up-current finger dock. A little forward throttle as we were pushed downstream saw us slide right in to the utter amazement of the dock hand.

Chapter 2: Preparing for an Emergency

"It was a dark and stormy night", a turn of phrase first penned by Washington Irving in 1809 and later used by Charles Schulz's beagle Snoopy, is one of the first things that comes to mind when thinking back on boating and anchoring emergencies. Yes, problems do come up during daylight hours, but they are usually easier to spot and deal with as, or even before, things get critical. At night, when visibility is poor and reaction times are longer, 'problems' can quickly escalate into an emergency situation. However, even on a 'dark and stormy night' most problems can be resolved and disaster averted with just a little advance planning. (Has the advance planning thing started to sink in?)

> *"The time for taking all measures for a ship's safety is while still able to do so. Nothing is more dangerous than for a seaman to be grudging in taking precautions lest they turn out to have been unnecessary. Safety at sea for a thousand years has depended on exactly the opposite philosophy."*

Admiral Chester W. Nimitz

Dragging Anchor

In the middle of one night, while anchored in a protected harbor we thought we knew well, a storm came up. It instantly produced a heavy chop across a wide fetch from a direction opposite to where we anchored. We dragged anchor – right into a mooring field. (Yes, at that time we still had a CQR as our primary anchor) Before we knew it, our chain rode became entangled in another boat's mooring. We had to sever its bridle and tie that boat off to our own under some pretty extreme circumstances. We then found safe refuge and re-anchored. The next morning, we brought the other boat back to the mooring field and notified the marine police.

306

Hooking Rules ⚓ Anchoring Etiquette

That night we reaffirmed the value of not panicking and to having flashlights and knives handy on deck... as well as having a plan for an escape route to an alternative spot.

This looks like a really bad situation. There's one line going straight down off the starboard side, another trailing to port and the boat appears to be heading rather quickly toward the bridge. What to do? Read on.

"Oh no, we're dragging!" is one of the worst things to hear someone say in the middle of the night. Most of us have at one time dragged anchor, and we are sure it was never a pretty sight. The most important advice we can give is to stay calm and think things through. Believe it or not, if you do this one thing, and don't freeze up or panic, you are likely to have plenty of time – if you are prepared.

Assuming that you have set your anchor well and that it is indeed the right one for your boat and the bottom, the primary cause for dragging would be a weather change. Instead of being snugly at anchor in the lee of an island, the wind has shifted 180 degrees and there is now a significant fetch to windward of your boat. A chop builds up causing your boat to pitch violently. This motion is transferred to your anchor, which may be dislodged resulting in your boat dragging towards shallow water.

Alex and Daria Blackwell

So, before things get bad, make it a habit to survey the anchorage as soon as you are settled. Choose the direction you want to exit in if trouble develops well before dark! Observe potential alternate anchoring spots, obstacles, and boats. *Plan your exit strategy!* Write it down in the logbook. Discuss it with your crew.

Perhaps the most important thing to remember is a little saying we like, "When in doubt, check it out." That is, if you think your anchor may be dragging, check it! Usually you will get tipped off by a change in the motion of the boat.

One evening while having cocktails in a busy anchorage we watched a boat move slowly past us. It was approaching another vessel. There was nobody visible aboard the dragging boat, and the people on the other boat were tending their barbeque and quite oblivious to their impending problem. So, we shouted and yelled, and in the end sounded five short blasts (emergency) on our horn while broadcasting a Sécurité message on the VHF.

To our sheer amazement, the owners of the dragging boat appeared and started shouting at the people barbequing downwind from them that they had to move. Finally, the boat that was dragging realized their mistake – that it was indeed their boat dragging anchor. They relented, pulled anchor and retreated into a far corner of the rather large bay. There they re-anchored away from the center of activity. We just hope they saw this as a lesson and learned from it!

If your anchor does drag, the number one thing to do is stay calm and work as a team. Start the engine immediately as soon as you've ascertained that there are no lines trailing in the water behind you. Start motoring slowly in the direction of the anchor and away from danger. One person heads for the bow and takes up the rode as fast as possible. Avoid letting the rode drop behind the boat at all cost because a situation that is bad can get much worse if your prop is fouled rendering your boat inoperable. As soon as the anchor is up, move to a safer location and re-anchor.

Hooking Rules ⚓ Anchoring Etiquette

To make things easier, keep essential tools on deck. Hand signals are hard to see at night and voices impossible to hear over the roar of the wind. Keep FRS radios (walkie-talkies), flashlights, spotlights, signal devices, and knives on deck.

If another boat comes adrift, sound an alarm to alert others in the anchorage. More importantly, be prepared to help. There is a lot you can do with a small dinghy.

Dinghy brigade to the rescue!

This boat dragged its CQR anchor through a busy anchorage in Dominica before being rescued and tied to a mooring by the dinghy brigade.

Of interest is that the bottom in this harbor is crisscrossed with furrows dug by dragging anchors. The guide book states that the holding in this anchorage is "poor". When we dove on our scoop type anchor, we noted that it had "moved" a total of about 5 inches in three weeks of shifting, sometimes strong winds. We found the holding to be excellent.

Chapter 3: Freeing Your Boat from a Grounding

There is nothing good to be said about running aground. The only certainty is that it will happen to every boater and has almost certainly happened to every seasoned skipper. A grounding can range from just skimming the mud in a channel, to discovering an uncharted obstruction (like a rock), to the worst case of going hard aground – your boat comes to an abrupt halt, then lists over to one side and will not budge.

As always, preparation is key. Your first actions are to ensure the safety of your crew – were there any injuries, and is this a life-threatening situation? After that you must check that the hull is intact, and that your boat will not sink when you refloat her. Naturally, if they have not done so already, everyone should don their life jackets immediately.

Hooking Rules ⚓ Anchoring Etiquette

Grounding in Soft Mud

The most common grounding, at least for us with a deep draft, seems to be soft mud. Here your boat often comes to a relatively gentle stop. Often it is a small speed bump that the boat skips over. Sometimes, however, your boat will come to a full stop.

Our first choice, when running aground in soft mud, is always to go hard astern, though if your boat has a long blade rudder this may not be a wise choice. Otherwise we try to spin out of our predicament. We do this by alternating forward and reverse thrusts with our engine and by turning the helm hard over in alternate directions with each burst of thrust. As our boat kicks out to port in reverse and to starboard when in forward with the prop walk, we are usually able to reverse our direction and then go back the way we came. See the chapter on maneuvering in tight places for more on prop walk.

Tides

Let us not forget that a boat can also wind up high and dry with the tide going out from underneath her. If you are on a falling tide and catch it early enough, you may just be able to motor out – as long as you know where deeper water is to be found. That is why entering an unknown anchorage on a falling tide can be a tricky decision.

If you are indeed already hard aground, your options are to wait until the tide comes back in, try to refloat your boat, or kedge her off.

Refloating

Now comes the part where you need to know your boat. Is there an angle of list where she draws less because of a shift in her buoyancy and may float free? If heeled way over, a sailboat with a keel, for example, will draw much less than if straight upright.

Many powerboats have similar characteristics, though perhaps not quite so pronounced. You may thus merely need to shift ballast (people

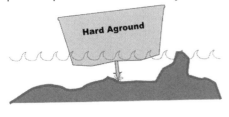

and objects) to reduce your draft and minimize the grip of what you landed on.

For boats with a mast, you can also leverage the mast as a fulcrum to heel your boat over and dramatically reduce your draft. Attach the kedge rode to a halyard and pull the boat over. A large dinghy can even achieve this as long as the rope coming from the mast to is long enough. This same principle can be used by adding weight to the end of the boom and bringing it out perpendicular to the boats beam.

Just be mindful that the force exerted on the mast is not so strong as to damage the mast or its rigging.

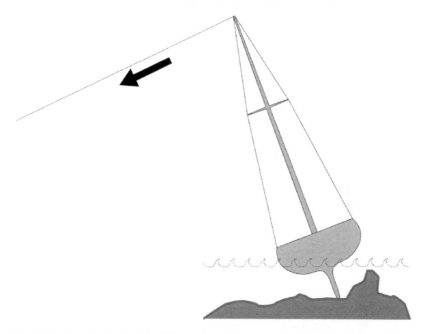

Attach a long rope to a halyard to utilize maximum leverage to heel your boat over and reduce its draft – just be mindful of potential damage to the mast and rigging.

Kedging

Your boat is aground, and you have done all you can to refloat her as per the preceding and you need a little more help. Kedging is in most cases your best approach, as pulling by another boat may not exert enough force. Evaluate whether your chances are better by trying to move your boat forward or astern. It is better to swing the boat while doing this as this tends to break the connection to the bottom more readily.

Alex and Daria Blackwell

Using your dinghy, another boat or even by diving, bring an anchor and a long and strong rode out away from your boat. Once this anchor or rope is securely connected to the bottom, a boulder, or some other big heavy object, start cranking it in using your windlass or a winch. Block and tackle will also work here – anything that will multiply the force with which you are pulling.

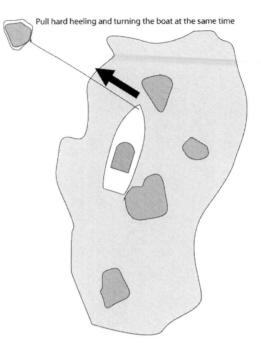
Pull hard heeling and turning the boat at the same time

Once free, go below decks and inspect your boat from stem to stern for leaks or other damage. Check for loose or dislodged equipment, damaged through hulls, loosened or damaged keel bolts, etc. It is also advisable to inspect her by diving as well. Your rudder or propeller may be damaged and repairable but may fail catastrophically if used too soon.

Any boat that is seriously grounded should be fully inspected by a yard or surveyor qualified to detect problems.

Part 7: 'Hooking Rules!' –
Anchoring Etiquette

At home, social etiquette is something one learns from one's parents. Most people grow up learning to eat politely, each culture in its own way. In the Western World, they should be fairly well versed in table etiquette, whatever about the finer points of each culture's different adaptations. Then again, in some people's minds, this might be deemed antiquated; they might maintain that most kids don't need to be formally taught manners anymore.

Not everyone grows up boating. Therefore, many people have not acquired a finer sense of what is right and wrong on the water. Unless you are a Robinson Crusoe anchored off a deserted island on your own, you need to know etiquette. We all do. No, we are not the 'Miss Manners' or 'Emily Posts' of anchoring, but we have picked up a few behavioral observations that we can share with you as suggestions.

What is etiquette other than a code, written or unwritten, that governs the expectations of behavior according to the contemporary conventions and social norms. Many, though not all, laws that govern us today are based in some way on common sense and established practice. Anchoring etiquette is no exception, and though some of this, too, has passed into law, more remains unwritten. In any case, there are some things one should or must comply with when coming into an anchorage and dropping a hook. The same goes for what one does once securely attached to the bottom. When there is no written rule or law, common sense and etiquette will often dictate who has the rights if and when a dispute arises, and rest assured that it will.

There you are relaxing after a long passage (okay, so you only motored an hour to get there). It is a beautiful calm and sunny day. You are about to go swimming and peace and harmony abounds. That is until your soon-to-be intimate neighbor arrives. He is at the wheel and clearly having a bad day based on the loud expletives emanating from the cockpit. His tender mate is on the foredeck jostling with the anchor and associated hardware. She, too, has good lung capacity.

They entered the anchorage with just the right amount of steam to bury their large stern and kick up a wake that would surely wake the dead. And, as surely as the sun will set in the west, they have your full and undivided attention.

Now that they are here, they parallel your boat and then angle inward as they pass your bow. All thoughts about relaxing evaporate as you hear a chain clanking and see a yard sale worth of tackle unceremoniously being shoved overboard – right in line with your anchor.

The good news is that their boat stays put. The bad news is they never set their anchor. Instead they brought up some cocktails and fired up their barbi directly upwind of your boat. The plume drifts towards you, and their boat is likely to do so as well.

But it does not end there, heavens no! Ambiance is required and they crank up the stereo – a good high-amp sound system must be used to its max. You just know that later the cell phone will come out beeping some annoying and repetitive sound, and only if you are lucky will it be replaced by shouting of "Can you hear me now?" when one of them responds to the incessant phone's demands as the dog barks in answer from the cockpit.

Hooking Rules ⚓ Anchoring Etiquette

Then come the toys – and they have them all. The jet skis (personal watercraft) start buzzing, the ski boat uses your boat as a rounding mark and the chopper is just waiting for take-off.

Then later on, the sun has set, dinner is done, and the stars decorate the firmament while their underwater lights keep the fish awake below. The floodlights come on, and the bravado starts anew. Yes, you guessed it. They have drifted over towards your boat. You are able to see the whites of their eyes without the need for optical magnification with your binoculars. "What are you doing so close to my boat?" he shouts in your direction. There goes any chance for a peaceful evening.

This is, of course, an extreme, fictitious, example we created to highlight some of the inconsiderate and even rude behaviors that qualify for breach of etiquette. We all have true stories on this line to recount. Frankly, had we in fact experienced just the beginnings of this scenario, we most assuredly would have left for a more peaceful spot long before it got this far. On the other hand, if we had stayed and that friendly neighbor's boat had hit ours, he would clearly be at fault, though it would have been a tedious and heated process to get to that understanding.

The 'Rules of the Rode' – Hooking dos and don'ts

Of course, the COLREGS (the Collision Regulations, or Rules of the Road) apply in anchorages as well as when a vessel is underway. Stay away from channels and government marks and avoid restricted zones! Be sure to turn on your all-around white anchor light at night or display a black ball during the day when anchored to comply with the law.

The number one rule of anchoring is simple:

The first boat anchored sets the precedent for how subsequent boats anchor in that anchorage.

317

Alex and Daria Blackwell

After that, it comes down to common sense and respect. So beyond the cardinal rule, there are five simple things to consider when coming into an anchorage or picking a spot. All of these 'rules' were violated in the opening story.

- ⚓ Wake
- ⚓ Proximity
- ⚓ Sound
- ⚓ Sight
- ⚓ Smell

Let's take a closer look at each.

Chapter 1: The Cardinal Rule – The First Boat Sets the Precedent

The cardinal rule is in fact quite simple. If you arrive in an anchorage and the first one there is a cabin cruiser yawing widely and they have 200 feet of rope rode out in five feet of water, they have set the precedent. Any subsequently arriving boats will need to give them room. Remember that moorings, fish floats, traps and pots were there before any day tripper.

This 'rule' is actually written into Admiralty case law:

"A vessel shall be found at fault if it ... anchors so close to another vessel as to foul her when swinging ... (and/or) fails to shift anchorage when dragging dangerously close to another anchored vessel. Furthermore, the vessel that anchored first shall warn the one who anchored last that the berth chosen will foul the former's berth."
(U.S. Decision No. 124-5861 — 1956).

Anchoring etiquette dictates that the use of an anchorage is on a first come, first served basis. The first boat has the right to anchor whichever way they please, putting out one or two anchors, in whatever configuration with as much scope as they deem appropriate. Everyone else is obligated to avoid interfering with the first boat.

Boats coming later have to respect the space needs and swing radii as well as other attributes of those already anchored. This includes but is not limited to the obvious considerations: type of boat, method of anchoring, selection of location, and behavior of the boaters.

Of course, if you are the fiftieth boat in the anchorage, you cannot know who got there first. You should treat all those who were there before you as setting the precedent.

Alex and Daria Blackwell

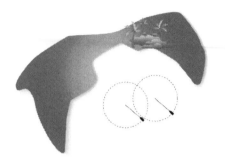

The boat that gets there first sets the precedent for method of anchoring, location, and swing radius among other things.

If, for example, several power boats have rafted together and set out two anchors in a 'V' to reduce swing radius, then dropping a single anchor nearby may cause you to swing in very different patterns. Simply stated, match your technique to what others are doing, and don't be afraid to ask what your potential neighbor has done. If you do not like the situation or what the boat that got there first has done in anchoring, find another spot.

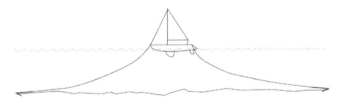

If the boat that arrived first set the precedent for bow and stern anchoring, then all other vessels arriving later should do the same to preserve the same pattern of boat motion in the harbor.

In a large and relatively uncrowded anchorage there is not much of an issue as you can easily find another spot where you will not be afoul of another vessel. In most anchorages, however, anchoring too close or in such a way that could cause a potential problem is not acceptable.

Hooking Rules ⚓ Anchoring Etiquette

How Much Rode?

In trying to match the other boats' technique, you will want to let out a comparable amount of rode to match their scope. The angle the rode makes at the surface of the water if the rode is fully stretched out is a quick indicator of how much rode your potential neighbor has out. (see chapter on scope) The more acute the angle is, the greater the scope. Don't be afraid to ask if you are not sure how to estimate. If boats already in the anchorage do not have enough scope, give them a wide berth, especially if your spot is downwind of them. If you cannot go elsewhere, consider speaking with your new neighbors about adding more scope for safety.

Similarly, if someone comes in to the anchorage after you and anchors too close or does not use enough scope, it is fair for you to address them, politely asking them to move or let out more rode as the case may be. In fact, according to the US Admiralty decision cited above, you are required to do so should there be a possibility of interference.

By the same token, if you get to an anchorage first and the anchorage starts to get crowded, don't be a hog with 10:1 scope. Reduce to a reasonable scope such as 5:1 under stable weather conditions. Actively try to help newcomers find a good spot rather than accusing them of infringing on your rights. Not only is it the right thing to do, it could save someone a night of distress – often you. Don't forget that *what goes around comes around*, and you may be the one in need next time.

If Things go Bump in the Night

Whether you are the first to arrive or the last does not matter if you start to drag your anchor. Now yours is the burdened vessel in the eyes of the law and you must keep clear of all other boats.

Alex and Daria Blackwell

Even with the newer anchors, conditions may arise causing you to drag anchor. It is how you handle the situation that makes the difference. If letting out more scope doesn't stop the dragging, the best thing to do is to move to a spot with a better bottom or to switch anchors to one that might work better for the given bottom type. Too many skippers delay the decision to move until they're bearing down onto other boats, and perhaps causing a chain reaction of dragging anchors from which it is very difficult to recover.

It is also common courtesy to alert your neighbors if you notice something amiss. If you see a boat dragging, hail them either on the radio or by shouting, sounding your horn or getting over to them via dinghy. Blue water cruisers routinely help each other out using their dinghy to push or pull a boat out of harm's way, going over to assist with pulling up or re-setting an anchor, and standing by to help in any way. It is common courtesy and most appreciated.

Chapter 2: Wake – Mind Your Effect on Entering an Anchorage

Entering an anchorage or mooring area is like moving into a new neighborhood. You want your neighbors to like you. Enter at slow speed (<5 knots) to avoid making a wake. Anchorages are no wake zones. And remember, even a dinghy can throw a considerable wake

Any wake is a serious sleep deterrent at best and a hazard in the galley and elsewhere at worst. People don't want dishes flying off the salon table, hot soup burning their hands, or bodies being flung against the rigging or off the boat – not to mention items hurtling on deck causing damage to their vessel. Throwing a wake is a serious offense in many anchorages. In places marked as no wake zones, the harbormaster can give you a citation that will cost you money. If you are determined to have been driving recklessly and endangering the safety of others, in the U.S. you can be charged up to $5000 in fines and serve jail time as well. So, in this case, a matter of etiquette can also be a matter of the law if the behavior crosses the line of common sense.

A dingy passing an anchorage

Alex and Daria Blackwell

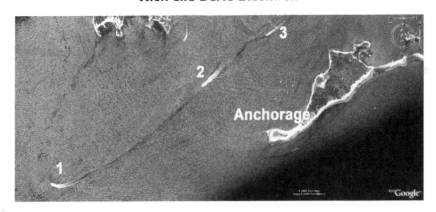

In this satellite image from Google Earth, it is easy to see how the wake from successive speed boats (1, 2 & 3) is affecting a popular nearby anchorage

In a reverse situation, there is one particular anchorage we know where there is a slalom ski run set up at one end. It is, in fact, well-marked. Vessels anchored nearby must thus accept the fact that their tranquility is liable to be disturbed if and when early morning skiers arrive. The skiers' territory was there first.

A massive wake in an anchorage is more than a nuisance, it can be downright dangerous.

Chapter 3: Proximity – Give Your Predecessors (and Yourself) Room

Cruise through the anchorage before selecting your spot. Observe how other boats have anchored. Imagine what the anchorage will look like when the tide goes out or comes in.

When you see a spot you like, check around for proximity of other anchored vessels. How close are the boats next to the spot you are eying? Review where anchored boats are in relation to what you see on the chart. Are there obstructions? Might they have a generator or air conditioning on board that would create noise during the night? Does it look like a situation with party potential, such as a raft up? Do they have anchors out in configurations that would create markedly different swing patterns than you are contemplating?

The full text of the Admiralty ruling regarding anchoring also discusses proximity. Although this specifically refers to leaving an engineless sailboat enough room to maneuver, the same applies to large power vessels such as ferries in the preceding image.

Alex and Daria Blackwell

The boats here have swung around and are now clearly too close.
This will soon be a problem for their owners.

Drive into the spot you are contemplating and look all around. Does it feel like there will be enough space when you drop back after letting out your rode? Be sure that you won't be too close if something changes, like the wind direction, current direction, or height of the tide.

If you set your anchor and observe that you are too close to another vessel, it is incumbent upon you to pull it back up and move. If the people on the boats near where you have positioned yourself are glowering at you, that is usually a clue to anchor elsewhere. If they tell you that your vessel is too close, you are obliged to move.

We also keep an eye on boats that arrive after we do. Why? Because of the magnet effect. Even though most boats are made of wood or plastic, if you drop a hook in the water in a secluded anchorage you are bound to attract the only other boat to come in. Yes, they will do a nice circle around your boat, perhaps wave to you, and then drop their anchor right next to you – never over on the other side of the bay.

Hooking Rules ⚓ Anchoring Etiquette

A lovely yawl anchored on her own in an empty bay.

In one case, we watched as a powerboat demonstrated the magnet effect to a classic yawl. In a wide expanse of bay with almost no boats, it dropped anchor right next to the yawl and then disgorged three jet skis, which buzzed the yawl like angry bugs.

A power boat demonstrating the 'magnet effect' and anchoring right next to a yawl in a wide-open anchorage.

Alex and Daria Blackwell

If you were there first, it is your right to speak to the skipper of a boat that arrives after you and ask him or her to move if you feel there is potential for danger. Remember, if your property, your safety or your sanity are at risk, you have the right and the obligation to ensure the best possible outcome.

Then again, sometimes it is simply not worth it, and moving on is the easier way to go. The yawl moved on that day... and so did we.

In the end, boating etiquette is pretty simple. It is a matter of being a good neighbor. Keep that in mind, and you will be welcome in any anchorage.

Chapter 4: Sound – Disturbing the Peace

Please remember that sound travels far over water. Voices, music, engine noise, especially outboard motors – and that includes dinghies, go-fast boats, ski boats, jet skis, generators, barking dogs, and the dreaded 'ringing phone' are all examples of the most egregious disruption of anchorage serenity. It is easy to see that common sense can prevail in predicting what will not be appreciated and protecting the serenity for the common good.

Noise comes in many shapes and sizes. A group of revelers who party actively well into the night can be as annoying as any jet ski, unless of course you are part of the party. So where is the happy medium? You can invite neighbors to the party, accept that people won't be happy with you in the morning, or temper your volume along the way. Your choice.

That is not to say that you should not enjoy a good party. If you are planning a raft up or just an evening of revelry with friends, try to be the first in the anchorage. As before, the first boat sets the precedent and that can apply to the use of the anchorage as well. People who see a raft up expect some degree of rowdiness, although excess can be hard to tolerate for anyone. There are also certain anchorages where raft ups are common, and people expect laughter, voices, music and BBQ scents to be wafting throughout. It can be easier to anchor in such a designated party place if you are planning a party where a certain set of behaviors is anticipated and often shared.

Let us consider some other particularly annoying things that can happen in an anchorage. You wake up one morning hearing a dog barking incessantly. It is Sunday and he wants to go, but his master is sleeping in. You want to sleep in, too, but there is no visible sign of activity on board. What to do? Calling on the VHF won't do it because they are most likely not listening. We have actually stopped by an offending vessel in our dinghy under the pretense of finding out if the

329

dog is in some kind of trouble. We managed to make our point without causing aggravation.

If you need to run a generator, be aware that even that noise carries great distances over water. Respect the fact that most cruisers appreciate tranquility. Many people do not realize that a generator can be very disturbing to fellow cruisers who do not have such mechanical gear on board. Sailors in small vessels have little aboard to make noise. Anchoring a power vessel close by that has constant refrigeration or air conditioning that requires the constant running of an engine is inconsiderate. As always, try to anchor near vessels similar to your own. They will be less likely to notice or take offence to this type of disturbance, as like you they are accustomed to it.

One of our friends almost came to fisticuffs with another friend over this issue. One had a trawler the other a racer-cruiser sailboat. They rafted together for the night. At 6 am the trawler fired up its generator to heat water and charge batteries. The sailors were so incensed they never spoke to the trawler folks again. They have told the story many times, yet never mentioned it to their former friends. The problem with that is that the trawler folks probably had no idea how disturbing their generator could be to others.

Hooking Rules ⚓ Anchoring Etiquette

A Word on Civilized Communication during Maneuvers

Be aware when anchoring (especially during the early evening hours), that almost everyone else in the anchorage will be observing you (as discreetly as possible, of course). It is just the way it is. You will do it too. Remember that it is not the anchoring, or the need to re-anchor, which separates the beginners from the experts. It is the amount of

yelling and chaos that breaks out between the person handling the anchor, and the person maneuvering the boat. Boating is the only sport which has generated T-shirts that proclaim, "Don't yell at me!" and classes called "Nobody yells." One can be pretty confident in stating that anchoring has been responsible for many of the verbal tirades. The point here is to avoid yelling in the anchorage. Everyone will hear, and no one will be impressed.

To avoid the embarrassing shouting, we have several suggestions for communications. Most important, develop a set of hand signals to communicate with one another well in advance. When you have someone on the bow working the anchor (we prefer the strong male in that department even though we now have a windlass and we both have to know how to use it) and the other person aft at the helm, it may be difficult to be heard above the roar of the engine. We usually use simple hand signals to let each other know of obstructions, intentions, and speed or course changes.

Alex and Daria Blackwell

We also use walkie-talkies (handheld radios) that are available relatively inexpensively at most sporting goods stores. These radios are especially useful when the wind is really blowing, and your words are scattered from the bow before they have a chance to leave your tongue. We also use them to communicate from below decks to topside, like on night watch when we need to rouse a sleeping mate.

Some commercially available walkie-talkies

In the US the walkie-talkies are FRS and GRMS radios. These are not legally usable in the UK and Europe; the EU equivalent is the PMR446 (Pan European Radio system) which uses similar (often the same) models as FRS but chipped for a different frequency. The best for use aboard are the ones with headsets that are also muffled against extraneous noise, as wind can interfere with voice transmission.

The other great reasons to have these radios are that, apart from the GMRS radios, you don't need a license and they are legal for use on shore as well as for keeping in touch with the dinghy brigade. Don't forget, that VHF radio is for use solely on the water, ship to ship and only with special permit from land to water as in a marina dock house. The newer GMRS

radios have a much greater range and can be used to communicate ship to shore as well – but only where permitted.

Wings has been using headsets for communication during anchoring for years. You never hear them entering an anchorage.

333

Alex and Daria Blackwell

Radios for on board, ship-to-ship and ship-to-shore communication

FRS For use in the US and Canada only. Inexpensive, no license, 2-mile range (0.5 watts power), invaluable if you drag in the pitch dark night. You may use these on your boat, ship-to-ship, ship-to-shore and on shore. (Plenty of range for most boats).

PMR446 Pan European Radio system which uses similar (often the same) models as FRS but chipped for a different frequency. Inexpensive, no license, 2-mile range (0.5 watts power), invaluable if you drag in the pitch dark night. You may use these on your boat, ship-to-ship, ship-to-shore and on shore. (Plenty of range for most boats).

GMRS For use in the US only – illegal in many other places. A little more expensive, up to 25-mile range (up to 5 watts power), requires FCC license ($85 fee) in the US, some with integral GPS, FRS and weather radio. You may use these on your boat, ship-to-ship, ship-to-shore and on shore.

VHF A ship's station license required in most places. In US, an operator's license is not required. In Europe and elsewhere, you are required to have an operator's license with DSC training. Frequencies vary between US, Canadian, and International waters. Ship stations may communicate with other ship stations or coast stations primarily for safety, and secondarily for navigation and operational efficiency. Casual conversation is discouraged. All users of marine radio are responsible for observing federal communications and Coast Guard requirements.

Chapter 5: Smell – Sharing is Not Always Desirable

Barbecues light up in every anchorage and most people don't mind the smell of burgers on the grill. But if you have an excessively smoky meal to cook or fish on the grill, being upwind of a boatload of vegetarians may be cause for strong sentiments. In general, there is not a lot you can do except, of course, where possible avoid anchoring directly upwind of another vessel. This also prevents the potential for dragging down onto that vessel.

Sharing is not always a good thing, especially when you are upwind of other vessels and cooking something particularly odiferous.

Pump Out Religiously

There is nothing more disconcerting than an idyllic setting marred by boaters who, inconsiderately and against the law, refuse to use a holding tank and pump-out stations. Instead, they turn their heads overboard and ruin a pristine environment. What a joyous thought to send your children swimming in proximity to such environmentally caring neighbors.

That goes for any environmentally unfriendly refuse and discharge. Do not empty your bilge in small coves where small leaks causing oily discharge can harm the sanctuary. Do not feed the birds and do not throw anything overboard, including biodegradable waste. This is not only a matter of etiquette and good environmental practice, but in many places, it is also against the law.

Chapter 6: Lights – After Dark, Seeing the Light

Light can be an annoyance at best and a hazard at worst. If you come into an anchorage at night and find that you must use a search light to find an opening, do not shine the light directly at other people's boats. And never shine the light into people's faces. You will blind them with the light. If they happen also to be underway as you are searching for the right spot, they will be incapable of maneuvering safely and may not see you coming.

 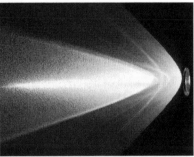

Spotlights and other bright lights can be annoying and can quickly blind a person

Etiquette in the anchorage dictates that one should never shine a light directly into other people's boats unless there is an emergency. Common sense dictates respecting the privacy of your neighbors in the anchorage. If you are driving around in your dinghy trying to find your boat and using your flashlight as your navigation light and search light, please be considerate.

Other than the required all-round white anchor light, it is entirely up to your discretion as to what other lights you leave on at night aboard your vessel.

Chapter 7: Dinghy Etiquette – A Tender is a Boat

Shore leave is a wonderful thing. It can be lots of fun, but getting back to your boat late at night, or worse yet in the fog, can be a little challenging. Especially if the engine cuts out, you forgot oars, and the tide is heading out... but that is another story.

A more common scenario is a shore party that had a lovely evening, toasted the season's bounty in good company and is now having a jovial return to the mother ship. They are speeding through the anchorage, forgetting that dinghies often throw a bigger wake than their big sisters. They are shouting over the roar of the engine, having forgotten how far sound carries over the water, and they buzz boats, searching for the one they belong to and cannot find. Gone is the serenity of the anchorage in one ungracious moment.

Dinghy etiquette is no different from big boat etiquette. Drive slowly without creating a wake, speak softly, do not shine lights directly into other vessels, and find your boat with some degree of accuracy to disturb as few neighbors as possible.

Hooking Rules ⚓ Anchoring Etiquette

If you are using your dinghy at night to go ashore or to visit others in the anchorage, consider doing so using oars and not your outboard. If you are rowing around the anchorage and see people on deck, you should be friendly but not intrusive unless encouraged, of course. Some boaters are friendly and like to socialize, while others are reflective and just want to be left alone.

Tradition dictates that if you approach another vessel you should do so on the starboard side six to ten feet away. If you strike up a conversation and you recognize by their attitude that they really aren't interested, just move on. Similarly, if you approach a friend's vessel and they are not on deck, approach from the starboard side and call out, "Ahoy, 'vessels name'." If they do not respond, move on. If they come on deck and respond, proceed as instructed. It is courteous to request permission to tie up and come aboard even if invited for a potluck dinner in advance. Don't go knocking on the hull or ports except in an emergency situation.

When going ashore, it is often the case that there is already another boat tied to a bollard or cleat when you get there. It is not only poor form, but also asking for trouble if you tie your dock line over the top of the other boat's. Instead, always try to tie it under theirs.

That way, if the other boat departs before you do, which may be likely since they got there first, they will not have to untie and retie your boat. Not only is it courteous for them not to have to do so, but it is also in your interest, as you do not know what knot (if any) they might tie.

Chapter 8: Adhering to the COLREGS

Even when anchored, you are required to adhere to the internationally-mandated rules of the road. The most significant rules pertaining to anchoring are staying away from restricted zones, never anchoring in marked channels, never tying up to government navigational marks like red or green buoys or lighthouses and using the proper night lights and day shapes.

In designated anchorages, you are not required to use the standard signals, but you may do so if you choose. We always use an all-around white light at night and black ball during the day. Each of our boats has had scars to prove that someone had not seen it during the night. Sometimes this was just an inexplicable black scuff mark, and at other times we found a deep gouge in the paint. And, when a fishing trawler t-boned our anchored boat a while back, the first question asked by our insurer and by the police was whether we had an anchor ball up. "Yes, no problem."

Although this is less a matter of etiquette and more a matter of adhering to law, etiquette is preserved when you adhere to the law. You won't be in the way of vessels navigating tight channels, you won't be obstructing their view of markers or even dragging them off station, and you will be easier to see if you are well lit.

Polluting waters is against several US and international laws. The Refuse Act of 1899 prohibits the throwing, discharging, or depositing of any refuse matter of any kind (including trash, garbage, oil, or any other liquid pollutants) into the waters of the U.S.

The MARPOL Annex V international law restricts overboard dumping of garbage. The U.S. law of Annex V prohibits all dumping of plastic trash and limits the overboard dumping of other garbage. Violators caught dumping may be assessed a civil penalty up to $25,000.

Hooking Rules ⚓ Anchoring Etiquette

The Federal Water Pollution Control Act prohibits the discharge of hazardous substances or oils into U.S. navigable waters. If you witness a boat discharging oil or hazardous substances into the water (or if yours does) you must notify the U.S. Coast Guard. You must give the following information: (1) location, (2) source, (3) size, (4) color, (5) substance, and (6) time observed.

Though not governed by law in all places but increasingly true of many places, you may not pump sewage overboard in coastal waters. All recreational boats with toilet facilities must have a working marine sanitation device (MSD) on board in US waters. The Coast Guard must certify all installed MSDs.

Certainly, it is a breach of etiquette in the worst regards to pump out in a pristine anchorage where people swim, animals live, and sensitive ecosystems are trying to survive. It is also unacceptable to throw anything overboard, including scraps of food which not only introduce non-native elements to the local waters but may offend people on nearby boats and shore.

Chapter 9: Etiquette Afield – When You Go Far and Wide

When chartering or sailing to remote destinations such as reef sites and island paradises, never drop an anchor on anything but sand! Anchoring on coral is a violation of almost every nation's regulations, not to mention the local customs.

Many places have now put in moorings in ecologically sensitive zones. Always use the mooring balls if you can. If you can't use a mooring because someone got there before you or whatever other reason, then verify that you are over clear sand before dropping your anchor.

It is no fun appearing in court next to the drug smugglers in handcuffs. Even that is probably better than having operators of the myriad of dive and fishing boats who make a living on the reef desiring to 'discuss' anchoring etiquette with you first-hand.

Damage to coral from anchors is one of the reasons why National Marine Sanctuaries have been established. Both international and local regulations prohibit anchoring inside sanctuary boundaries. So, know the local regulations before you anchor there. A good place to start is often the cruising guides.

Make sure you get permission before picking up a guest mooring if it is not designated as a public mooring. It may be reserved for another boater arriving later or it may be unsuitable for your vessel. Then again, consider rafting up with a vessel that arrived before you. If you ask politely, you may have a great experience and make new friends.

There are also many places where anchoring may not be allowed. Although these may not necessarily be marked on the available charts, there may well be local or national regulations dictating this. The onus is on the master of the vessel to familiarize himself or herself with these regulations beforehand.

Hooking Rules ⚓ Anchoring Etiquette

The state of Florida in the US has been testing a pilot program and enacting legislation limiting or restricting anchoring in certain areas. To familiarize yourself with the current status of anchoring in Florida, visit the BoatUS.com/gov pages. For information on anchoring restrictions elsewhere, check the noonsite.com website.

Chapter 10: The Golden Rule and Parting Thoughts

Anchoring etiquette requires invocation of the Golden Rule – you know, that you treat others the way you like to be treated yourself. It all boils down to that simple consideration. With that in mind, chances are you will always be welcome, allowing you to go wherever and whenever, leaving a clean wake and a clean conscience behind, and making friends along the way. Respect goes a long way in that regard.

According to The Annapolis Book of Seamanship by John Rousmaniere, yachting is older than almost every other outdoor sport, including golf. It is associated with longstanding traditions which have evolved from necessity, circumstance and to some degree ceremony. Boating etiquette has developed not to put restrictions on your horizons but to establish a standard set of practices that instill confidence.

Your fellow boater is someone you may need to call on in times of distress or need, as in grounding, anchor failure, or any number of other reasons – like when you have run out of ice or sugar. It is consequently wise to maintain good rapport by abiding to accepted traditions and applying common sense in questionable situations. Privacy, courtesy, respect and mutual aid are the cornerstones of boating etiquette.

"The clink of an anchor-chain,
the 'Yo-Ho!' of a well-timed crew,
the flapping of huge sails –
I love all these sounds."

John 'Rob Roy' MacGregor

Hooking Rules ⚓ Anchoring Etiquette

Top 10 Rude Behaviors

*That Show Disrespect and Breech of
Etiquette in an Anchorage*

1. *Anchoring too close to another vessel which got there first*

2. *Dumping anything overboard, including scraps, bilge water, or holding tanks*

3. *Creating a wake in an anchorage*

4. *Shouting above engine noise*

5. *Anchoring with different configuration than other vessels within swing radius*

6. *Playing loud music within hearing distance of others*

7. *Shining a spotlight directly at anchored vessels or keeping bright lights on all night*

8. *Running a generator (or other equipment) very early in the morning or late into the night*

9. *Constant noise (dog barking for prolonged periods, cell phone ringing incessantly, etc.)*

10. *Anchoring upwind of anchored vessels (and barbecuing odiferous meals on deck)*

Appendix

Glossary of Nautical and Anchoring Terms

Abaft	Behind you when you are facing forward
Abeam	Imaginary line amidships at right angles to keel of vessel
ABYC	American Boat and Yacht Council, Inc.
Admiralty law	Maritime law according to the British Admiralty; the law of the seas
Adrift	Floating without anchoring or direction
Afloat	On the water
Aft	The section of a vessel to the rear of amidships and near the stern
Aground	Touching bottom
Amidships	The center portion of a vessel
Anchor	An object made to grip the sea bottom and, by means of a chain or rope, hold a boat in a desired position
Anchorage	A suitable place in which vessels may anchor, often a customary or designated harbor area
Anchor locker	A compartment used to store the rode and sometimes the anchor
Astern	Direction toward the stern of or behind the vessel
Athwart	Anything placed across the boat from side to side such as a bench across the stern
Aweigh	An anchor when it is off the sea bottom
Bail	To remove water from a boat by bailer or pump
Bar	Shoal of sand or mud on which a vessel can run aground
Beacon	Signal mark on land or a post or buoy placed over a shoal or bank to warn vessels of shallows
Beam	Vessel's width amidships
Bearing	Direction or point of the compass at which an object is seen
Bilge	Lower interior part of a vessel's hull

Happy Hooking ⚓ The Art of Anchoring

Bimini	Framed canopy, usually of canvas, that protects the bridge and/or cockpit from sun and rain
Bow	Forward part or front pointy end of the boat
Bow roller	A mechanism at the bow which guides a chain or rope rode and allows it to be eased overboard or hauled aboard without damaging the hull. Many of these also provide storage for the anchor when not in use
Bridge	Control station from which a large boat is navigated
Bulkhead	Vertical partition in a boat.
Buoy	A floating object showing navigation channels or marking prohibited areas on the water
Cabin sole	Floor of the cabin
Capsize	To turn over, bottom side up
Cast off	To undo all mooring lines in preparation for departure
Catenary	The theoretical effect of a chain sagging that prevents it from pulling an anchor out in a swell
Chafe	The breakdown of rope fibers caused by friction of a rope moving against a hard edge
Chart	A detailed map of a body of water that contains piloting information
Chart Datum	The datum to which soundings on a chart are referred. It is usually the Mean Lower Low Water.
Chocks	Guides through which a rode can be passed to keep it aligned properly at the bow
Chop	Short, steep waves creating erratic motion
Claw	Category of anchors designed to catch seabed rather than dig into it
Cleat	A piece of hardware with projecting ends to which lines are made fast
Cockpit	An indented space on a deck in a boat for the use of the helmsman and crew; usually either aft or center
Cockpit sole	Floor of the cockpit
COLREGS	The International Regulations for Preventing Collisions at Sea 1972 (COLREGS) are published by the International Maritime Organization (IMO), and set out, inter alia, the "rules of the road" or navigation rules to be followed by ships and other vessels at sea in order to prevent collisions between two or more vessels
Companionway	A hatch or entrance from the deck to the cabin
Compass	Instrument showing the heading of a vessel, can be magnetic or electronic

347

Crown	The base of an anchor where the fluke (s) connect to the shank
Current	Movement of the water in a horizontal direction
Davit	A crane that projects over the side or stern of a ship and is used as a hoist
Dead ahead	In a direction exactly ahead
Depth sounder	Electronic instrument, measuring the time a sound wave takes to go from the sounder probe to the bottom and return, then displaying the result in feet, fathoms, or meters. The true depth to the bottom must take the position of the sounder on the hull into account.
Dinghy (dink)	A small boat used as a tender to deliver people and cargo from ship to shore
Displacement hull	Type of hull that plows through the water even when more power is added
Downwind	A direction with the wind to leeward
Draft	The depth of the vessel measured from the water line vertically to the lowest part of the hull or keel
Drag	How much force it takes to make the anchor drag along the bottom or pull out altogether.
Ebb	An outgoing tide
Etiquette	A code of practice, written or unwritten, that governs the expectations of behavior according to the contemporary conventions and social norms.
Fathom	A linear nautical measurement for indicating water depth equal to six feet
Fenders	Objects placed along the side of the boat to protect the hull from damage
Fetch	The distance across the water that wind can travel unobstructed by land
Flare	Pyrotechnic signaling device to indicate distress
Fluke	A projection or blade on an anchor intended to dig into the seabed; hook anchors have two or more flukes, while fluke anchors have two blades
Following sea	Waves or swell from astern
Fore	Located at the front of the vessel; fore cabin is toward the bow, the opposite of aft cabin; foredeck is the forward part of the main deck.
Forward	Toward the bow
Freeboard	The vertical distance measured from the waterline to the gunwale at the side

Happy Hooking & The Art of Anchoring

Galley	The boat's kitchen
Give-way vessel	Vessel which must stay clear of vessels that have the right-of-way
Gunwale	The upper edge of a boat's side at the deck - pronounced "gunnel"
Ham	Amateur radio (also called ham radio) with designated High Frequency radio bands for purposes of private recreation, non-commercial exchange of messages, experimentation, self-training, and emergency communication.
Hail	Call to another vessel
Harbor	A protected area where vessels may anchor, moor or dock
Hatch	An opening in the boat's deck
Hawse pipe	The steel pipe through which the hawser or anchor rode passes; located in the ship's bow on either side of her stem. See also Navel pipe
Head	A marine toilet
Head sea	Waves coming from the direction in which a vessel is heading
Heading	The compass direction in which a vessel is pointed at any given moment
Helm	The wheel or tiller by which a ship is steered
HF Radio	High Frequency radio. See also Ham and SSB
High tide	Highest normal level of depth reached
Holding power	The amount of force or load an anchor can withstand before being pulled out of the seabed; some anchors are classified as HHP (high holding power) or SHHP (super high holding power) for certification and comparison purposes
Holding tank	Storage tank for sewage
Hook	An implement used to secure a vessel to the bottom of the seabed; a hook style anchor
Hull	The main structural body of a vessel, excluding superstructure, masts, sails or rigging
Inboard	Inside or more toward the center of a vessel
Inland Rules	Rules of the road that apply to vessel operating in harbors, rivers, lakes, and inland waterways
ICW	Intracoastal Waterways (ICW) are interconnected bays, rivers and canals along the coasts (such as US Atlantic and Gulf of Mexico coasts) that allow vessels to transit without heading into the open sea
Jetty	A structure projecting out from the shore to protect a harbor against surge by current or tide
Kedge	An anchor used to pull one's boat off a shallow when aground

Keel	The main structural member of a vessel, the backbone; the lateral area beneath the hull to provide steering stability and reduce leeway
Kellet	A weight suspended from a road that helps to prevent wraps of the rode around the keel in changes of wind or current, especially in light air
Knot	A configuration of a rope or ropes that allows two ropes to be tied together or one to perform a desired function such as securing a boat to a dock or anchor. Also, a unit of speed equal to one nautical mile (6,076.10 feet) an hour.
Latitude	Geographic demarcation north or south of the equator
Launch	(1) To put a vessel into the water; (2) a small open boat, mainly used for transportation between a vessel and shore
Lee	The side opposite to that from which the wind blows
Leeward	Situated on the side turned away from the wind. (Opposite of windward.)
Line	A rope used aboard a ship
List	Leaning to one side, often caused by imbalance in stowage, water ingress or wind
LOA	Length over all; the maximum length of a vessel's hull, excluding projecting spars or rudder
Load	The amount of horizontal force exerted by the action of wind and wave on the structures of a boat
Locker	On board storage compartment or closet
Log	A record or diary of a vessel's journey. The Ship's Log was originally actually a piece of wood dropped overboard to record speed. v. to record
Longitude	Geographic demarcation east or west of the prime meridian
Lubber's line	A mark or permanent line on a compass that shows the course of the boat.
Making way	Making progress through the water
Marina	A place providing secure moorings or dock space for pleasure boats and usually offering service facilities, such as fuel and showers
Mayday	A radio distress call, from the French m'aidez (help me); SOS in Morse Code
Mean High Water, MHW	The observed average of all the high-water heights
Mean Higher High Water, MHHW	The observed average of the higher high-water height of each tidal day

Happy Hooking ⚓ The Art of Anchoring

Mean Low Water, MLW
> The observed average of all the low water heights

Mean Lower Low Water, MLLW
> The observed average of the lower low water height of each tidal day

Midships — The center of the boat

Moored — Anchored or made fast to a pier or wharf

Mooring — Permanent ground tackle

Mooring field — Place where vessels are kept on secure permanent moorings

Nautical mile — 6076.12 feet, or 1852 meters, an international standard; the geographical mile, the length of a minute of latitude along the meridian at latitude 48°

Navel pipe — The steel pipe on the ship's deck through which the anchor rode passes that leads down to the anchor locker; also known as spurling pipe. See also: Hawse pipe

Navigation Rules — The "Rules of the Road" governing navigation lights, vessels meeting or passing, sound signals, distress signals and anchoring; COLREGS

Offshore — Out of sight of land

Outboard — Powerboat having an engine outside the hull

PFD — Personal Flotation Device

Pier — Permanent structure extending into navigable water, used as a landing place for craft or for recreational and commercial purposes, such as a fishing pier

Pitch — (1) Independent movement of the bow and stern up and down due to wave action
(2) The theoretical distance advanced by a propeller in one revolution

Plow — UK = Plough, an anchor designed like two convex plowshares meant to dig into the seabed

Port — The left side of the boat when you are facing the bow, also a destination or harbor

Propeller — Mechanism that pushes water aft to propel a boat

Pulpit — The forward railing structure at the bow

Rafting up — Tying up to an anchored vessel without having to anchor

Relative bearing — A direction in relation to the fore-and-aft line of a vessel

Rode — A chain, rope, cable or combination of these used to secure a boat to an anchor

Alex and Daria Blackwell

Rules of the Road	The nautical traffic rules for preventing collisions on the water (COLREGS)
Samson Post	Post used for tying off the anchor rode.
Scope	The length of the anchor rode relative to the depth of the water measured from the deck of the vessel.
Scupper	A hole allowing water to run off the deck
Seacock	A through-hull valve, a shut-off on a plumbing or drain pipe between the vessel's interior and the sea
Sea kindly	Comfortable motion in rough seas
Seaworthy	Fit or safe for an ocean passage
Set	(1) An anchor that has grabbed the seabed and stopped the boat from moving (2) The effect a current has on the course of a vessel underway
Setting ability	The ease with which an anchor grabs a seabed
Shank	The shaft or stem used to pull an anchor to set it
Slip	A berth for a boat, usually between two piers
Snubber	A length of stretchy material, such as rope or rubber that adds elasticity to a chain rode. Also called a strop, nipping line, or mooring compensator
Spurling Pipe	The steel pipe on the ship's deck through which the anchor rode passes that leads down to the anchor locker; also known as navel pipe. See also: Hawse pipe
SSB	Single side band long-range radio. See also Ham.
Stand-on vessel	The vessel with the right-of-way
Starboard	The right side of the boat when you are facing the bow
Stock	A stabilizing arm perpendicular to the shank on some anchors that provides roll stability and helps orient it properly for setting
Stern	The aft or back end of the boat
Stow	To put in the proper place
Swamp	To fill with water coming in over the gunwales
Swing radius	The radius of the circle your boat will make around the anchor when the tide or wind direction changes
Tender	A small boat which accompanies a larger vessel and is used to transport persons and gear between the vessel and shore. Dinghy

Happy Hooking & The Art of Anchoring

Transom	The transverse planking which forms the after end of a square-ended boat
Trim	To arrange weights in a vessel in such a manner as to obtain a desired balance of draft at bow and stern and side to side
UKHO	United Kingdom Hydrographic Office
Underway	Vessel in motion when not moored, at anchor, made fast to the shore, or aground
USCG	United States Coast Guard
Vessel	Any watercraft capable of being used as a means of transportation on the water
VHF	Very High Frequency electronic radio communications and direction-finding system
Wake	Waves created by vessel motion. Track that a boat leaves behind it when moving on the water.
Way	Making progress through the water; headway when going forward and sternway when going backwards
Weigh anchor	To raise the anchor in preparation for departure
Windlass	A manual, hydraulic or electric winch used to retrieve the rode and weigh anchor
Windward	Situated on the side closest to the wind. (Opposite of leeward.)
Yaw	To swing erratically; back and forth motion made by boats at anchor

Alex and Daria Blackwell

Factors to Keep in Mind When Anchoring

	How to find out	*What to do*
Type of bottom (soft mud, hard, sand, rocks, etc.)	Look on the chart (paper or chart-plotter if you are in high enough magnification); bottom is marked: M, h, S, rky, S sh, etc. Use Chart no. 1 to interpret what they mean.	Choose the recommended anchor for the type of bottom.
Location of nearby obstacles	Drive in a circle that represents your expected swing radius	Avoid anchoring close to other boats, mooring buoys, marker buoys, fish stakes, or anything that your boat could hit if you swing 360 degrees
Depth	Determine the height of the tide now and compare it to the depth (MLW) marked on the contour lines around your selected anchorage.	Note if the tide is coming in or going out. Anchor in depth that will ensure you will have plenty of water at low tide and plenty of scope on your rode at high tide.
Contour of bottom	Check for consistent depth (within a couple of feet) in the vicinity of where you drop anchor.	Avoid sloping bottoms. Your anchor will not hold if sliding down-hill.
Wind/weather	Listen to marine weather forecasts (e.g., NOAA weather radio VHF channels 01-07 or Channel 16 advisories)	Pick a spot where you will be sheltered from wind and waves throughout the predicted pattern for the night. On a hot night, pick a spot where you will find a cooling breeze.
Currents	Watch the marker buoys to see if they're being pulled in a certain direction and observe how the water is moving in your selected spot. Realize that when the tide goes against the wind, a chop is likely to develop. Prepare for a full tide cycle.	If there is a strong current, set two anchors, or set an anchor in a location where it will have plenty of room to reset if it pulls up. Set your anchor alarm on your chart-plotter. Assign anchor watch duty. Add a weight to a rope rode to avoid wrapping the keel during slack water.

354

Neighbors	If someone comes in after you've anchored, and they drop their hook too close to you.	Politely suggest that they may be too close when the tide/wind shifts and perhaps would like to reconsider. If they don't move, you will have to decide if it is worth moving yourself for peace of mind.
Dragging	If you notice a boat dragging anchor in your vicinity.	Blow your horn with five short blasts, repeat as needed. If no one is aboard, consider using your dinghy to keep the boat from damaging other vessels and to reset their anchor. Consider tying the breakaway vessel side by side with another.
Rafting-up	Raft-ups, potluck dinners or social gatherings are always fun. You can pre-arrange this with your friends or hoist a cocktail flag and hail your neighbor – you never know.	Prepare fenders and dock lines, hail your anchor boat and discuss intentions, come alongside slowly, throw lines and secure, then adjust position to account for obstructions like spreaders.

White Seahorse Publishing

About the Authors

Captains Daria & Alex Blackwell

Daria and Alex Blackwell are lifelong sailors and passionate cruisers. They have completed three Atlantic crossings and have spent years cruising the coasts of the Americas and Europe, as well as the Bahamas, the Caribbean islands, and the Atlantic islands, most recently double-handing on their vintage 57-foot Bowman ketch, *Aleria*. Alex holds a USCG Master's license with sailing and towing endorsements. Daria holds a USCG OUPV Captain's license.

The Blackwells are members of the Ocean Cruising Club, Seven Seas Cruising Association, Irish Cruising Club, American Yacht Club, and Mayo Sailing Club. They are the SSCA cruising station for Ireland, OCC Port Officers for the west of Ireland, and TransOcean eV base for Ireland. Daria is Vice Commodore of the OCC and Alex is OCC Regional Rear Commodore for Ireland.

Evenings at anchor are prime creative times for Alex

White Seahorse Publishing

Daria and Alex are frequent contributors to sailing publications on both sides of the Atlantic, writing about technology, cruising, as well as their sailing adventures for publications such as *Yachting World, Cruising World, Yachting, Classic Boat, Cruising Outpost, Ireland Afloat, Offshore, Practical Boat Owner, Lats & Atts, Windcheck,* and numerous e-zines.

We hope to see you out there!

The Blackwells have adapted the content of *Happy Hooking* to other media and deliver live seminars at boat shows and sailing clubs, online webinars on behalf of the SSCA and Great Lakes Cruising Club, and a course on anchoring incorporated as a requirement for the NauticEd Bareboat certification program.

Daria doing some serious work

The Blackwells run the popular www.CoastalBoating.net, *"The boaters' resource for places to go and things to know"*. As founders of Sail4Kids Make a Memory Cruise, the Blackwells were recognized with prestigious awards by both American Yacht Club and the International Society for Perpetuation of Cruelty to Racing Yachtsmen.

The Blackwells have both enjoyed professional careers as copywriters, marketers and speakers. Alex was a partner in Starnet Media Group, a marketing support services firm. Alex's first book, *Oyster Delight by Jonathan Mite*, is a tribute to his lifelong interest in oysters, having launched an oyster hatchery in Ireland after being awarded a Master's degree in Fisheries Biology. Alex is President of Knowledge Clinic, Ltd.

White Seahorse Publishing

Among Daria's past accomplishments is management of advertising agencies, including as President of Dugan/Farley Communication, President of Bozell Global Healthcare and Managing Partner of S&H, Division of Y&R a WPP Company. She was also elected President of the

Editor and Cruising Kitty Onyx

Healthcare Businesswomen's Association, assisted in establishing the Europe Chapter, and was named 2011 HBA STAR for her contributions. Daria serves as CEO of Knowledge Clinic, Ltd.

When not out cruising, Daria and Alex currently live in Ireland. Sadly, Onyx, their editor and cruising kitty, has passed on to cruiser's heaven. She wrote a book about her adventures appropriately titled *Onyx the Cruising Kitty*. You can follow the Blackwells at *Aleria*'s Adventures on BlogSpot. You can connect with Alex and Daria on their Facebook page @CoastalBoating.net.

White Seahorse Publishing

Dear Reader:

Thank you very much for purchasing

Happy Hooking
The Art of Anchoring

We truly hope you enjoyed reading it
as much as we did writing it.

We greatly value your opinion.
Please be kind enough and post your thoughts about it on
www.amazon.com

Best regards

Also available from
White Seahorse Publishing

Self-Publishing for Success
Every book deserves to be published
Second edition

By Alex Blackwell

Do you have an idea for a book? Have you
been turned down or disappointed by
traditional publishers? Have you finished a
novel and are uncertain what the next steps
are in getting it into the hands of a reader? Or
are you an instructor or specialist and have
been asked about further reading? Alex
Blackwell has worked his way through all of
these scenarios. He has also been a book
printer and has self-published several of his
own fiction and non-fiction books.

As the saying goes, everyone has a book in them. Many have
even written one in whole or in part. Most have given up as the
publishing process proved either too daunting, or they were
flatly rejected by either a literary agency or a publisher. And then
there are all those who wrote just for the pleasure of it – a family
history, a memoir or biography, a personal poetry collection, or
just a cookbook for distribution to friends and family for
Christmas. All of these deserve to be published.

White Seahorse Publishing

Cruising the Wild Atlantic Way

By Daria & Alex Blackwell

The guide to the beauty and amenities of Ireland's Wild Atlantic West Coast

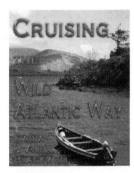

Whether travelling by road or boat, experience the true Ireland.

Ireland's untamed West Coast dotted with islands is one of the most challenging and daunting coastlines to sail. It can also be among the most rewarding if the weather cooperates and the mariner is well prepared for cruising this remote stretch of ocean. This island nation sits out in the North Atlantic which can stir up powerful fury.

Find out what it takes to sail the Wild Atlantic Way. Learn the secrets of how to prepare, where to stop, and how to thoroughly enjoy this unique cruising ground. Stretching from Donegal to Cork, it is the most unspoiled stretch of coastline in Europe. See a land as it was seen by explorers centuries ago, when roads didn't exist and the sea was the means by which to travel.

White Seahorse Publishing

Oyster Delight

By Alex Blackwell
with illustrations by John Joyce

"The Definitive Guide to enjoying oysters"

There has never been an oyster book like this one, Guaranteed. It covers just about everything an oyster lover would care to learn about this delectable little devil.

Written by a marine biologist who started an oyster hatchery in the West of Ireland and originally used a version of the cookbook to boost sales, it eventually grew to become this entertaining and most extraordinary, definitive guide to everything about oysters. And it is eminently readable, not like a cookbook at all, but informative and entertaining.

White Seahorse Publishing

Onyx: The Cruising Kitty

By Daria and Alex Blackwell

Onyx: The Cruising Kitty is a charming series of chronologically sorted short stories told in the voice of Onyx herself. In them she describes her adventures starting with when she chose her 'Peo-ple'. She then tells about how she got her sea legs and became a seafaring cruising kitty. Onyx has probably more sea miles under her paws than most sailors would ever dream of. She crossed the Atlantic three times and visited countless countries along the way.

The book is for all ages. It is easily read. It may be dipped into whenever the reader is in need of an uplifting story or devoured in one sitting.

"I'm Onyx, the Cruising Kitty.
I'm going to see the world.
But first I'll have to take a nap."

White Seahorse Publishing

The Naked Truth, a nautical murder mystery

By Daria Blackwell

In *The Naked Truth*, the Lynch's set out on the adventure of their lifetimes, having bought a sailboat, quit their high powered jobs in the City, sold their house, and cast off the lines. For the first time in their lives, they were free to do whatever they wanted, go wherever they pleased. They needed to restore their souls after a lifetime of servitude in the corporate concrete jungles. Sailing across oceans – just the two of them aboard – was exactly the kind of restorative adventure they craved.

Little did they know that the adventure was destined to take them to idyllic destinations with exquisite timing – timing that would set Jessica on a course to be the sole witness to a trail of brutal murders. Xander, distressed by Jessica's tormented ordeal and feeling helpless, discovers that he can help her decipher bizarre dreams that leave clues about the mysterious crimes.

They learn quickly to be careful of what they wish for, because no one can tell when their fortunes will change and who will be able to uncover the *naked truth*.

White Seahorse Publishing

The Butterfly Effect; It started on 9/11
Book 1 of the Butterfly Effect Series

By Alex Blackwell

The Butterfly Effect has been described as an *'addictive page turner'*. Once you pick it up you will find it hard to put down again.

September 11, 2001 will forever be etched into people's minds as 9/11. The intent was clearly to bring down the United States of America. But the momentum of the American machine is simply too great for an isolated event to bring it to its knees. Or is it?

Jason Geraghty lost his beloved wife on 9/11. She was working for a secret government agency in the north tower of the World Trade Center. In the certainty that this was the third and penultimate time the US Government had wronged him, his mission in life became creating an event that would actually bring down America.

White Seahorse Publishing

The Brotherhood; Acquisition of Power
Book 2 of the Butterfly Effect Series

By Alex Blackwell

Blending current events with historical fiction, this is a book you will want to read in one sitting!

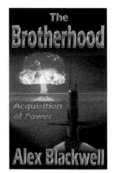

The sinking of the German Reich's greatest Battleship, the Bismarck, after a mere eight days at sea on her first assignment triggered a series of events that empowered the Bayer family to build a powerful business empire and create a brotherhood of like-minded German industrialists. Developing technology gives them the resources to acquire power greater than most countries in an audacious move. With this as a threat, world domination is in sight. However, the youngest of the Bayer dynasty, sees things differently: power must be used to be effective.

Dragged out of retirement, Jack O'D, who saved humanity in book 1 of the Butterfly Effect series, recruits Peter Blessingham, an ingenious computer hacker, into the biggest and most secretive intelligence-gathering organization in the world.

Can Peter and his team thwart the Brotherhood in their efforts? Can he stop the end of the world as we know it from happening?

Printed in Great Britain
by Amazon